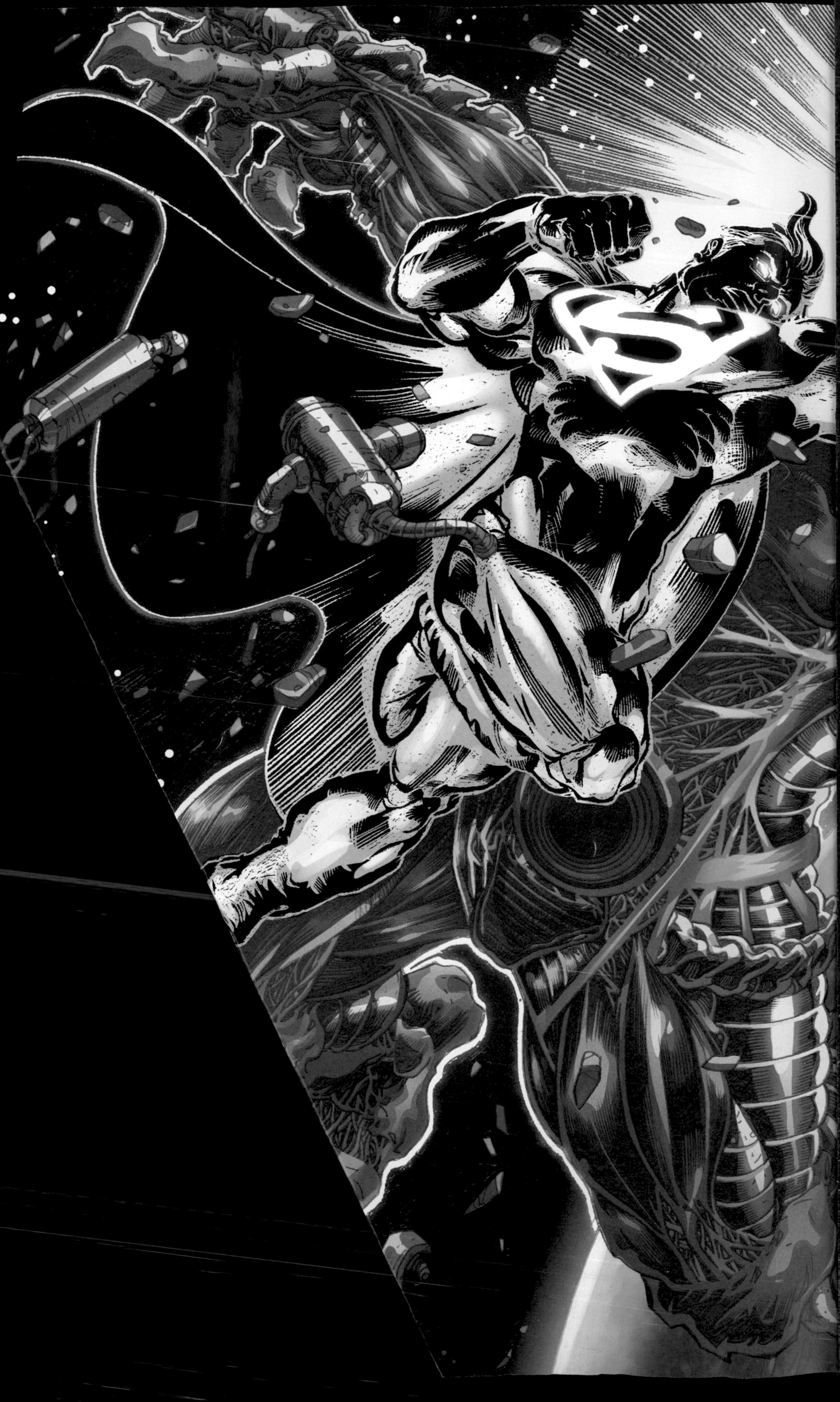

D0572682

DARKSEID WAR
POWER OF
THE GODS

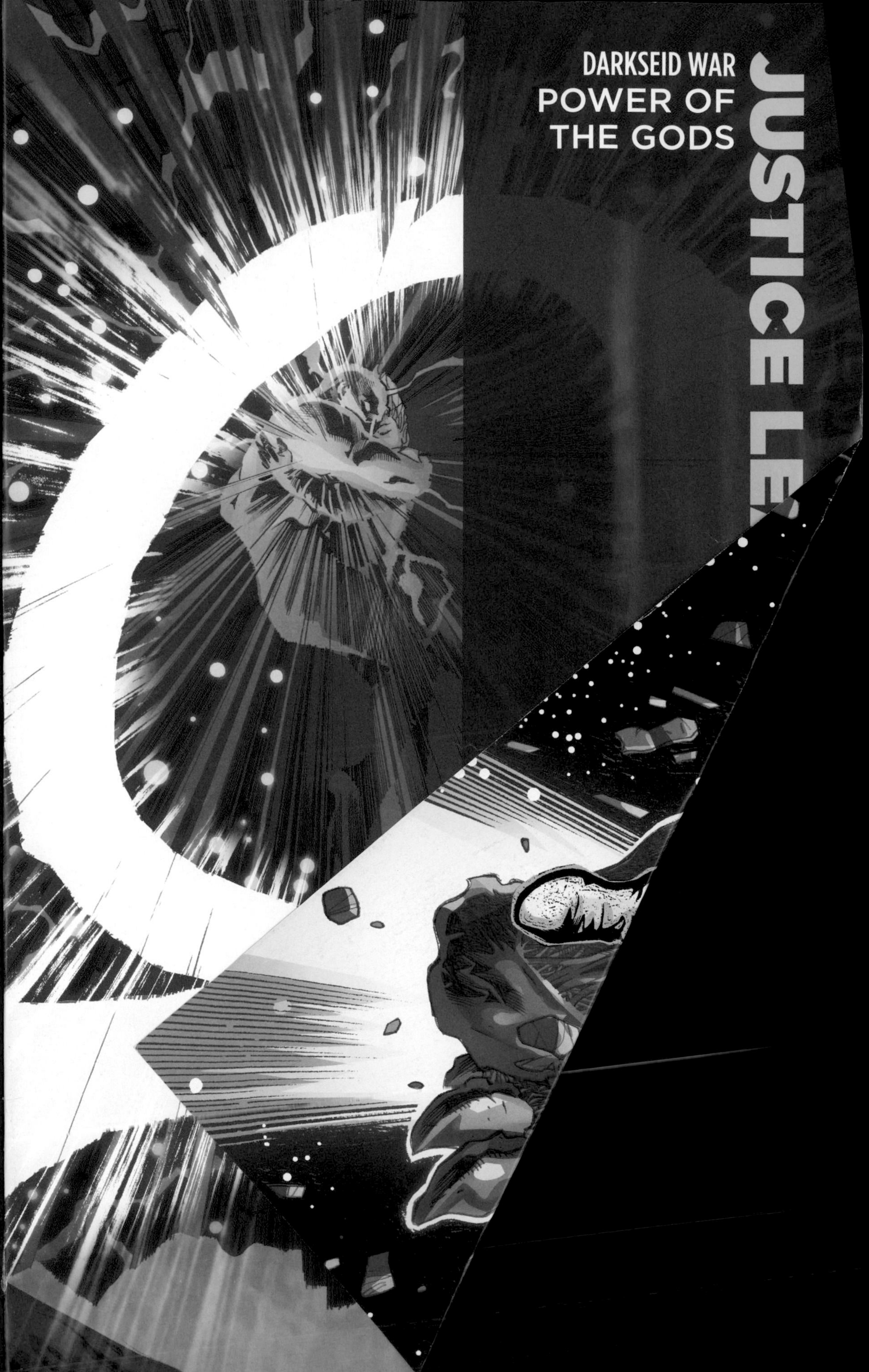
JUSTICE LE

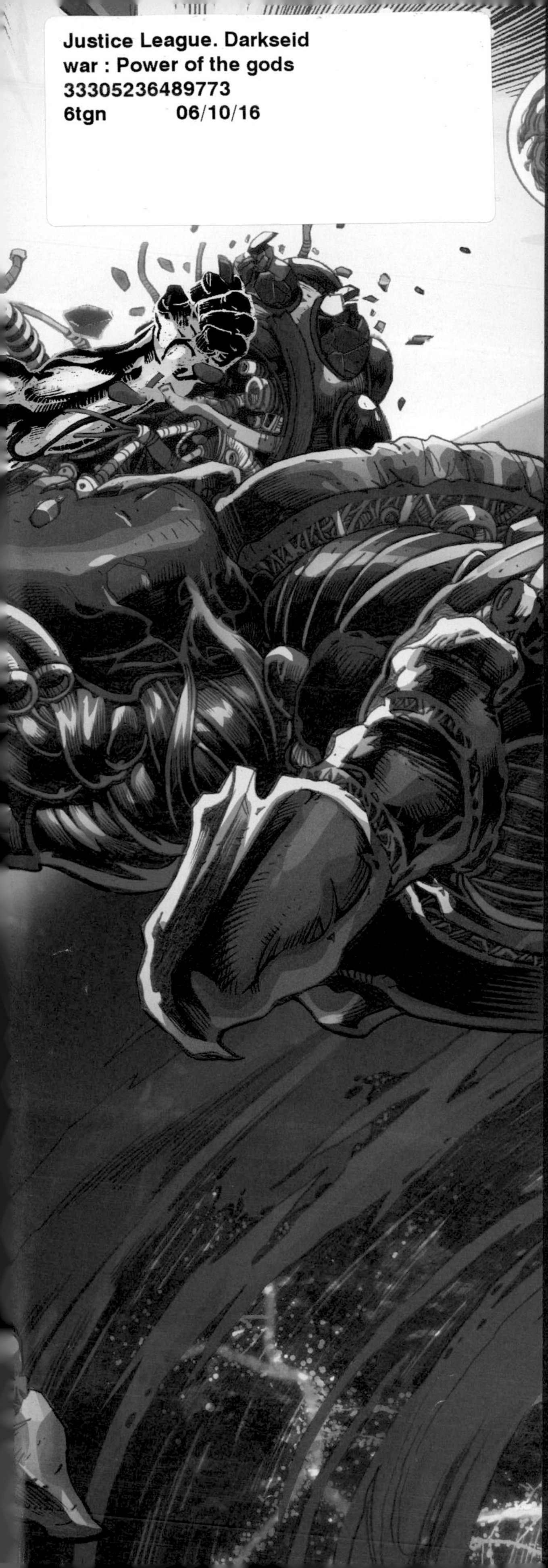

JUSTICE LEAGUE

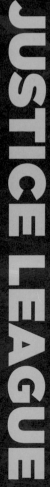

DARKSEID WAR
POWER OF THE GODS

COLLECTION COVER ART BY
FRANCIS MANAPUL

BATMAN CREATED BY
BOB KANE
WITH **BILL FINGER**

SUPERMAN CREATED BY
JERRY SIEGEL &
JOE SHUSTER
BY SPECIAL ARRANGEMENT
WITH THE JERRY SIEGEL FAMILY

BRIAN CUNNINGHAM Editor – Original Series
AMEDEO TURTURRO Assistant Editor – Original Series
JEB WOODARD Group Editor – Collected Editions
ROBIN WILDMAN Editor – Collected Edition
STEVE COOK Design Director – Books
DAMIAN RYLAND Publication Design

BOB HARRAS Senior VP – Editor-in-Chief, DC Comics

DIANE NELSON President
DAN DIDIO and JIM LEE Co-Publishers
GEOFF JOHNS Chief Creative Officer
AMIT DESAI Senior VP – Marketing & Global Franchise Management
NAIRI GARDINER Senior VP – Finance
SAM ADES VP – Digital Marketing
BOBBIE CHASE VP – Talent Development
MARK CHIARELLO Senior VP – Art, Design & Collected Editions
JOHN CUNNINGHAM VP – Content Strategy
ANNE DEPIES VP – Strategy Planning & Reporting
DON FALLETTI VP – Manufacturing Operations
LAWRENCE GANEM VP – Editorial Administration & Talent Relations
ALISON GILL Senior VP – Manufacturing & Operations
HANK KANALZ Senior VP – Editorial Strategy & Administration
JAY KOGAN VP – Legal Affairs
DEREK MADDALENA Senior VP – Sales & Business Development
JACK MAHAN VP – Business Affairs
DAN MIRON VP – Sales Planning & Trade Development
NICK NAPOLITANO VP – Manufacturing Administration
CAROL ROEDER VP – Marketing
EDDIE SCANNELL VP – Mass Account & Digital Sales
COURTNEY SIMMONS Senior VP – Publicity & Communications
JIM (SKI) SOKOLOWSKI VP – Comic Book Specialty & Newsstand Sales
SANDY YI Senior VP – Global Franchise Management

JUSTICE LEAGUE: DARKSEID WAR—POWER OF THE GODS

Published by DC Comics. Compilation and all new material Copyright © 2016 DC Comics. All Rights Reserved.

Originally published in single magazine form in JUSTICE LEAGUE: DARKSEID WAR—BATMAN, JUSTICE LEAGUE: DARKSEID WAR—FLASH, JUSTICE LEAGUE: DARKSEID WAR—SUPERMAN, JUSTICE LEAGUE: DARKSEID WAR—SHAZAM, JUSTICE LEAGUE: DARKSEID WAR—GREEN LANTERN, JUSTICE LEAGUE: DARKSEID WAR—LEX LUTHOR Copyright © 2015 DC Comics. All Rights Reserved. All characters, their distinctive likenesses and related elements featured in this publication are trademarks of DC Comics. The stories, characters and incidents featured in this publication are entirely fictional. DC Comics does not read or accept unsolicited submissions of ideas, stories or artwork.

DC Comics, 2900 West Alameda Avenue, Burbank, CA 91505
Printed by RR Donnelley, Salem, VA, USA. 3/18/16. First Printing.
ISBN: 978-1-4012-6149-8

Library of Congress Cataloging-in-Publication Data is available.

PEFC Certified

Printed on paper from
sustainably managed
forests and controlled
sources

PEFC
PEFC/29-31-75   www.pefc.org

PREVIOUSLY...

The last time the evil god Darkseid attacked Earth, the Justice League was formed to drive him back to Apokolips. Since then, the League has been on the lookout for any evidence of Apokolips technology being activated on Earth.

Now that time has come. A Boom Tube was opened, setting two of Darkseid's assassins loose on Earth. When the Justice League went to investigate, they were attacked by a woman called Grail. She claimed to be Darkseid's daughter and that she's come to Earth to kill her father.

Mister Miracle, the son of Darkseid's ancient enemy Highfather, spent his life on Apokolips before he learned how to escape. He tracked Darkseid's warriors to Earth and discovered their target—Myrina Black, a former Amazon warrior and Grail's mother. Black told Mister Miracle of her plan to lure Darkseid into a war with the Anti-Monitor on Earth. Millions could die, but Darkseid would ultimately fall. Horrified, Mister Miracle escaped to go warn the Justice League.

Under the control of Wonder Woman's lasso, the god Metron confessed that the information needed to stop the Anti-Monitor is in his omniscient chair. Consequently, Wonder Woman forcibly removed Metron, and Batman took his place on the Mobius Chair. Batman is now the **God of Knowledge**.

Meanwhile, Superman and Lex Luthor were ambushed by Lex's sister Lena, who declared allegiance to Darkseid and shot Lex before transporting both of them to Apokolips. With Superman's powers fading under the alien sun, Luthor dropped him in one of the planet's solar flame pits. Superman survived and became more powerful than ever...although his personality was changed, and he left Luthor to die on Apokolips. Superman is now the **God of Power**.

Back on Earth, Darkseid arrived to face the Anti-Monitor, with the Justice League caught in the middle. When Darkseid summoned the Black Racer, his enslaved embodiment of death, the Anti-Monitor took control of the Racer by bonding it to his own host—the Flash. Flash became the **God of Death** and killed Darkseid.

And then all hell broke loose...

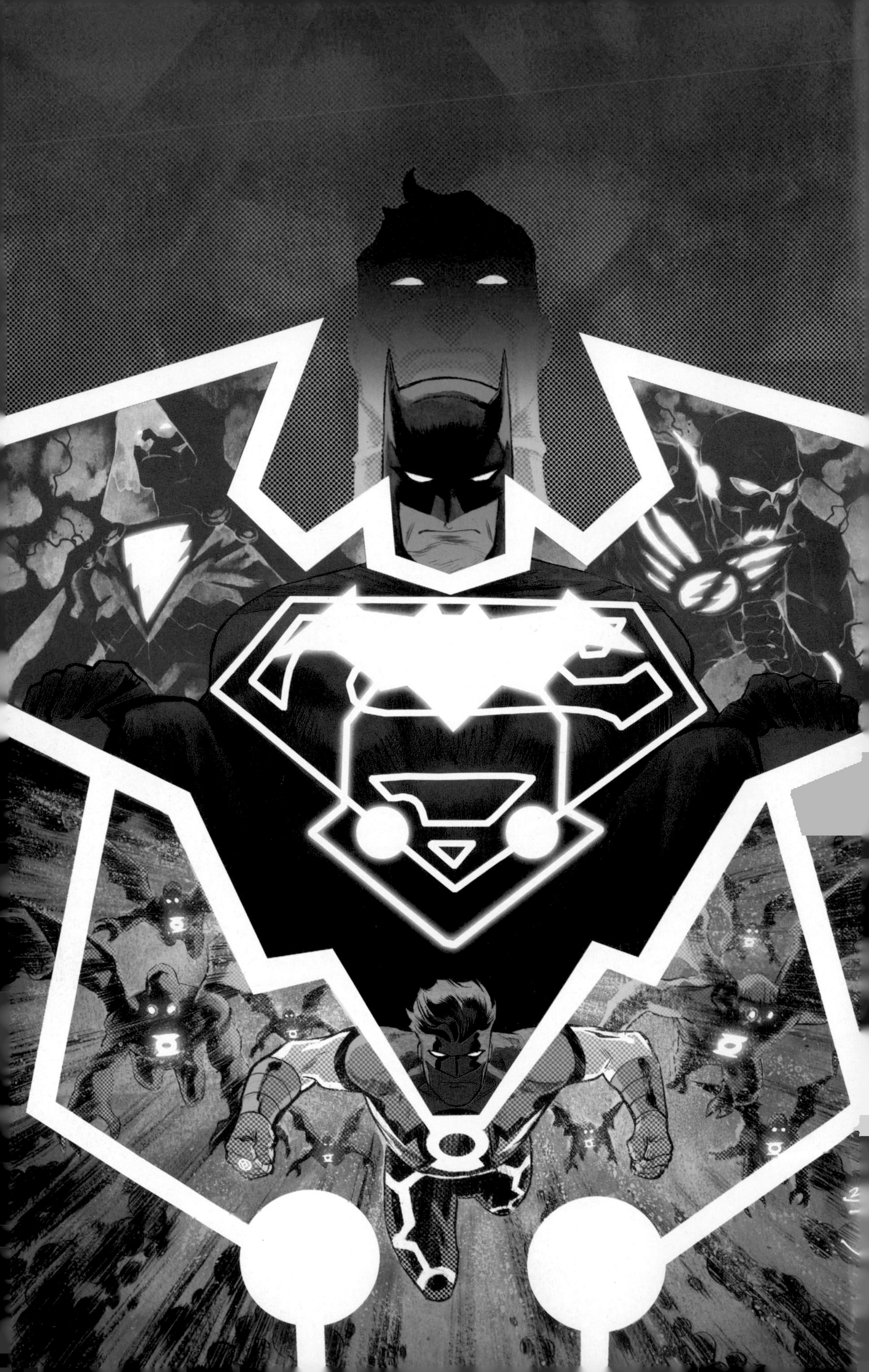

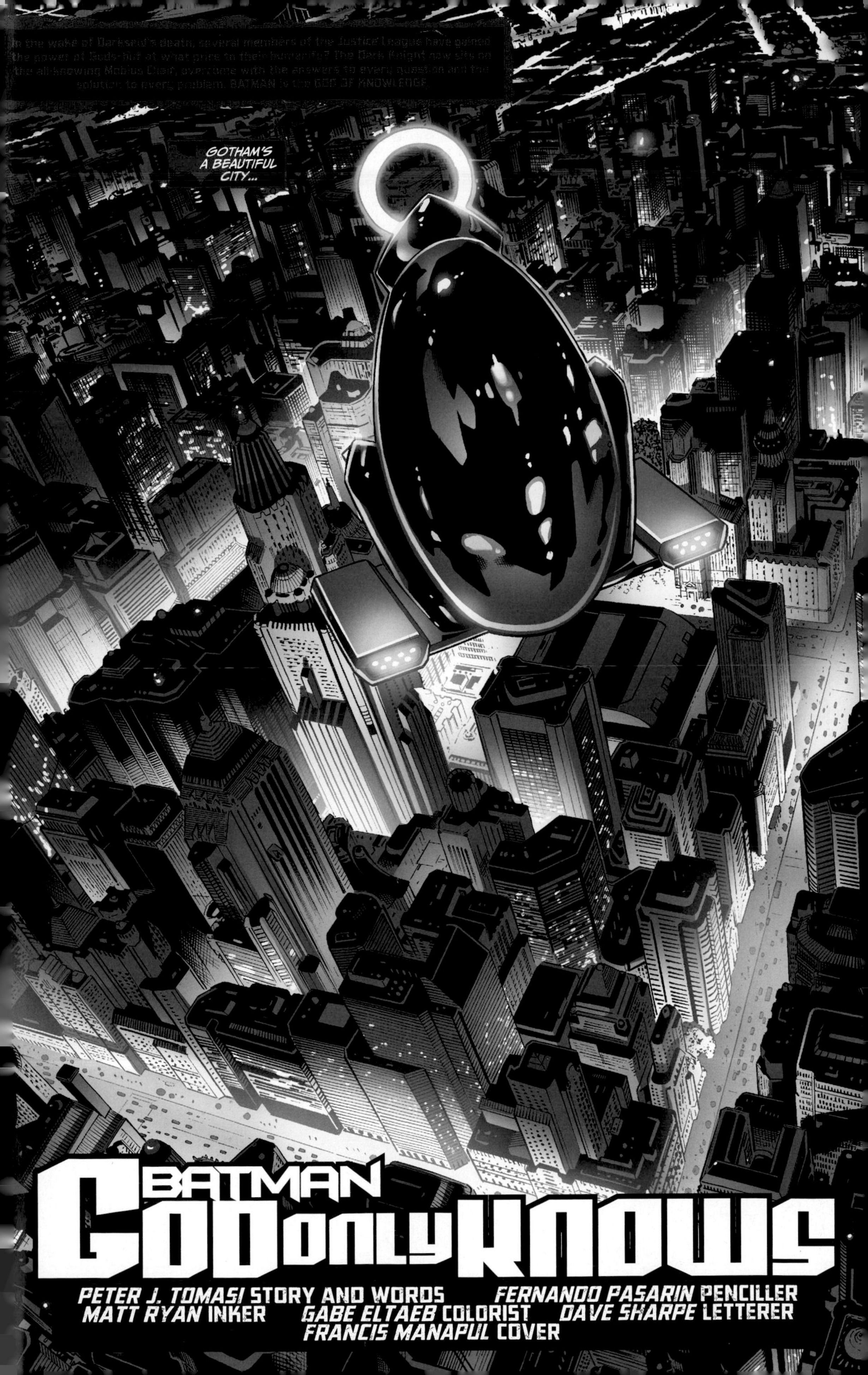
In the wake of Darkseid's death, several members of the Justice League have gained the power of Gods—but at what price to their humanity? The Dark Knight now sits on the all-knowing Mobius Chair, overcome with the answers to every question and the solution to every problem. BATMAN is the GOD OF KNOWLEDGE.
GOTHAM'S A BEAUTIFUL CITY...
BATMAN GOD ONLY KNOWS
PETER J. TOMASI STORY AND WORDS
FERNANDO PASARIN PENCILLER
MATT RYAN INKER
GABE ELTAEB COLORIST
DAVE SHARPE LETTERER
FRANCIS MANAPUL COVER

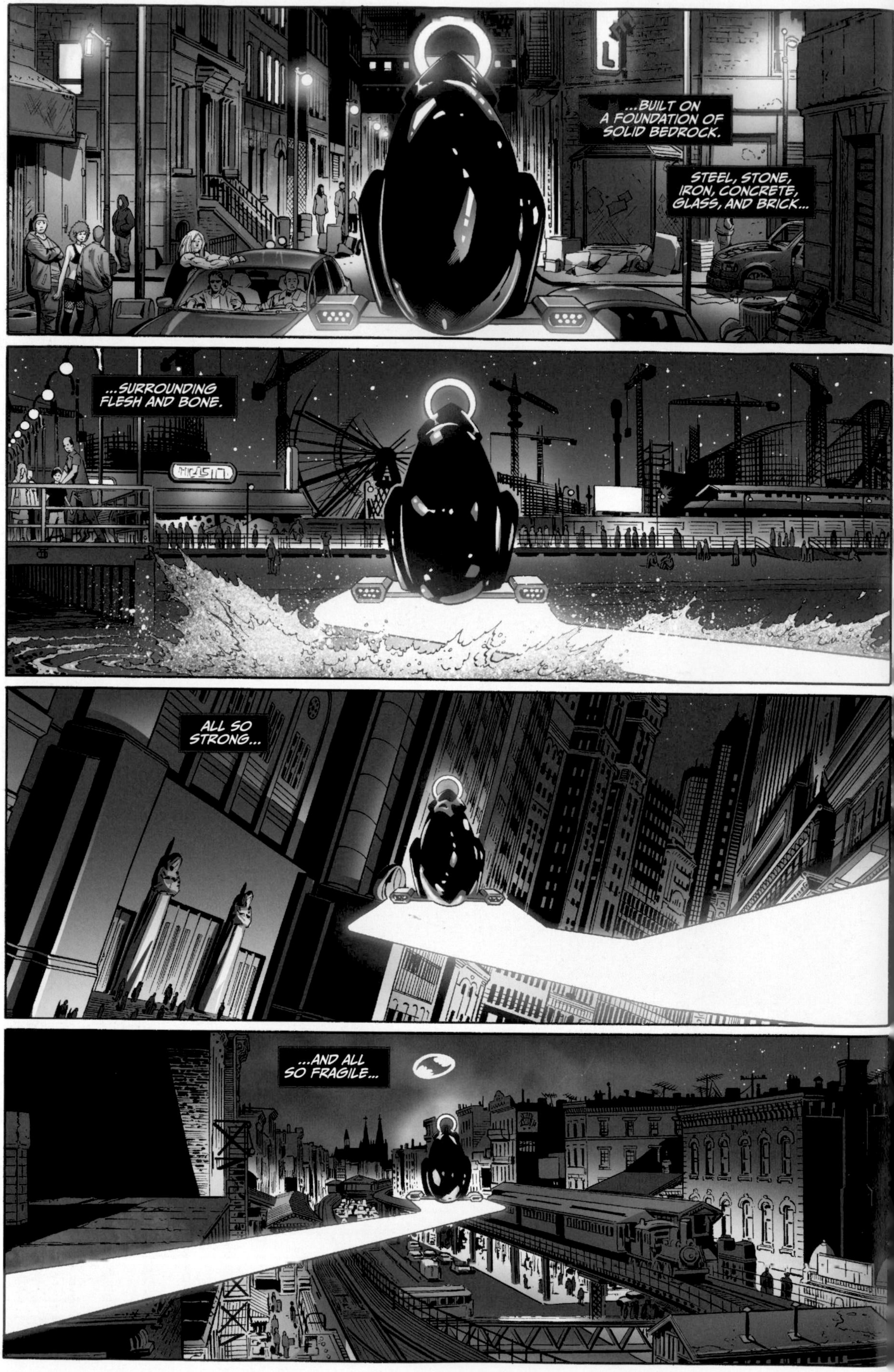
...BUILT ON A FOUNDATION OF SOLID BEDROCK.
STEEL, STONE, IRON, CONCRETE, GLASS, AND BRICK...
...SURROUNDING FLESH AND BONE.
ALL SO STRONG...
...AND ALL SO FRAGILE...

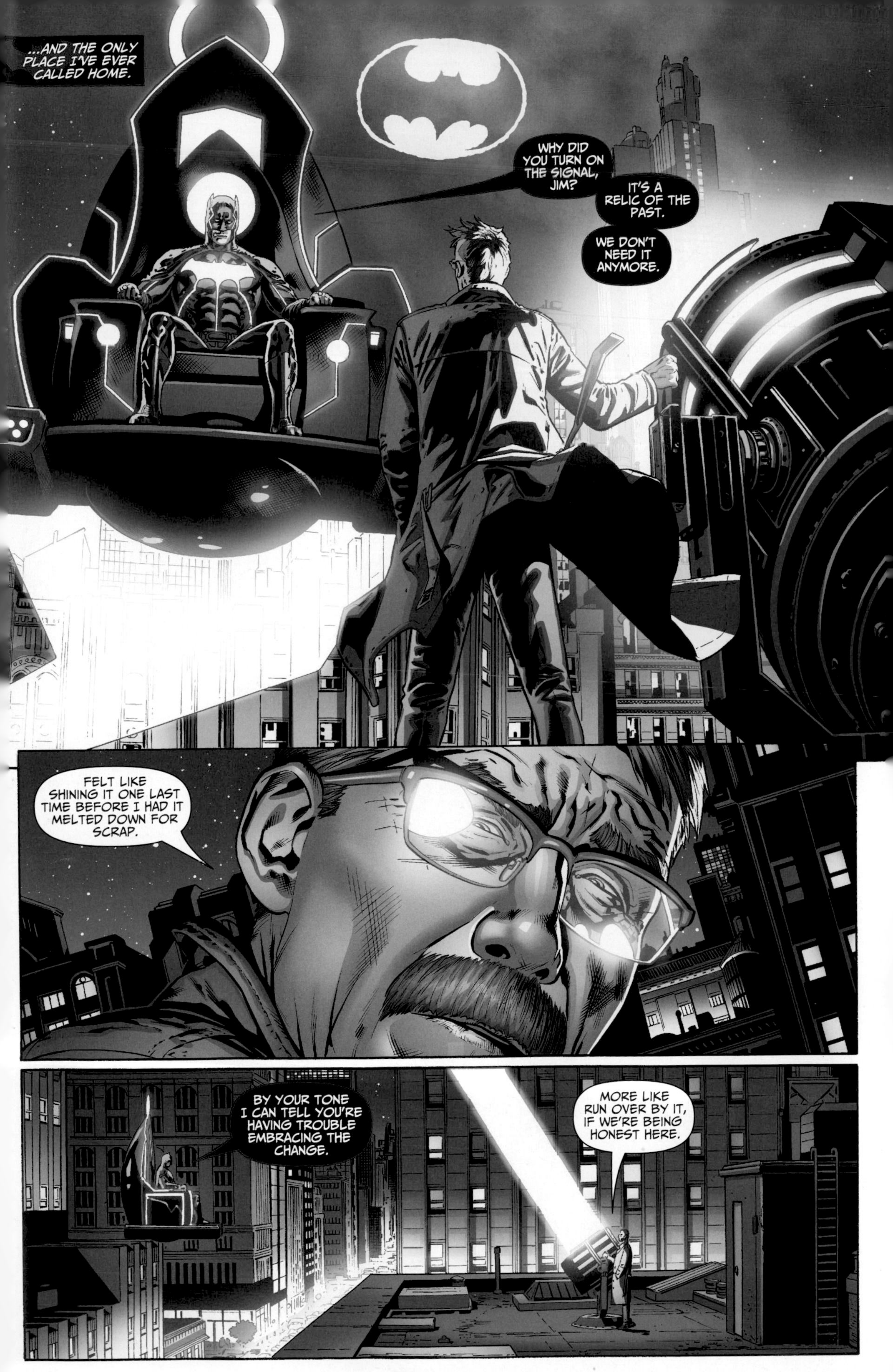
...AND THE ONLY PLACE I'VE EVER CALLED HOME.
WHY DID YOU TURN ON THE SIGNAL, JIM?
IT'S A RELIC OF THE PAST.
WE DON'T NEED IT ANYMORE.
FELT LIKE SHINING IT ONE LAST TIME BEFORE I HAD IT MELTED DOWN FOR SCRAP.
BY YOUR TONE I CAN TELL YOU'RE HAVING TROUBLE EMBRACING THE CHANGE.
MORE LIKE RUN OVER BY IT, IF WE'RE BEING HONEST HERE.

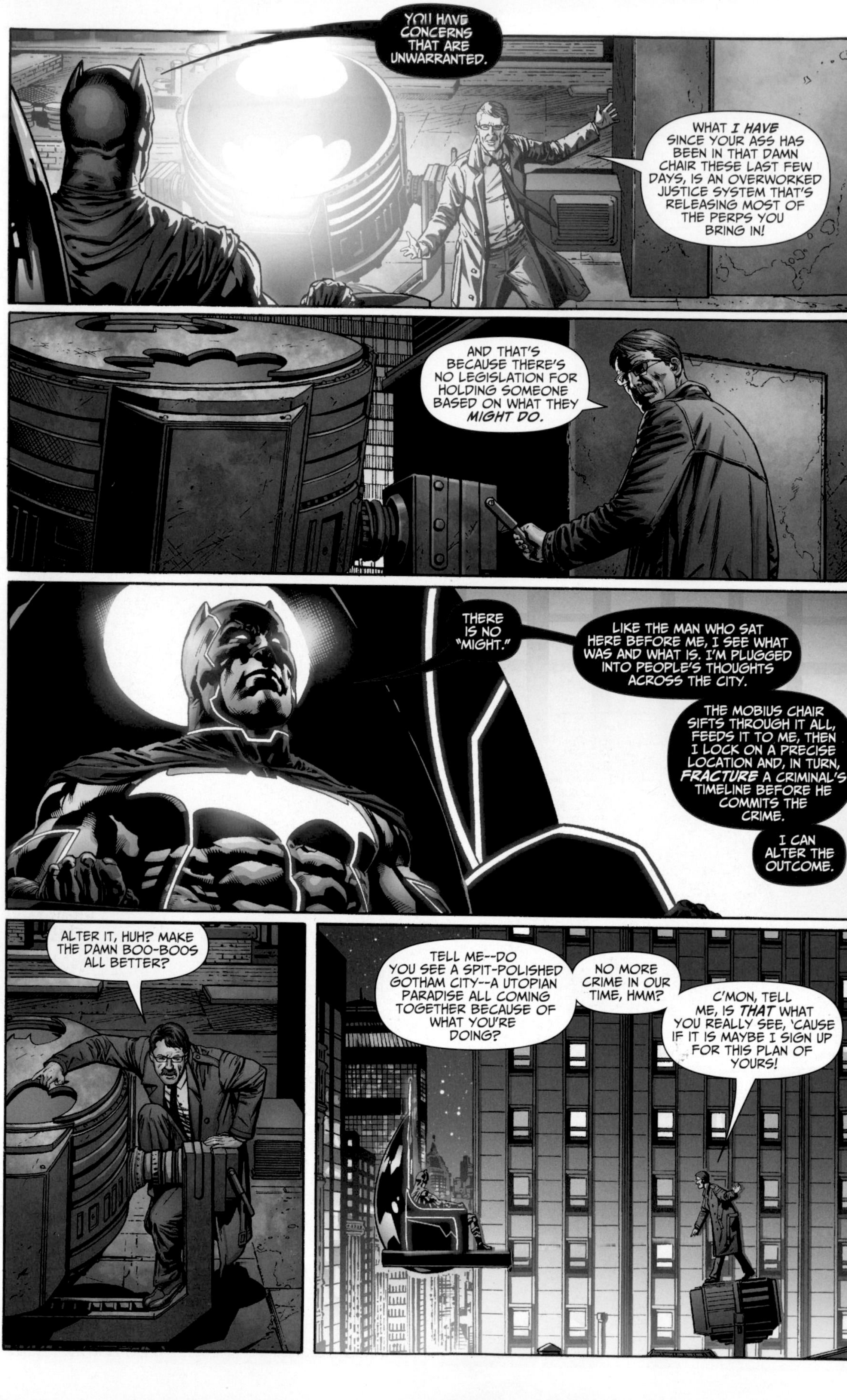
YOU HAVE CONCERNS THAT ARE UNWARRANTED.
WHAT I HAVE SINCE YOUR ASS HAS BEEN IN THAT DAMN CHAIR THESE LAST FEW DAYS, IS AN OVERWORKED JUSTICE SYSTEM THAT'S RELEASING MOST OF THE PERPS YOU BRING IN!
AND THAT'S BECAUSE THERE'S NO LEGISLATION FOR HOLDING SOMEONE BASED ON WHAT THEY MIGHT DO.
THERE IS NO "MIGHT."
LIKE THE MAN WHO SAT HERE BEFORE ME, I SEE WHAT WAS AND WHAT IS. I'M PLUGGED INTO PEOPLE'S THOUGHTS ACROSS THE CITY.
THE MOBIUS CHAIR SIFTS THROUGH IT ALL, FEEDS IT TO ME, THEN I LOCK ON A PRECISE LOCATION AND, IN TURN, FRACTURE A CRIMINAL'S TIMELINE BEFORE HE COMMITS THE CRIME.
I CAN ALTER THE OUTCOME.
ALTER IT, HUH? MAKE THE DAMN BOO-BOOS ALL BETTER?
TELL ME--DO YOU SEE A SPIT-POLISHED GOTHAM CITY--A UTOPIAN PARADISE ALL COMING TOGETHER BECAUSE OF WHAT YOU'RE DOING?
NO MORE CRIME IN OUR TIME, HMM?
C'MON, TELL ME, IS THAT WHAT YOU REALLY SEE, 'CAUSE IF IT IS MAYBE I SIGN UP FOR THIS PLAN OF YOURS!

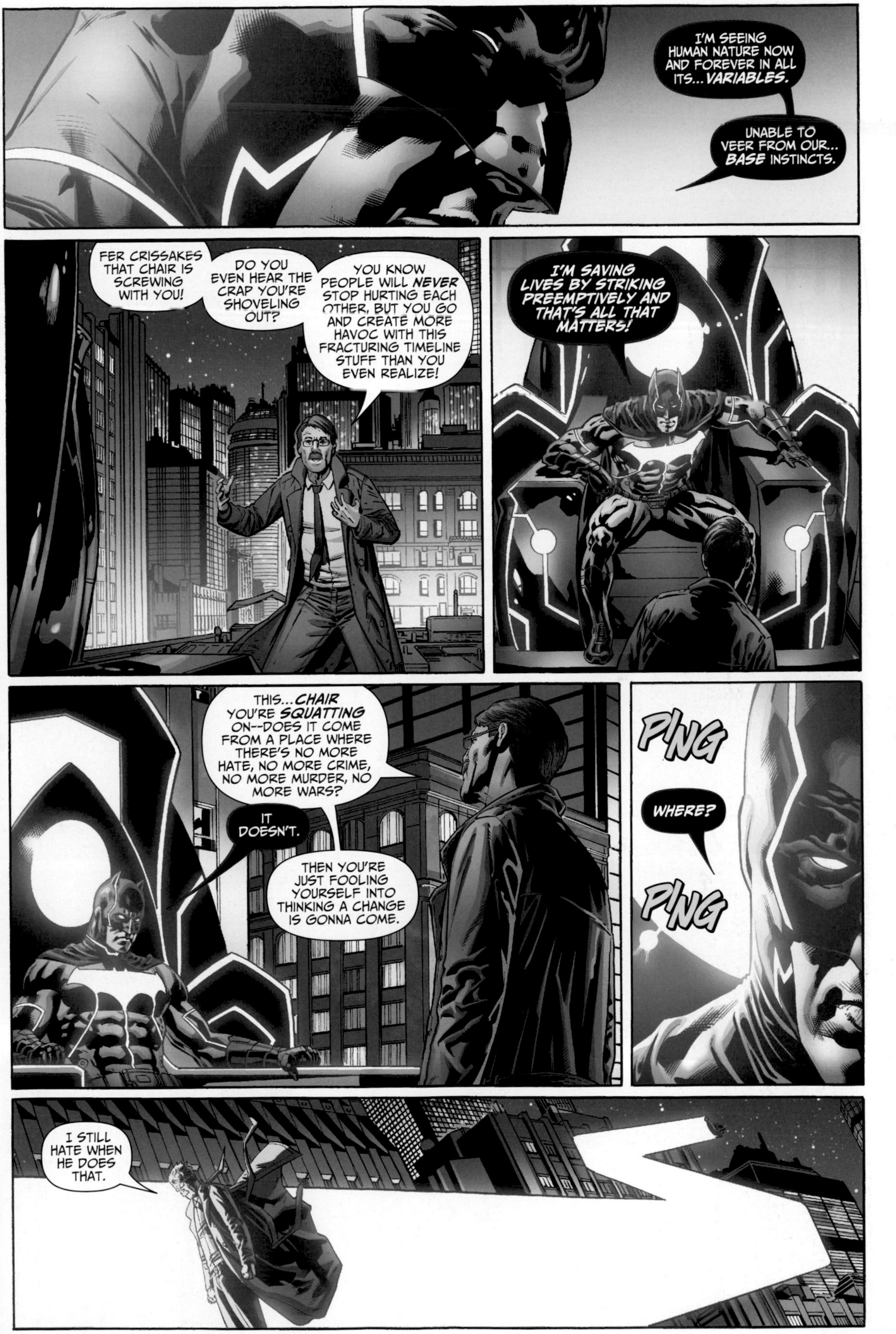

I'M SEEING HUMAN NATURE NOW AND FOREVER IN ALL ITS...VARIABLES.
UNABLE TO VEER FROM OUR... BASE INSTINCTS.
FER CRISSAKES THAT CHAIR IS SCREWING WITH YOU!
DO YOU EVEN HEAR THE CRAP YOU'RE SHOVELING OUT?
YOU KNOW PEOPLE WILL NEVER STOP HURTING EACH OTHER, BUT YOU GO AND CREATE MORE HAVOC WITH THIS FRACTURING TIMELINE STUFF THAN YOU EVEN REALIZE!
I'M SAVING LIVES BY STRIKING PREEMPTIVELY AND THAT'S ALL THAT MATTERS!
THIS...CHAIR YOU'RE SQUATTING ON--DOES IT COME FROM A PLACE WHERE THERE'S NO MORE HATE, NO MORE CRIME, NO MORE MURDER, NO MORE WARS?
IT DOESN'T.
THEN YOU'RE JUST FOOLING YOURSELF INTO THINKING A CHANGE IS GONNA COME.
PING
WHERE?
PING
I STILL HATE WHEN HE DOES THAT.

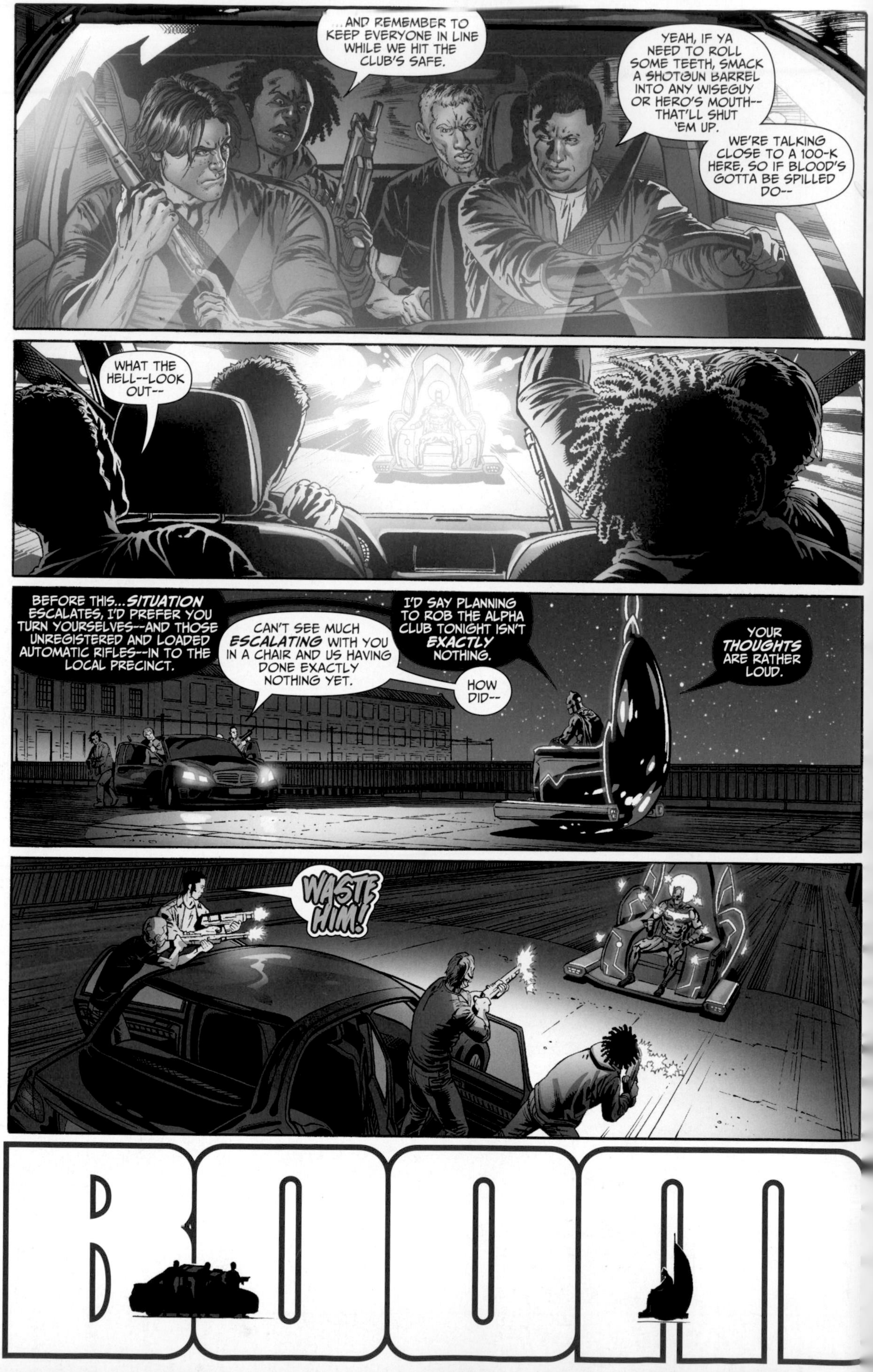
...AND REMEMBER TO KEEP EVERYONE IN LINE WHILE WE HIT THE CLUB'S SAFE.
YEAH, IF YA NEED TO ROLL SOME TEETH, SMACK A SHOTGUN BARREL INTO ANY WISEGUY OR HERO'S MOUTH-- THAT'LL SHUT 'EM UP.
WE'RE TALKING CLOSE TO A 100-K HERE, SO IF BLOOD'S GOTTA BE SPILLED DO--
WHAT THE HELL--LOOK OUT--
BEFORE THIS...SITUATION ESCALATES, I'D PREFER YOU TURN YOURSELVES--AND THOSE UNREGISTERED AND LOADED AUTOMATIC RIFLES--IN TO THE LOCAL PRECINCT.
CAN'T SEE MUCH ESCALATING WITH YOU IN A CHAIR AND US HAVING DONE EXACTLY NOTHING YET.
I'D SAY PLANNING TO ROB THE ALPHA CLUB TONIGHT ISN'T EXACTLY NOTHING.
HOW DID--
YOUR THOUGHTS ARE RATHER LOUD.
WASTE HIM!
BOOM

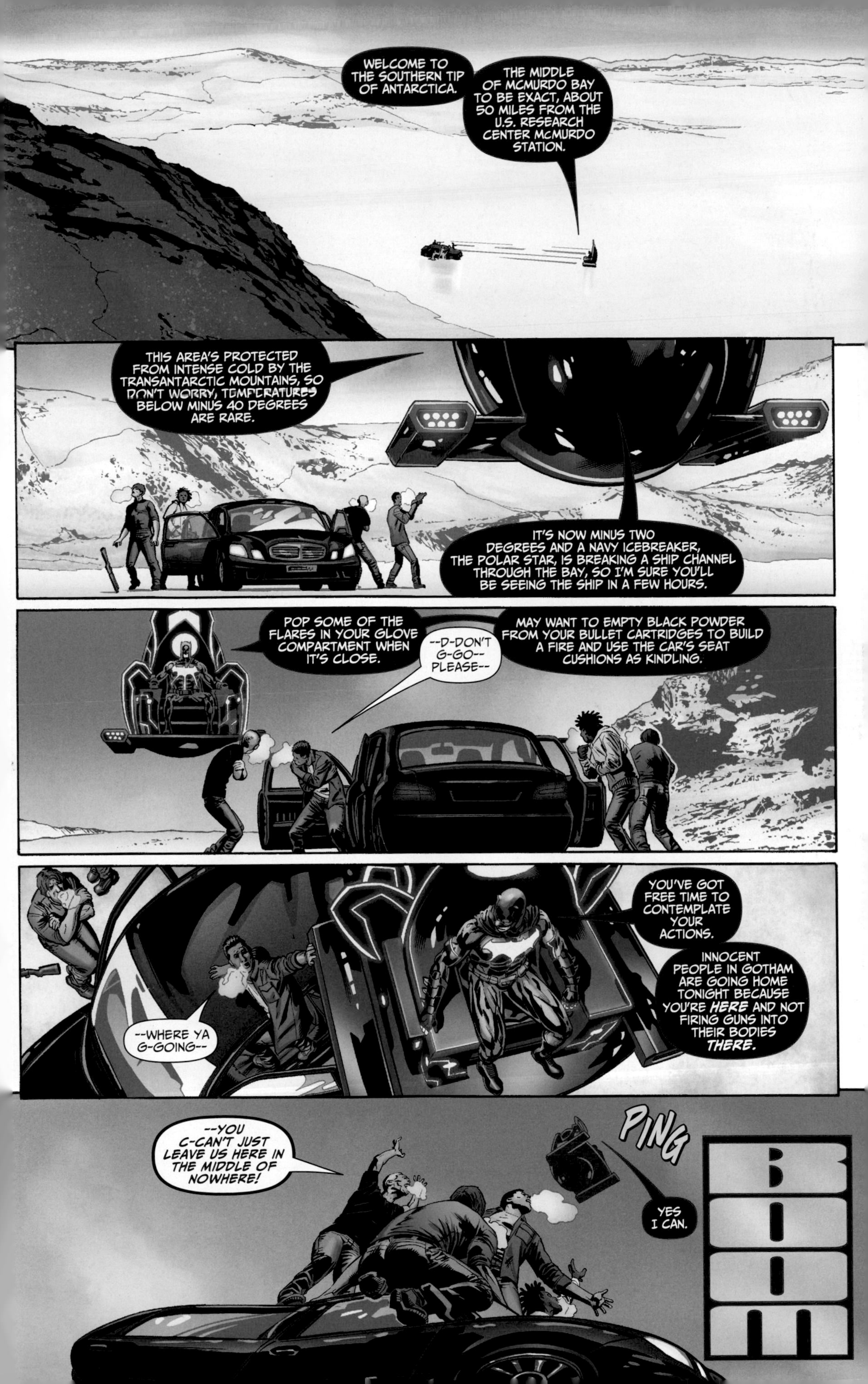
WELCOME TO THE SOUTHERN TIP OF ANTARCTICA.
THE MIDDLE OF MCMURDO BAY TO BE EXACT, ABOUT 50 MILES FROM THE U.S. RESEARCH CENTER MCMURDO STATION.
THIS AREA'S PROTECTED FROM INTENSE COLD BY THE TRANSANTARCTIC MOUNTAINS, SO DON'T WORRY, TEMPERATURES BELOW MINUS 40 DEGREES ARE RARE.
IT'S NOW MINUS TWO DEGREES AND A NAVY ICEBREAKER, THE POLAR STAR, IS BREAKING A SHIP CHANNEL THROUGH THE BAY, SO I'M SURE YOU'LL BE SEEING THE SHIP IN A FEW HOURS.
POP SOME OF THE FLARES IN YOUR GLOVE COMPARTMENT WHEN IT'S CLOSE.
--D-DON'T G-GO-- PLEASE--
MAY WANT TO EMPTY BLACK POWDER FROM YOUR BULLET CARTRIDGES TO BUILD A FIRE AND USE THE CAR'S SEAT CUSHIONS AS KINDLING.
YOU'VE GOT FREE TIME TO CONTEMPLATE YOUR ACTIONS.
INNOCENT PEOPLE IN GOTHAM ARE GOING HOME TONIGHT BECAUSE YOU'RE HERE AND NOT FIRING GUNS INTO THEIR BODIES THERE.
--WHERE YA G-GOING--
--YOU C-CAN'T JUST LEAVE US HERE IN THE MIDDLE OF NOWHERE!
PING
YES I CAN.
BOOM

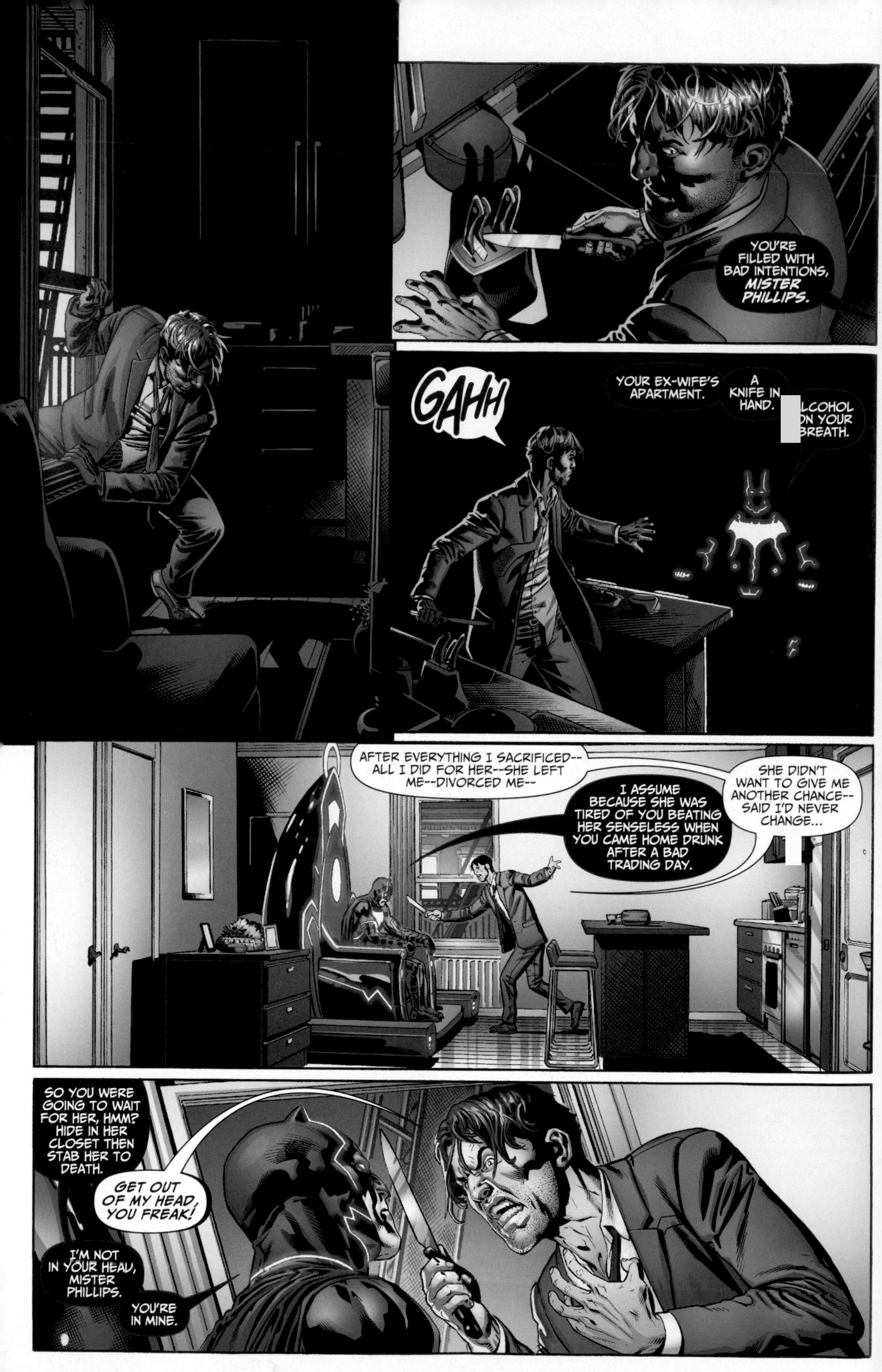
YOU'RE FILLED WITH BAD INTENTIONS, MISTER PHILLIPS.
GAHH
YOUR EX-WIFE'S APARTMENT.
A KNIFE IN HAND.
LCOHOL ON YOUR BREATH.
AFTER EVERYTHING I SACRIFICED-- ALL I DID FOR HER--SHE LEFT ME--DIVORCED ME--
SHE DIDN'T WANT TO GIVE ME ANOTHER CHANCE-- SAID I'D NEVER CHANGE...
I ASSUME BECAUSE SHE WAS TIRED OF YOU BEATING HER SENSELESS WHEN YOU CAME HOME DRUNK AFTER A BAD TRADING DAY.
SO YOU WERE GOING TO WAIT FOR HER, HMM? HIDE IN HER CLOSET THEN STAB HER TO DEATH.
GET OUT OF MY HEAD, YOU FREAK!
I'M NOT IN YOUR HEAD, MISTER PHILLIPS.
YOU'RE IN MINE.

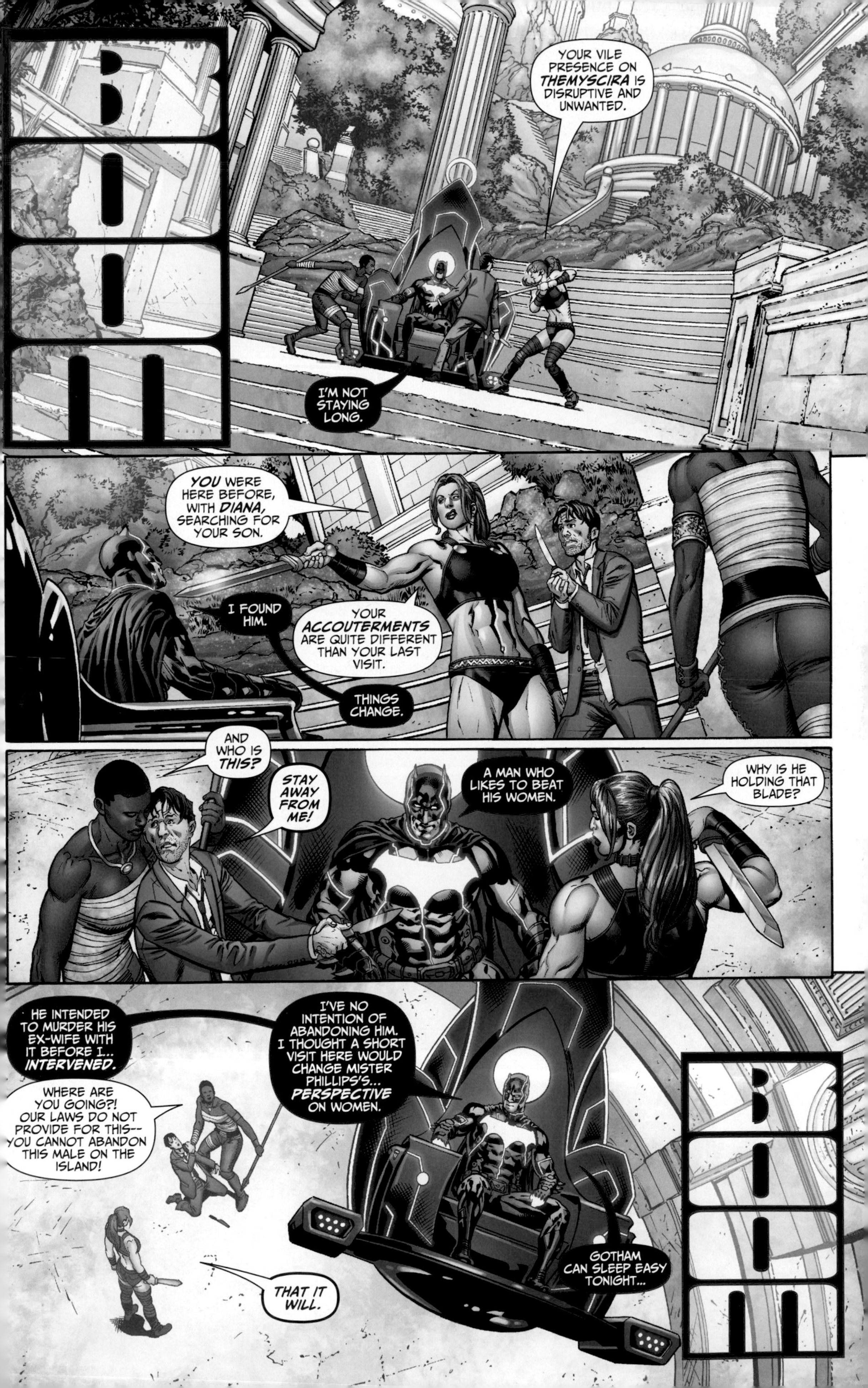
BOOM
YOUR VILE PRESENCE ON THEMYSCIRA IS DISRUPTIVE AND UNWANTED.
I'M NOT STAYING LONG.
YOU WERE HERE BEFORE, WITH DIANA, SEARCHING FOR YOUR SON.
I FOUND HIM.
YOUR ACCOUTERMENTS ARE QUITE DIFFERENT THAN YOUR LAST VISIT.
THINGS CHANGE.
AND WHO IS THIS?
STAY AWAY FROM ME!
A MAN WHO LIKES TO BEAT HIS WOMEN.
WHY IS HE HOLDING THAT BLADE?
HE INTENDED TO MURDER HIS EX-WIFE WITH IT BEFORE I... INTERVENED.
WHERE ARE YOU GOING?! OUR LAWS DO NOT PROVIDE FOR THIS-- YOU CANNOT ABANDON THIS MALE ON THE ISLAND!
I'VE NO INTENTION OF ABANDONING HIM. I THOUGHT A SHORT VISIT HERE WOULD CHANGE MISTER PHILLIPS'S... PERSPECTIVE ON WOMEN.
THAT IT WILL.
GOTHAM CAN SLEEP EASY TONIGHT...
BOOM

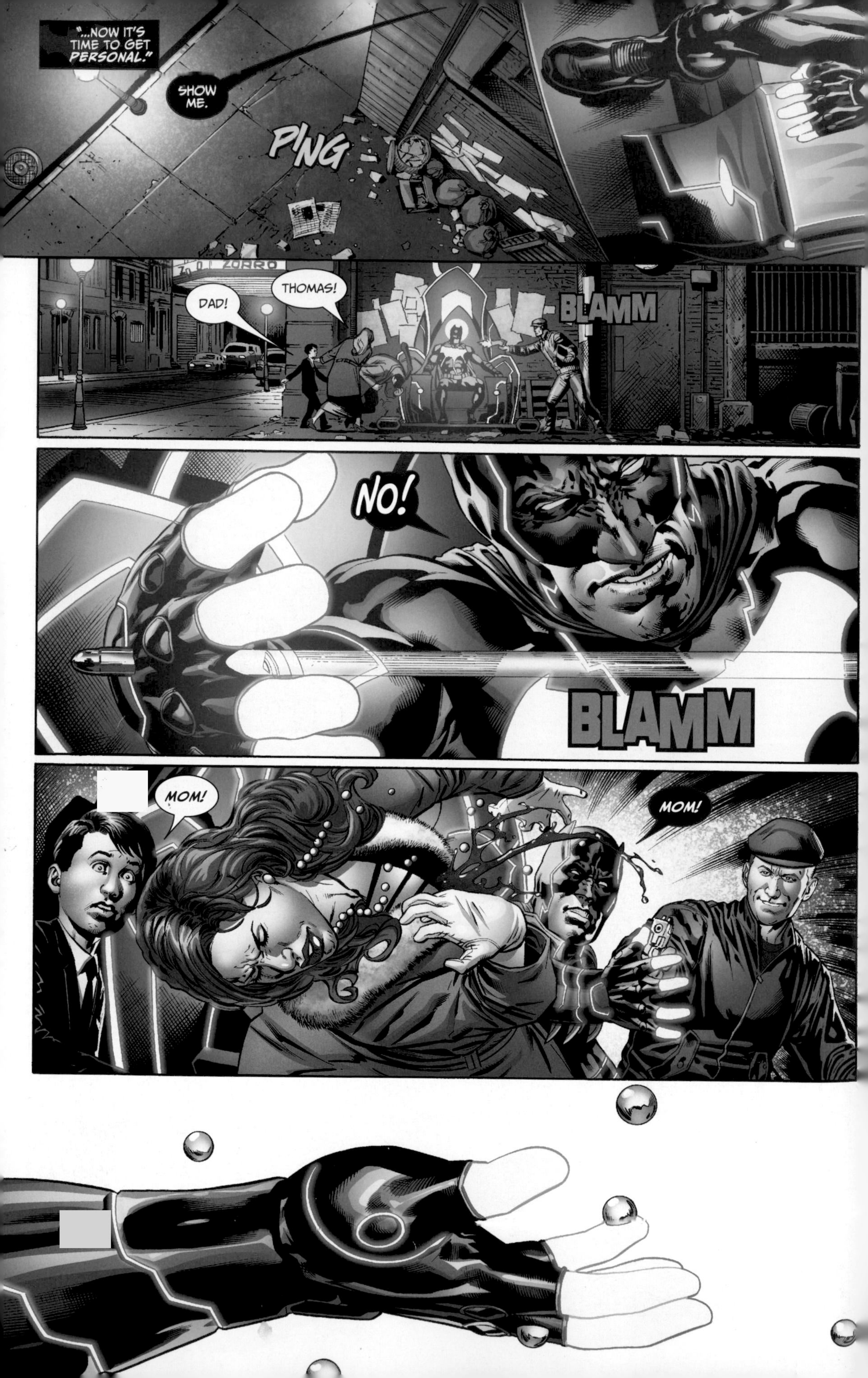
"...NOW IT'S TIME TO GET PERSONAL."
SHOW ME.
PING
ZORRO
DAD!
THOMAS!
BLAMM
NO!
BLAMM
MOM!
MOM!

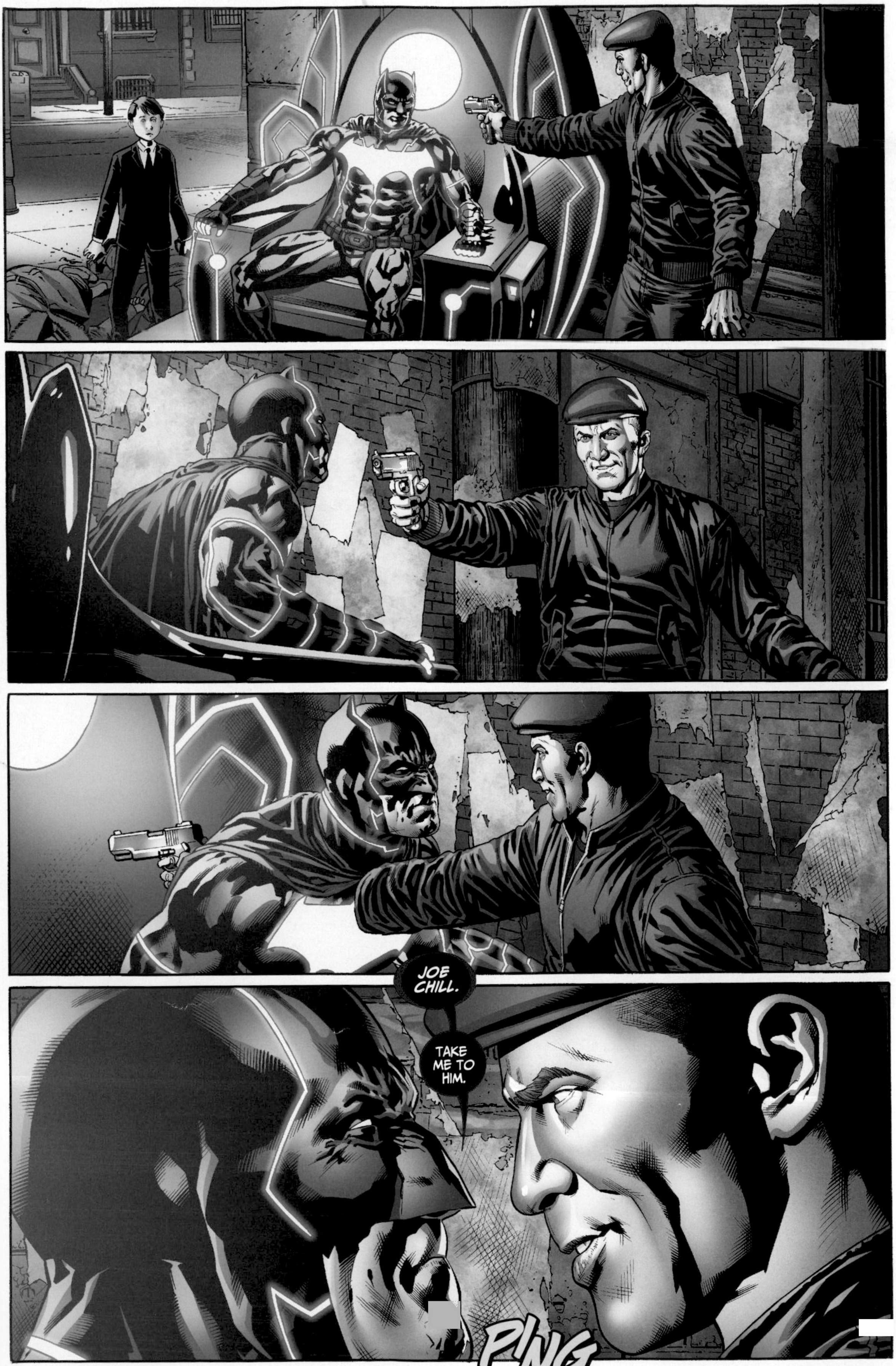
JOE CHILL.
TAKE ME TO HIM.
PING

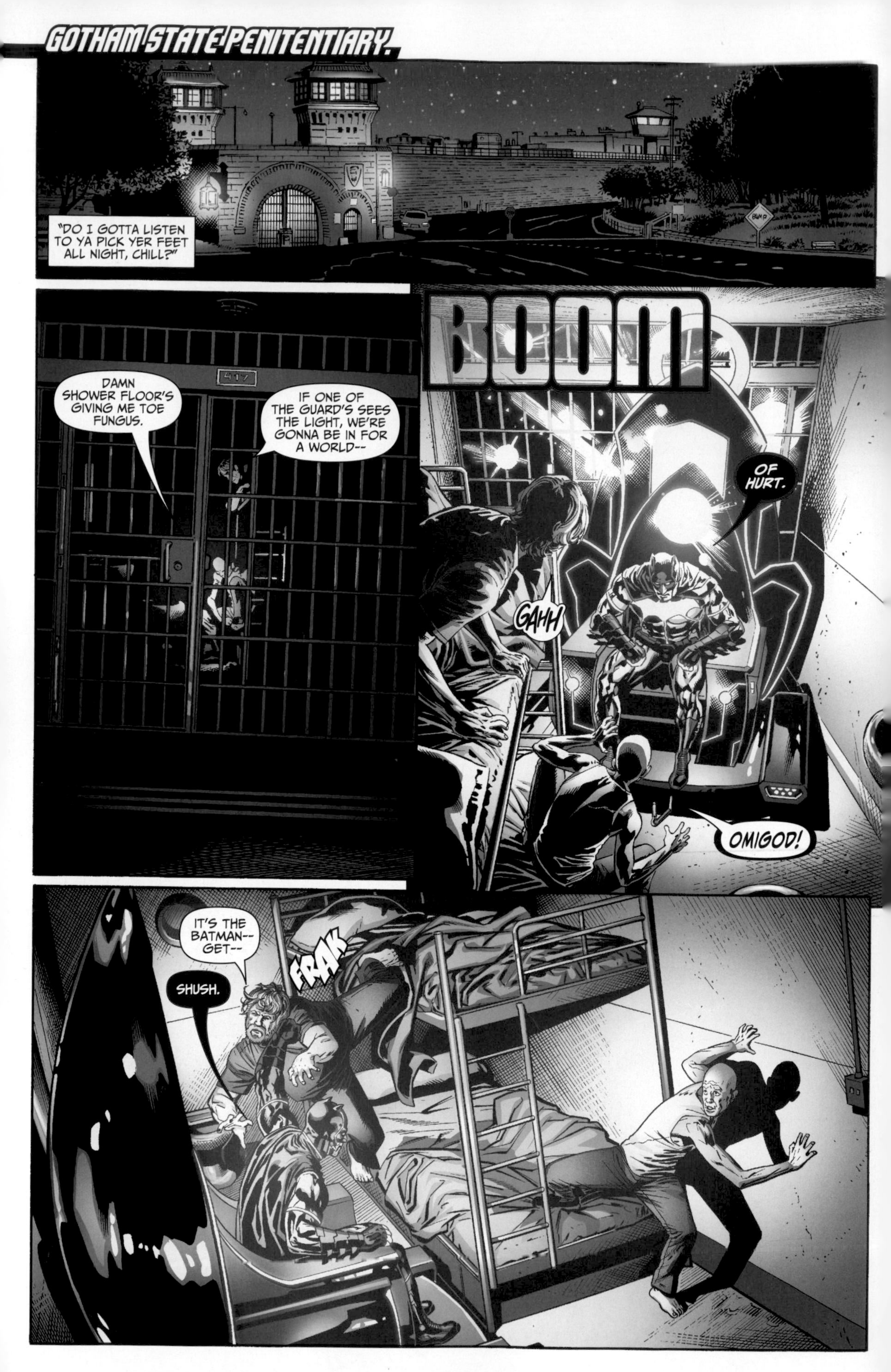
GOTHAM STATE PENITENTIARY.
"DO I GOTTA LISTEN TO YA PICK YER FEET ALL NIGHT, CHILL?"
DAMN SHOWER FLOOR'S GIVING ME TOE FUNGUS.
IF ONE OF THE GUARD'S SEES THE LIGHT, WE'RE GONNA BE IN FOR A WORLD--
BOOM
OF HURT.
GAHH
OMIGOD!
IT'S THE BATMAN-- GET--
FRAK
SHUSH.

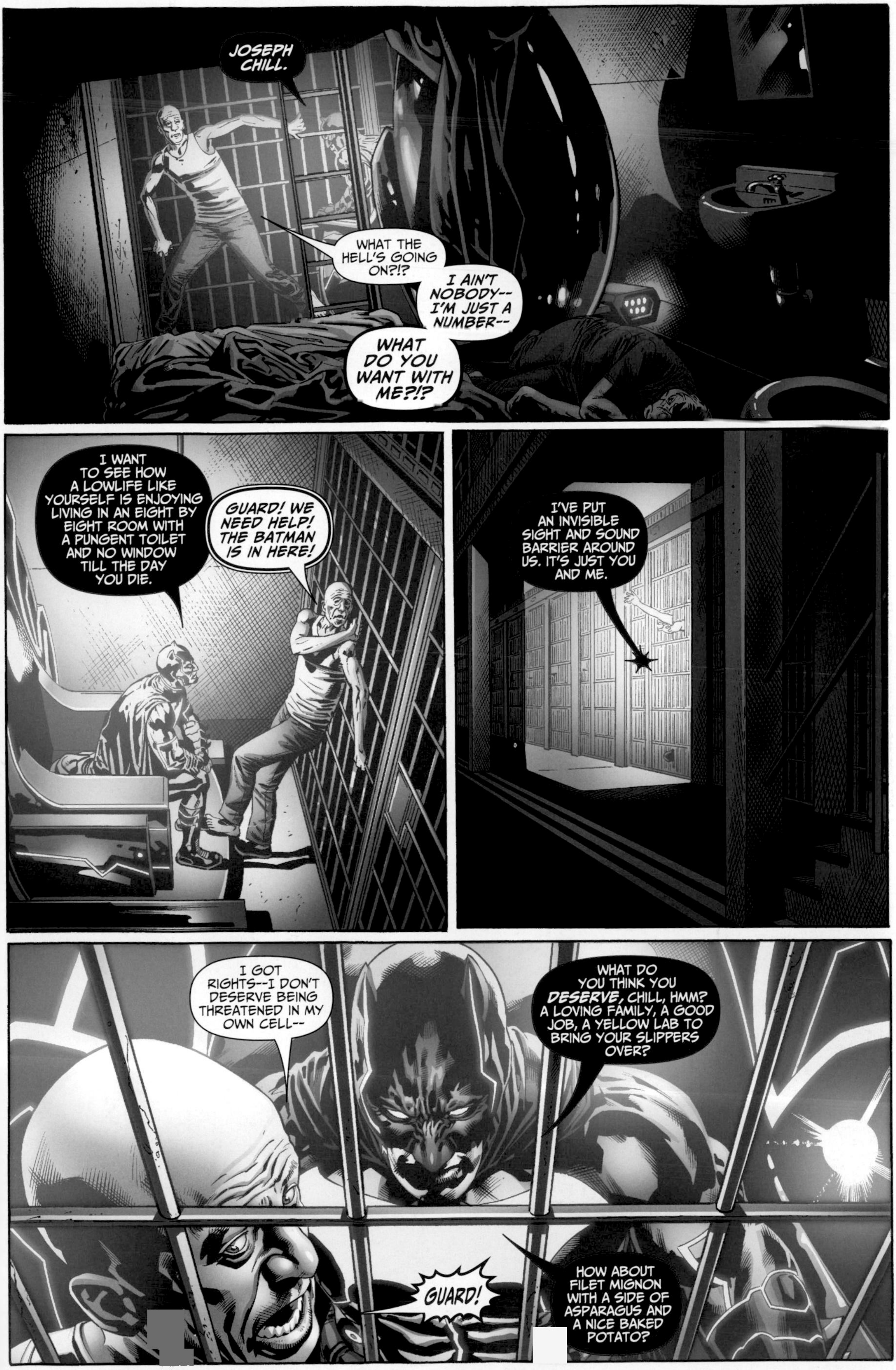
JOSEPH CHILL.
WHAT THE HELL'S GOING ON?!?
I AIN'T NOBODY--I'M JUST A NUMBER--
WHAT DO YOU WANT WITH ME?!?
I WANT TO SEE HOW A LOWLIFE LIKE YOURSELF IS ENJOYING LIVING IN AN EIGHT BY EIGHT ROOM WITH A PUNGENT TOILET AND NO WINDOW TILL THE DAY YOU DIE.
GUARD! WE NEED HELP! THE BATMAN IS IN HERE!
I'VE PUT AN INVISIBLE SIGHT AND SOUND BARRIER AROUND US. IT'S JUST YOU AND ME.
I GOT RIGHTS--I DON'T DESERVE BEING THREATENED IN MY OWN CELL--
WHAT DO YOU THINK YOU DESERVE, CHILL, HMM? A LOVING FAMILY, A GOOD JOB, A YELLOW LAB TO BRING YOUR SLIPPERS OVER?
GUARD!
HOW ABOUT FILET MIGNON WITH A SIDE OF ASPARAGUS AND A NICE BAKED POTATO?

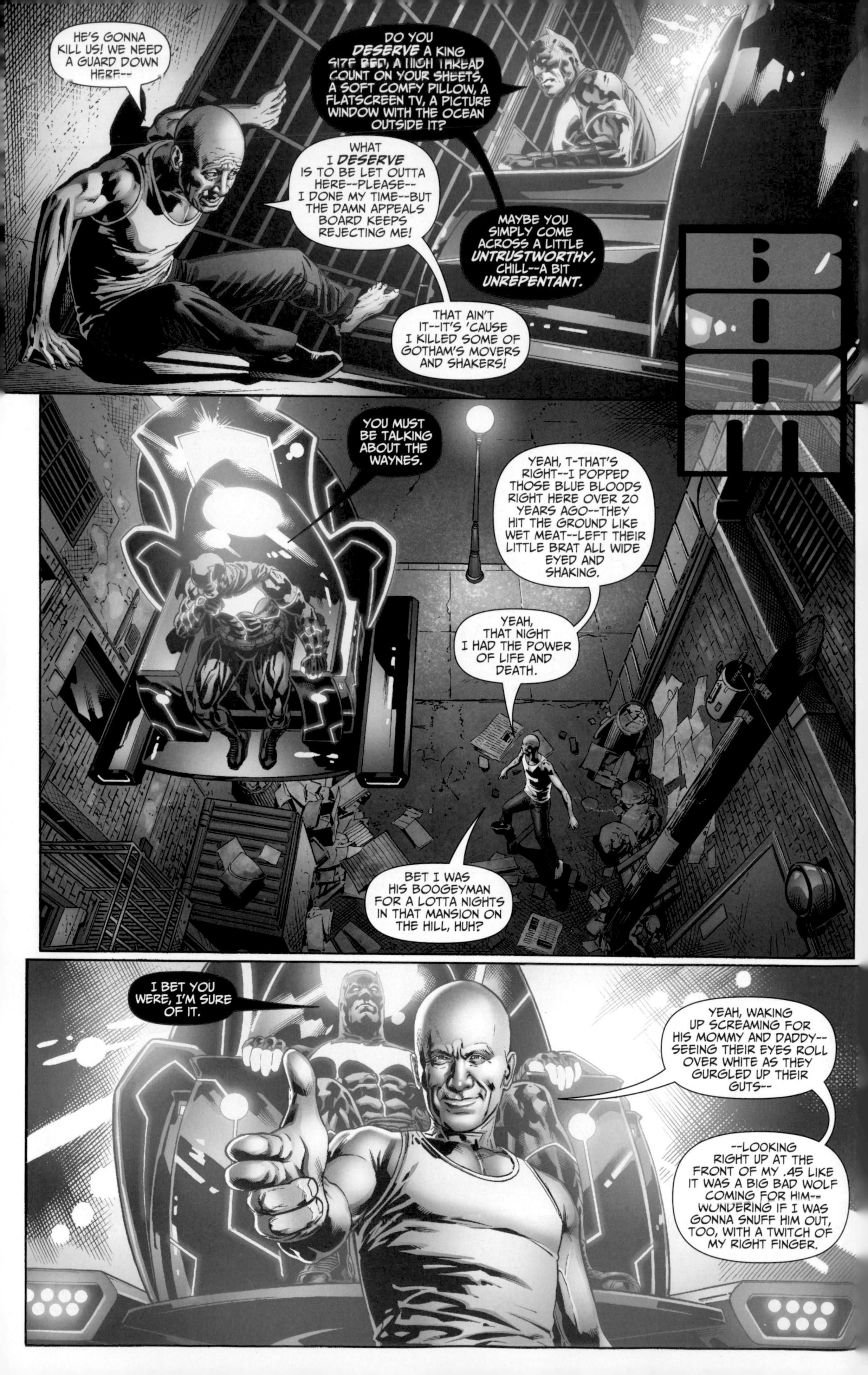
HE'S GONNA KILL US! WE NEED A GUARD DOWN HERE--
DO YOU DESERVE A KING SIZE BED, A HIGH THREAD COUNT ON YOUR SHEETS, A SOFT COMFY PILLOW, A FLATSCREEN TV, A PICTURE WINDOW WITH THE OCEAN OUTSIDE IT?
WHAT I DESERVE IS TO BE LET OUTTA HERE--PLEASE-- I DONE MY TIME--BUT THE DAMN APPEALS BOARD KEEPS REJECTING ME!
MAYBE YOU SIMPLY COME ACROSS A LITTLE UNTRUSTWORTHY, CHILL--A BIT UNREPENTANT.
THAT AIN'T IT--IT'S 'CAUSE I KILLED SOME OF GOTHAM'S MOVERS AND SHAKERS!
YOU MUST BE TALKING ABOUT THE WAYNES.
YEAH, T-THAT'S RIGHT--I POPPED THOSE BLUE BLOODS RIGHT HERE OVER 20 YEARS AGO--THEY HIT THE GROUND LIKE WET MEAT--LEFT THEIR LITTLE BRAT ALL WIDE EYED AND SHAKING.
YEAH, THAT NIGHT I HAD THE POWER OF LIFE AND DEATH.
BET I WAS HIS BOOGEYMAN FOR A LOTTA NIGHTS IN THAT MANSION ON THE HILL, HUH?
I BET YOU WERE, I'M SURE OF IT.
YEAH, WAKING UP SCREAMING FOR HIS MOMMY AND DADDY-- SEEING THEIR EYES ROLL OVER WHITE AS THEY GURGLED UP THEIR GUTS--
--LOOKING RIGHT UP AT THE FRONT OF MY .45 LIKE IT WAS A BIG BAD WOLF COMING FOR HIM-- WUNDERING IF I WAS GONNA SNUFF HIM OUT, TOO, WITH A TWITCH OF MY RIGHT FINGER.

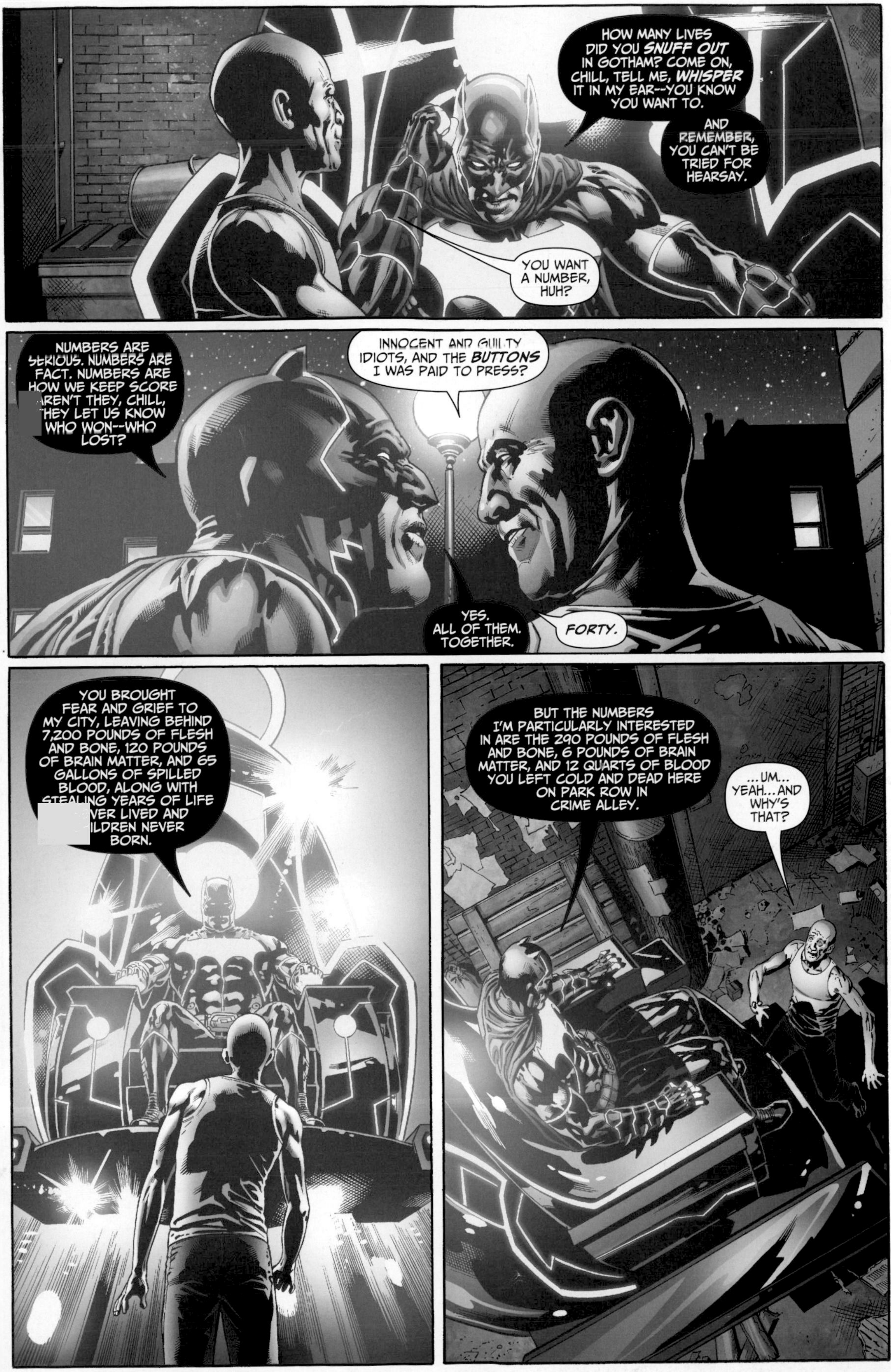

HOW MANY LIVES DID YOU **SNUFF OUT** IN GOTHAM? COME ON, CHILL, TELL ME, **WHISPER** IT IN MY EAR--YOU KNOW YOU WANT TO.
AND REMEMBER, YOU CAN'T BE TRIED FOR HEARSAY.
YOU WANT A NUMBER, HUH?
NUMBERS ARE SERIOUS. NUMBERS ARE FACT. NUMBERS ARE HOW WE KEEP SCORE AREN'T THEY, CHILL, THEY LET US KNOW WHO WON--WHO LOST?
INNOCENT AND GUILTY IDIOTS, AND THE **BUTTONS** I WAS PAID TO PRESS?
YES. ALL OF THEM. TOGETHER.
FORTY.
YOU BROUGHT FEAR AND GRIEF TO MY CITY, LEAVING BEHIND 7,200 POUNDS OF FLESH AND BONE, 120 POUNDS OF BRAIN MATTER, AND 65 GALLONS OF SPILLED BLOOD, ALONG WITH STEALING YEARS OF LIFE
VER LIVED AND
ILDREN NEVER
BORN.
BUT THE NUMBERS I'M PARTICULARLY INTERESTED IN ARE THE 290 POUNDS OF FLESH AND BONE, 6 POUNDS OF BRAIN MATTER, AND 12 QUARTS OF BLOOD YOU LEFT COLD AND DEAD HERE ON PARK ROW IN CRIME ALLEY.
...UM... YEAH...AND WHY'S THAT?

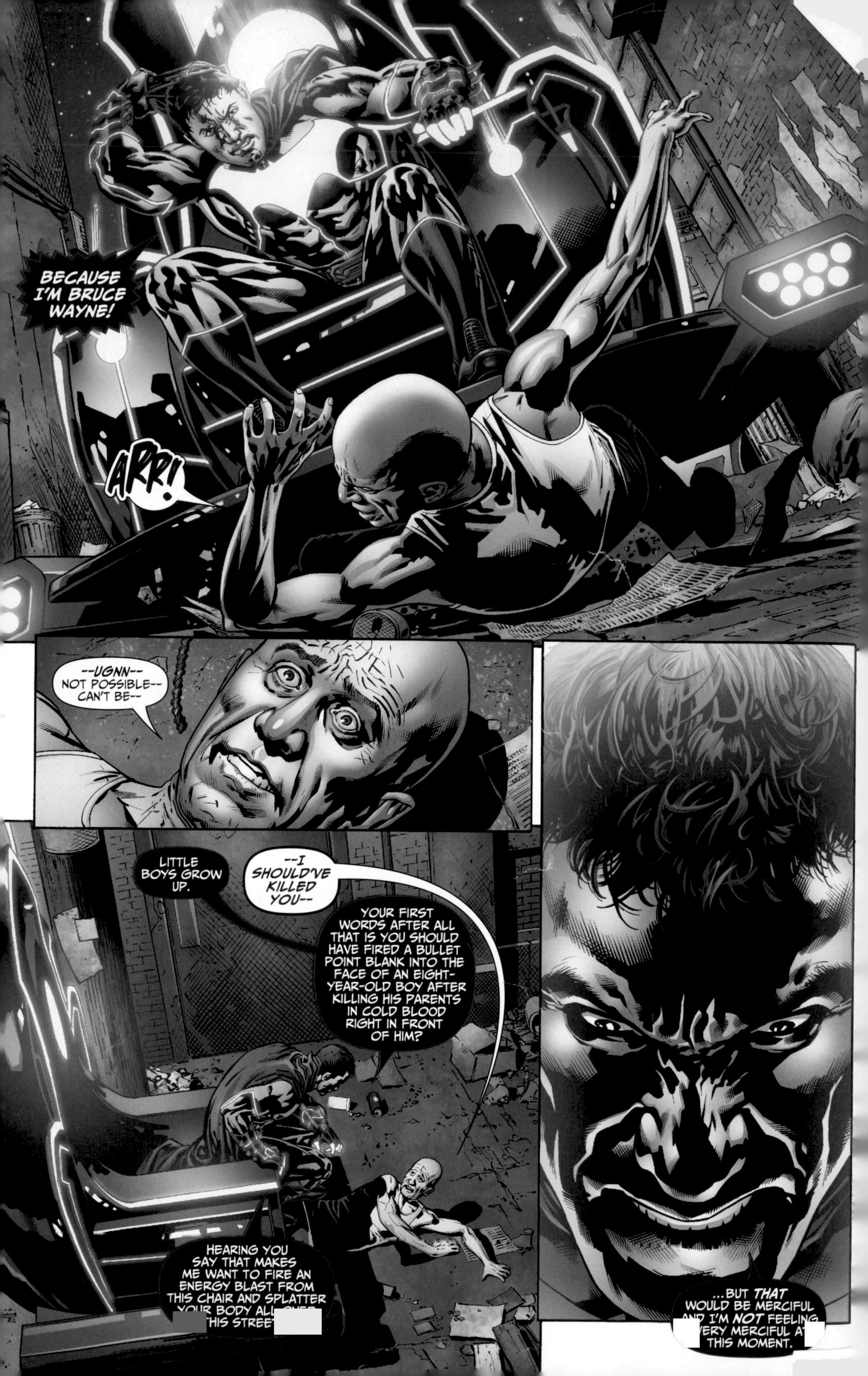
BECAUSE I'M BRUCE WAYNE!
ARR!
--UGNN-- NOT POSSIBLE-- CAN'T BE--
LITTLE BOYS GROW UP.
--I SHOULD'VE KILLED YOU--
YOUR FIRST WORDS AFTER ALL THAT IS YOU SHOULD HAVE FIRED A BULLET POINT BLANK INTO THE FACE OF AN EIGHT-YEAR-OLD BOY AFTER KILLING HIS PARENTS IN COLD BLOOD RIGHT IN FRONT OF HIM?
HEARING YOU SAY THAT MAKES ME WANT TO FIRE AN ENERGY BLAST FROM THIS CHAIR AND SPLATTER YOUR BODY ALL OVER THIS STREE
...BUT THAT WOULD BE MERCIFUL AND I'M NOT FEELING VERY MERCIFUL AT THIS MOMENT.

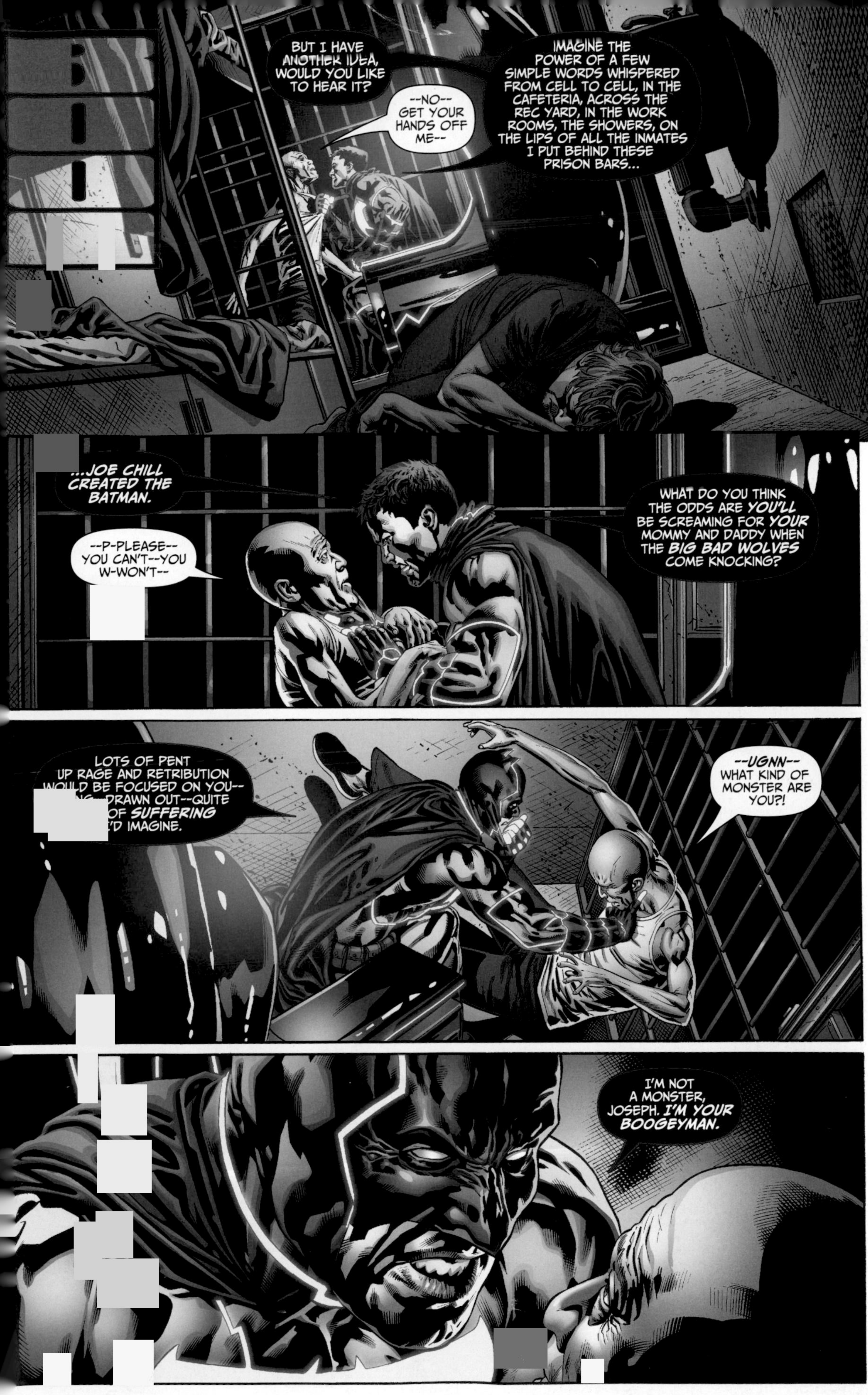
BUT I HAVE ANOTHER IDEA, WOULD YOU LIKE TO HEAR IT?
--NO-- GET YOUR HANDS OFF ME--
IMAGINE THE POWER OF A FEW SIMPLE WORDS WHISPERED FROM CELL TO CELL, IN THE CAFETERIA, ACROSS THE REC YARD, IN THE WORK ROOMS, THE SHOWERS, ON THE LIPS OF ALL THE INMATES I PUT BEHIND THESE PRISON BARS...
...JOE CHILL CREATED THE BATMAN.
--P-PLEASE-- YOU CAN'T--YOU W-WON'T--
WHAT DO YOU THINK THE ODDS ARE *YOU'LL* BE SCREAMING FOR *YOUR* MOMMY AND DADDY WHEN THE *BIG BAD WOLVES* COME KNOCKING?
LOTS OF PENT UP RAGE AND RETRIBUTION WOULD BE FOCUSED ON YOU-- DRAWN OUT--QUITE OF *SUFFERING* IMAGINE.
--UGNN-- WHAT KIND OF MONSTER ARE YOU?!
I'M NOT A MONSTER, JOSEPH. *I'M YOUR BOOGEYMAN.*

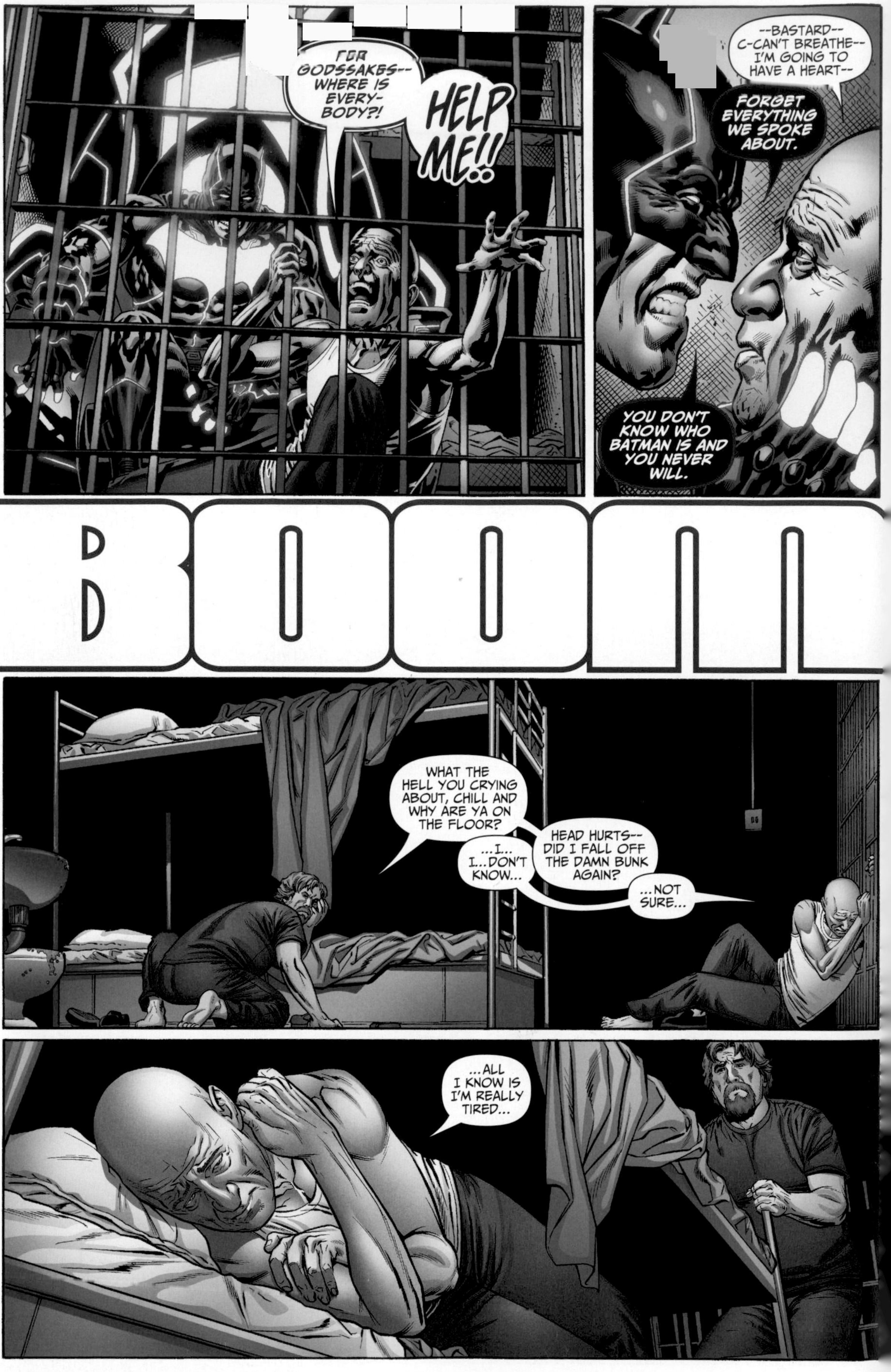
FOR GODSSAKES-- WHERE IS EVERY-BODY?!
HELP ME!!
--BASTARD-- C-CAN'T BREATHE-- I'M GOING TO HAVE A HEART--
FORGET EVERYTHING WE SPOKE ABOUT.
YOU DON'T KNOW WHO BATMAN IS AND YOU NEVER WILL.
BOOM
WHAT THE HELL YOU CRYING ABOUT, CHILL AND WHY ARE YA ON THE FLOOR?
HEAD HURTS-- DID I FALL OFF THE DAMN BUNK AGAIN?
...I... I...DON'T KNOW...
...NOT SURE...
...ALL I KNOW IS I'M REALLY TIRED...

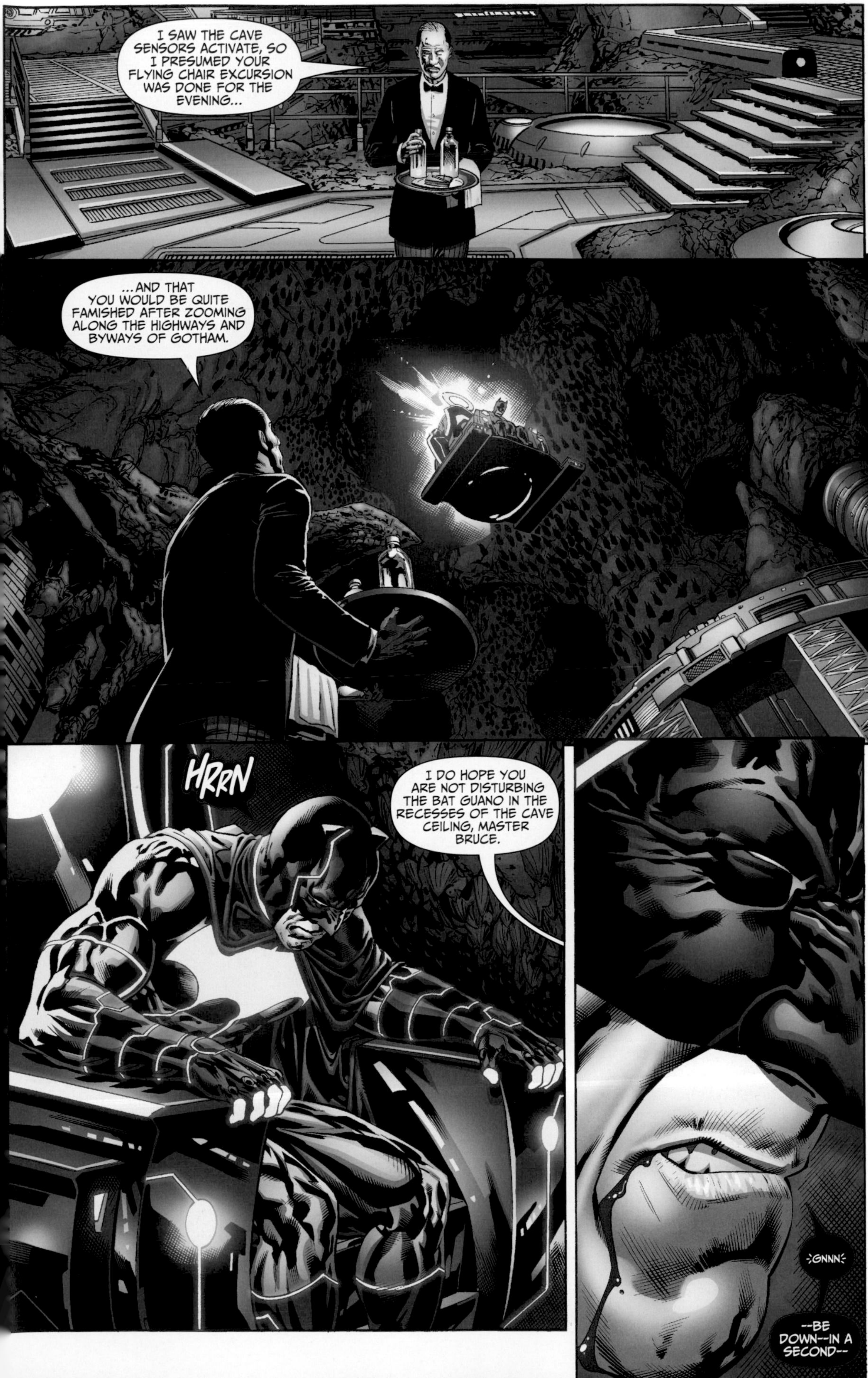
I SAW THE CAVE SENSORS ACTIVATE, SO I PRESUMED YOUR FLYING CHAIR EXCURSION WAS DONE FOR THE EVENING...
...AND THAT YOU WOULD BE QUITE FAMISHED AFTER ZOOMING ALONG THE HIGHWAYS AND BYWAYS OF GOTHAM.
HRRN
I DO HOPE YOU ARE NOT DISTURBING THE BAT GUANO IN THE RECESSES OF THE CAVE CEILING, MASTER BRUCE.
GNNN
--BE DOWN--IN A SECOND--

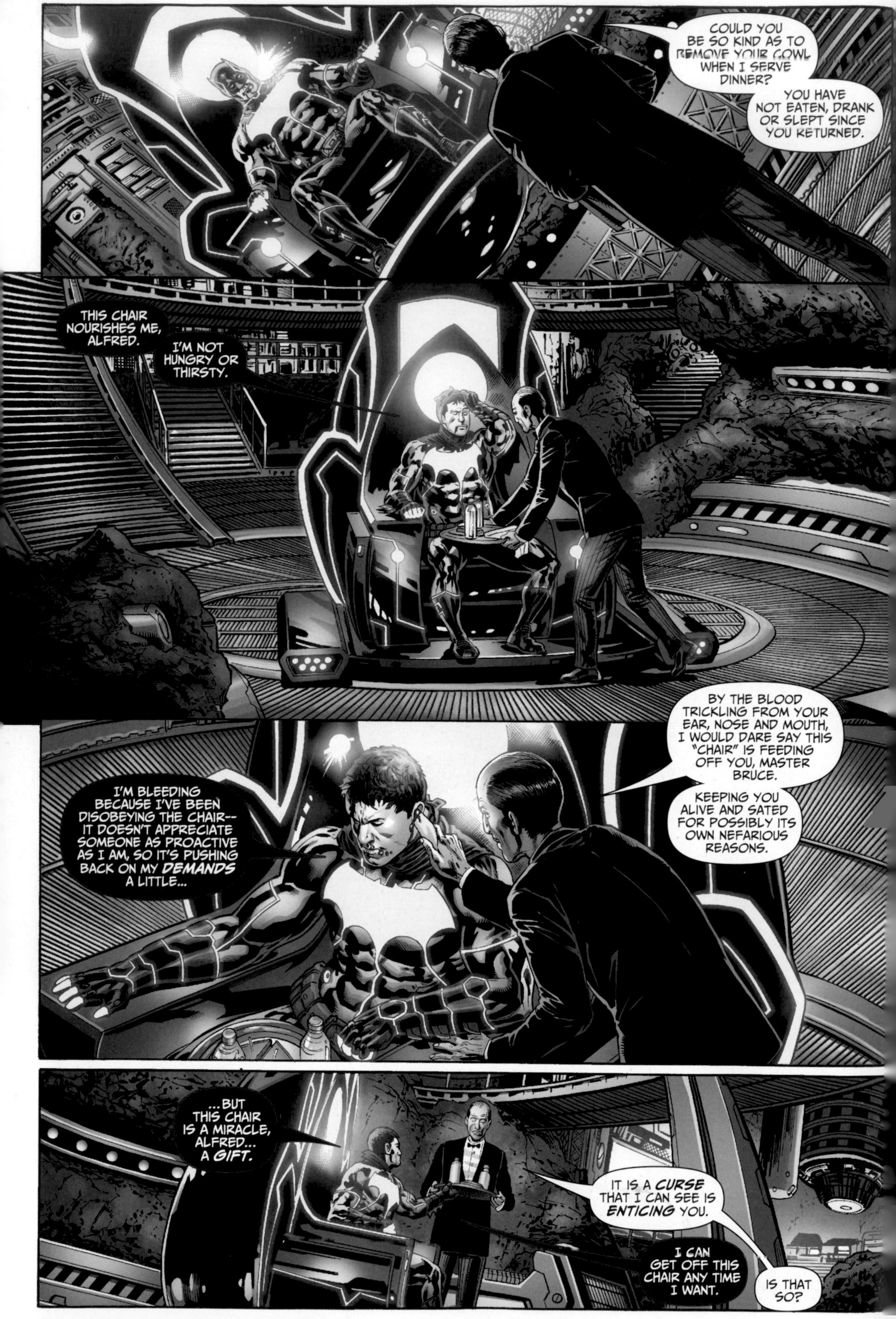
COULD YOU BE SO KIND AS TO REMOVE YOUR COWL WHEN I SERVE DINNER?
YOU HAVE NOT EATEN, DRANK OR SLEPT SINCE YOU RETURNED.
THIS CHAIR NOURISHES ME, ALFRED.
I'M NOT HUNGRY OR THIRSTY.
BY THE BLOOD TRICKLING FROM YOUR EAR, NOSE AND MOUTH, I WOULD DARE SAY THIS "CHAIR" IS FEEDING OFF YOU, MASTER BRUCE.
KEEPING YOU ALIVE AND SATED FOR POSSIBLY ITS OWN NEFARIOUS REASONS.
I'M BLEEDING BECAUSE I'VE BEEN DISOBEYING THE CHAIR-- IT DOESN'T APPRECIATE SOMEONE AS PROACTIVE AS I AM, SO IT'S PUSHING BACK ON MY *DEMANDS* A LITTLE...
...BUT THIS CHAIR IS A MIRACLE, ALFRED... A *GIFT*.
IT IS A *CURSE* THAT I CAN SEE IS *ENTICING* YOU.
I CAN GET OFF THIS CHAIR ANY TIME I WANT.
IS THAT SO?

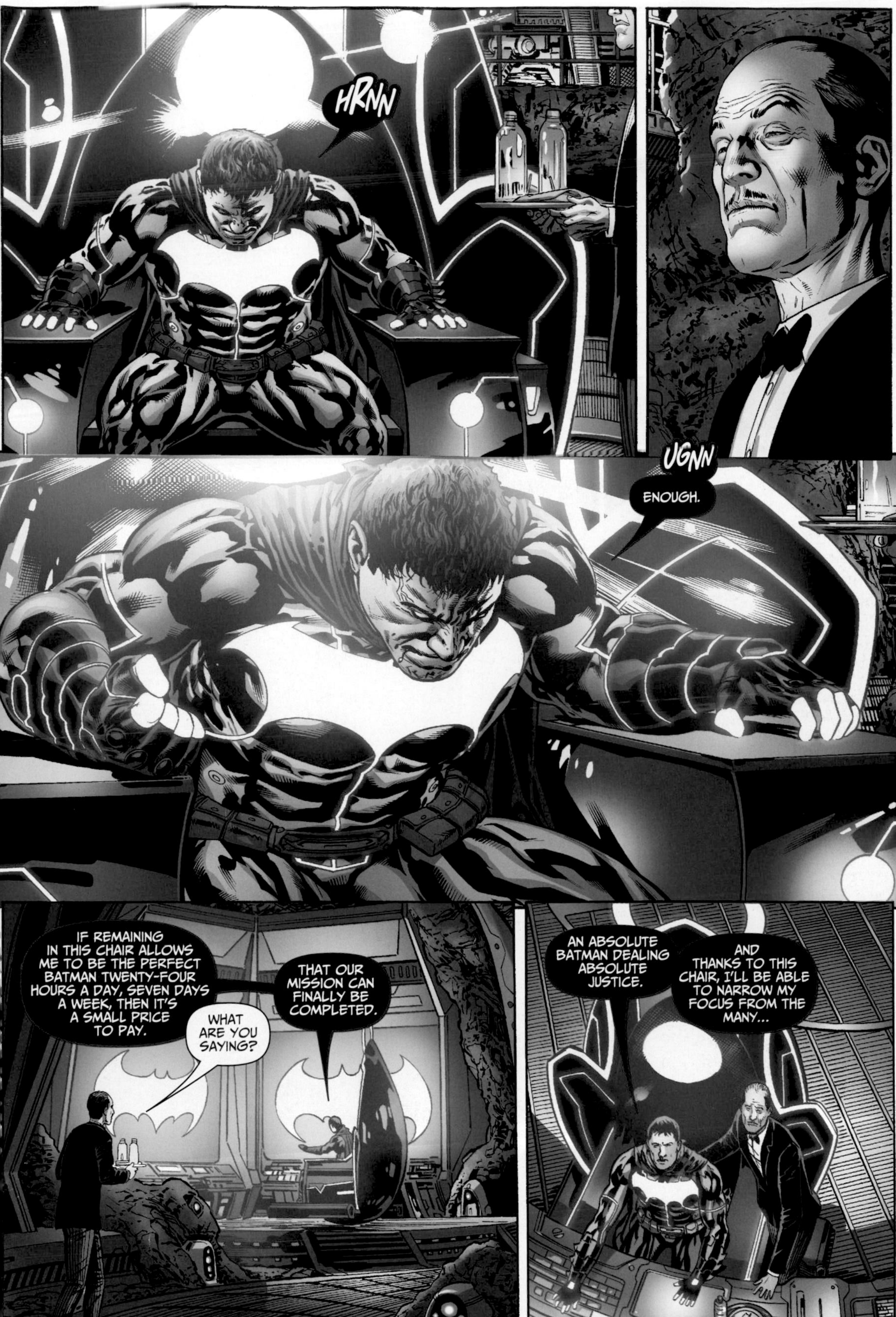
HRNN
UGNN
ENOUGH.
IF REMAINING IN THIS CHAIR ALLOWS ME TO BE THE PERFECT BATMAN TWENTY-FOUR HOURS A DAY, SEVEN DAYS A WEEK, THEN IT'S A SMALL PRICE TO PAY.
WHAT ARE YOU SAYING?
THAT OUR MISSION CAN FINALLY BE COMPLETED.
AN ABSOLUTE BATMAN DEALING ABSOLUTE JUSTICE.
AND THANKS TO THIS CHAIR, I'LL BE ABLE TO NARROW MY FOCUS FROM THE MANY...

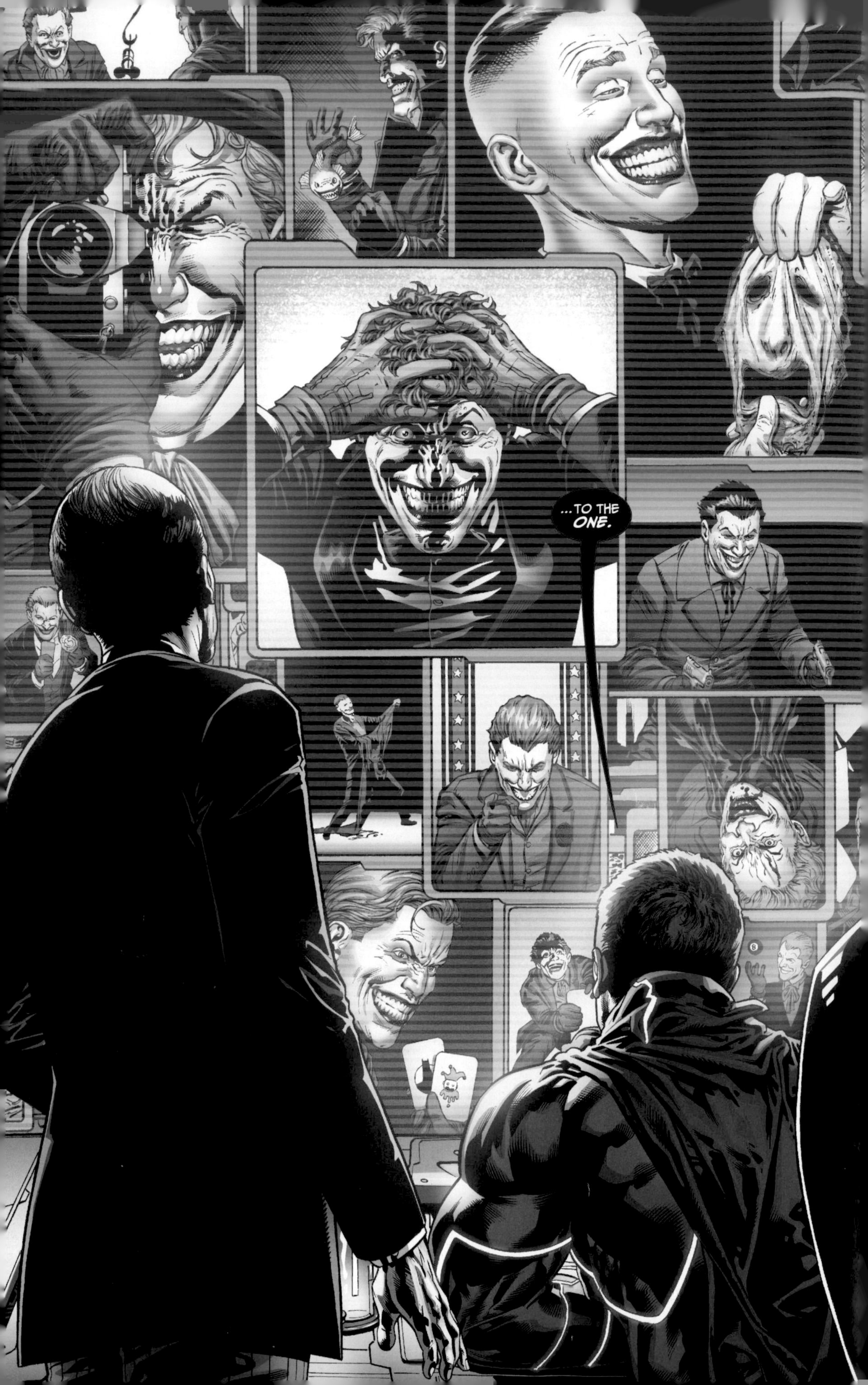
...TO THE *ONE.*

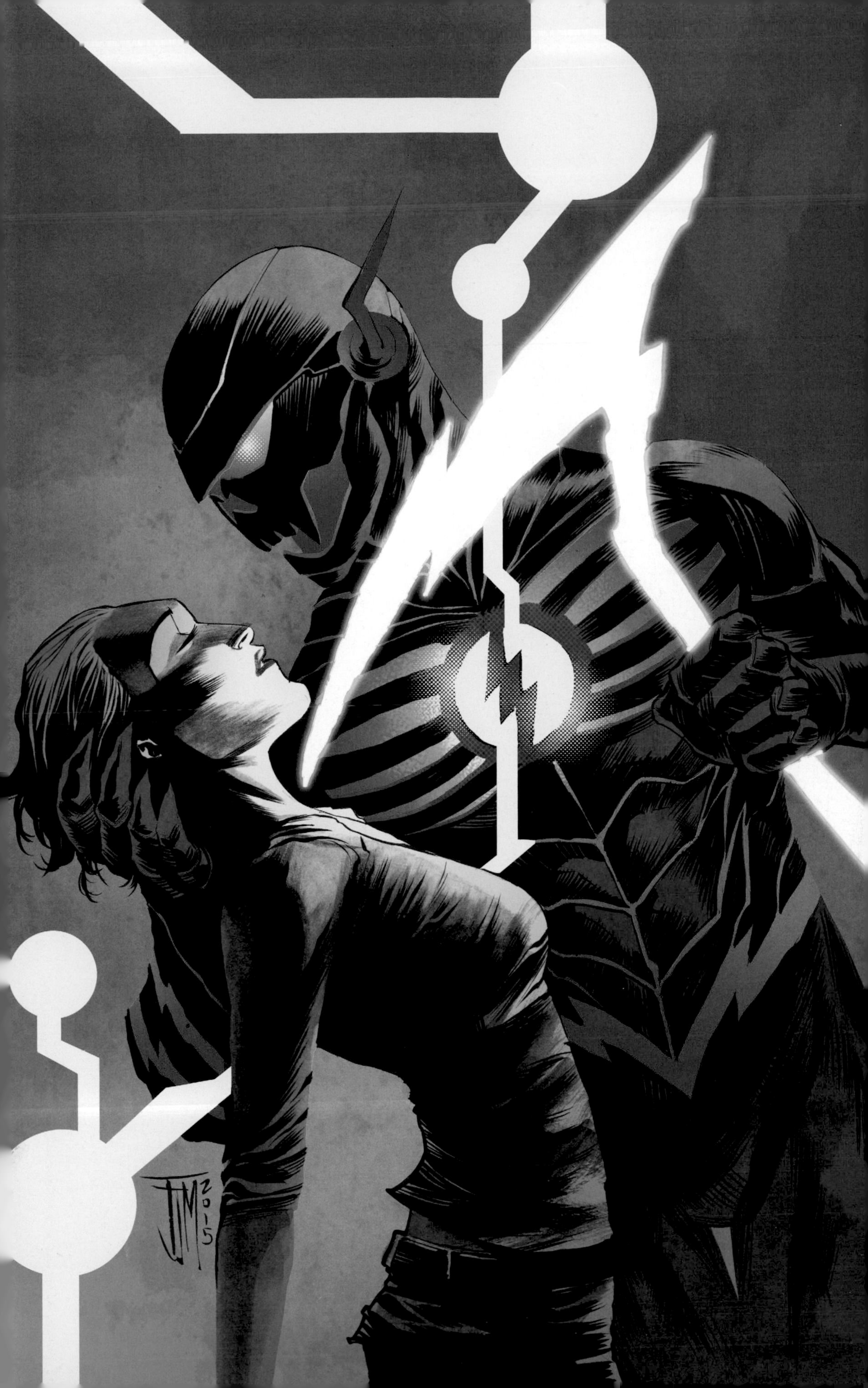

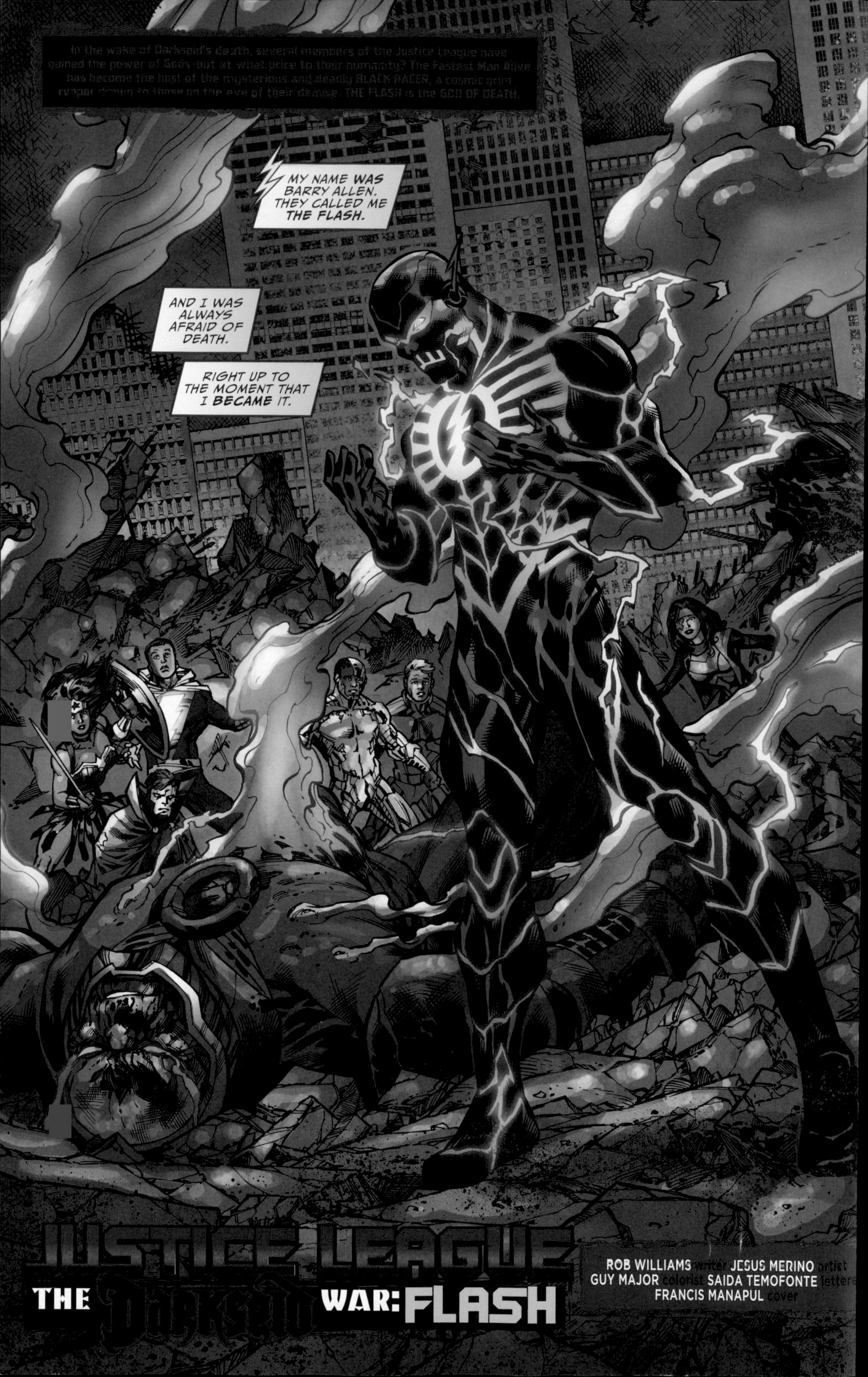
In the wake of Darkseid's death, several members of the Justice League have gained the power of Gods–but at what price to their humanity? The Fastest Man Alive has become the host of the mysterious and deadly BLACK RACER, a cosmic grim reaper drawn to those on the eve of their demise. THE FLASH is the GOD OF DEATH.
MY NAME WAS BARRY ALLEN. THEY CALLED ME THE FLASH.
AND I WAS ALWAYS AFRAID OF DEATH.
RIGHT UP TO THE MOMENT THAT I BECAME IT.
JUSTICE LEAGUE
THE DARKSEID WAR: FLASH
ROB WILLIAMS writer JESUS MERINO artist
GUY MAJOR colorist SAIDA TEMOFONTE letters
FRANCIS MANAPUL cover

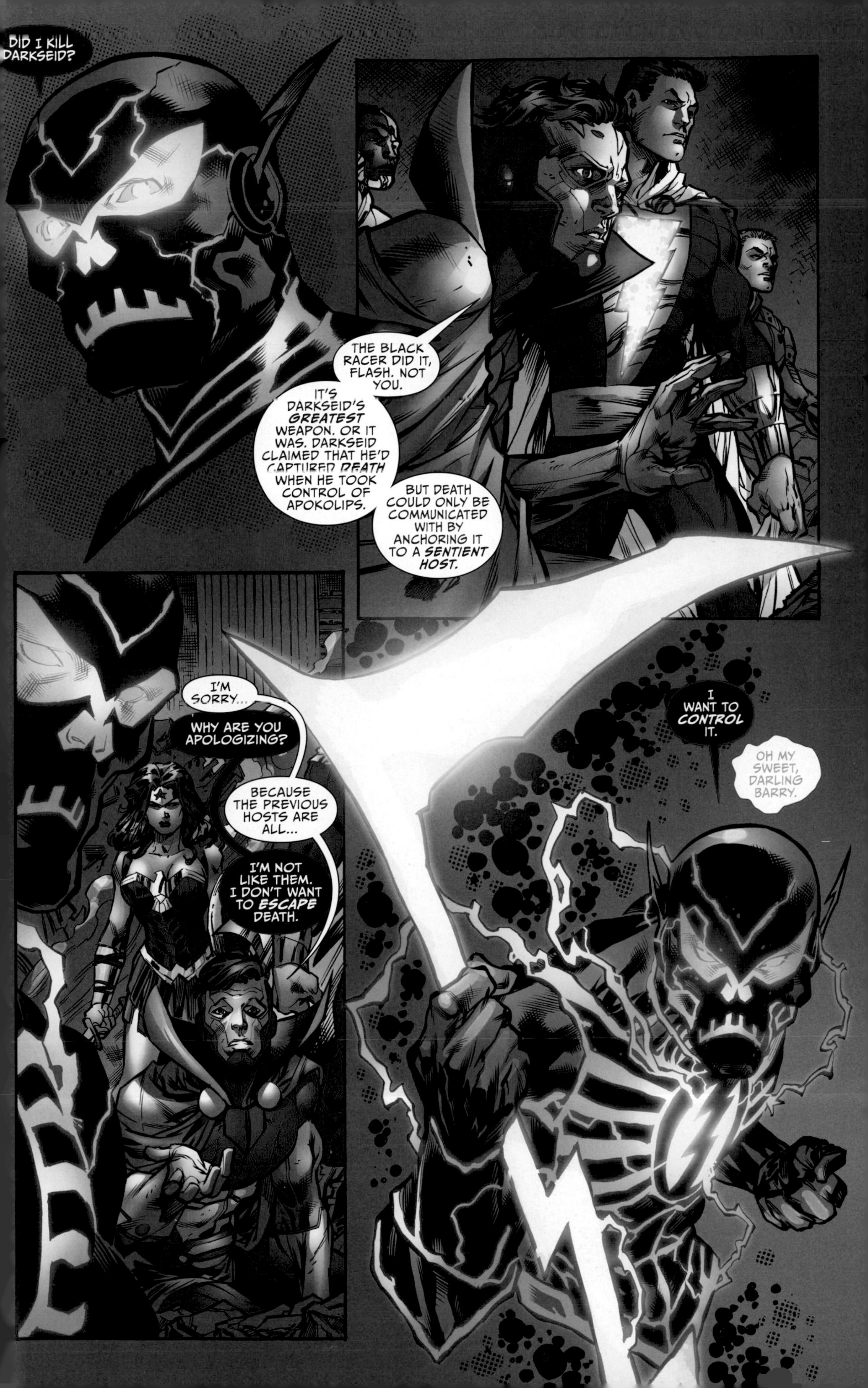
DID I KILL DARKSEID?
THE BLACK RACER DID IT, FLASH. NOT YOU.
IT'S DARKSEID'S GREATEST WEAPON. OR IT WAS. DARKSEID CLAIMED THAT HE'D CAPTURED DEATH WHEN HE TOOK CONTROL OF APOKOLIPS.
BUT DEATH COULD ONLY BE COMMUNICATED WITH BY ANCHORING IT TO A SENTIENT HOST.
I'M SORRY...
WHY ARE YOU APOLOGIZING?
BECAUSE THE PREVIOUS HOSTS ARE ALL...
I'M NOT LIKE THEM. I DON'T WANT TO ESCAPE DEATH.
I WANT TO CONTROL IT.
OH MY SWEET, DARLING BARRY.

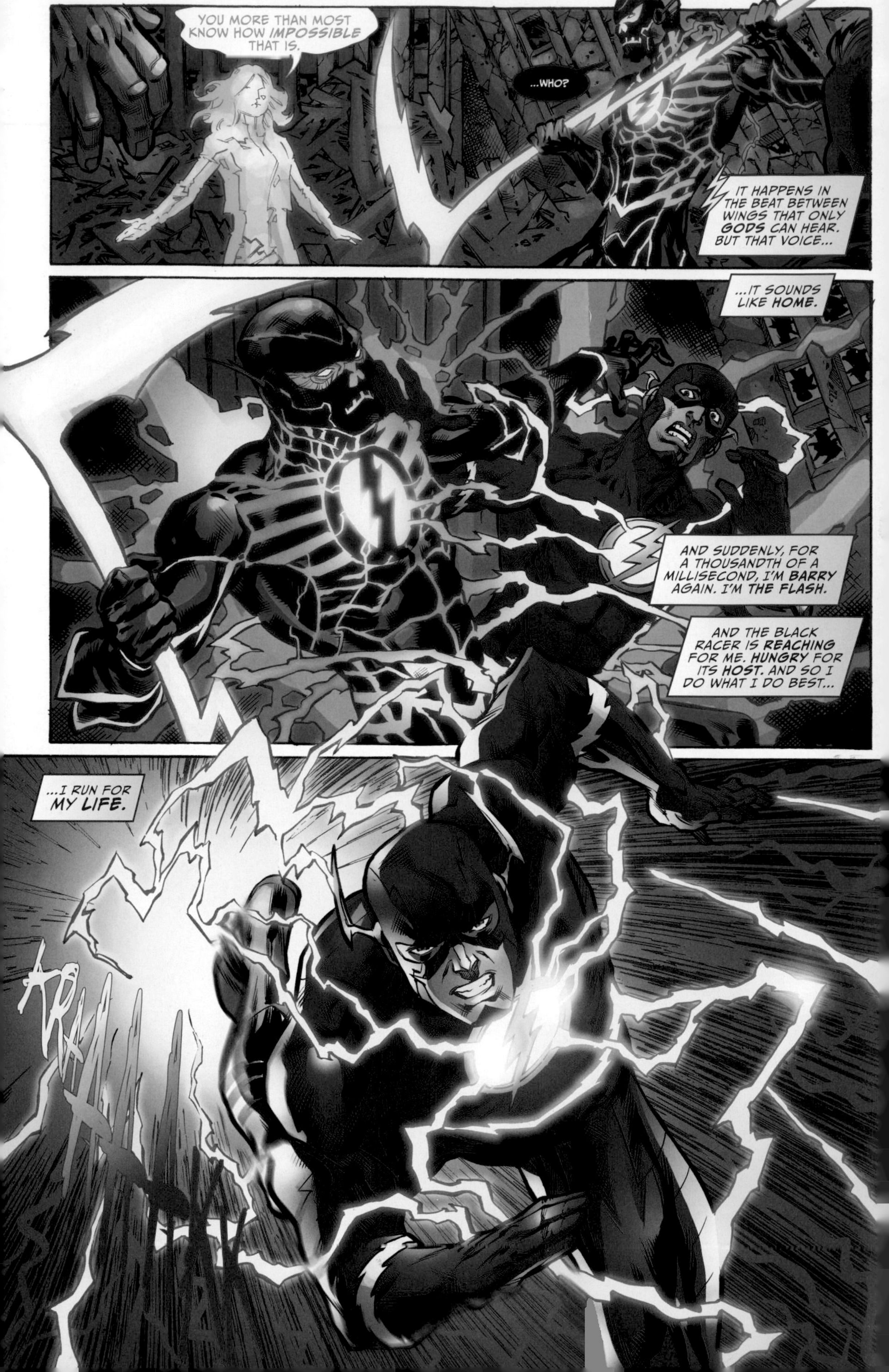

YOU MORE THAN MOST KNOW HOW IMPOSSIBLE THAT IS.
...WHO?
IT HAPPENS IN THE BEAT BETWEEN WINGS THAT ONLY GODS CAN HEAR. BUT THAT VOICE...
...IT SOUNDS LIKE HOME.
AND SUDDENLY, FOR A THOUSANDTH OF A MILLISECOND, I'M BARRY AGAIN. I'M THE FLASH.
AND THE BLACK RACER IS REACHING FOR ME. HUNGRY FOR ITS HOST. AND SO I DO WHAT I DO BEST...
...I RUN FOR MY LIFE.

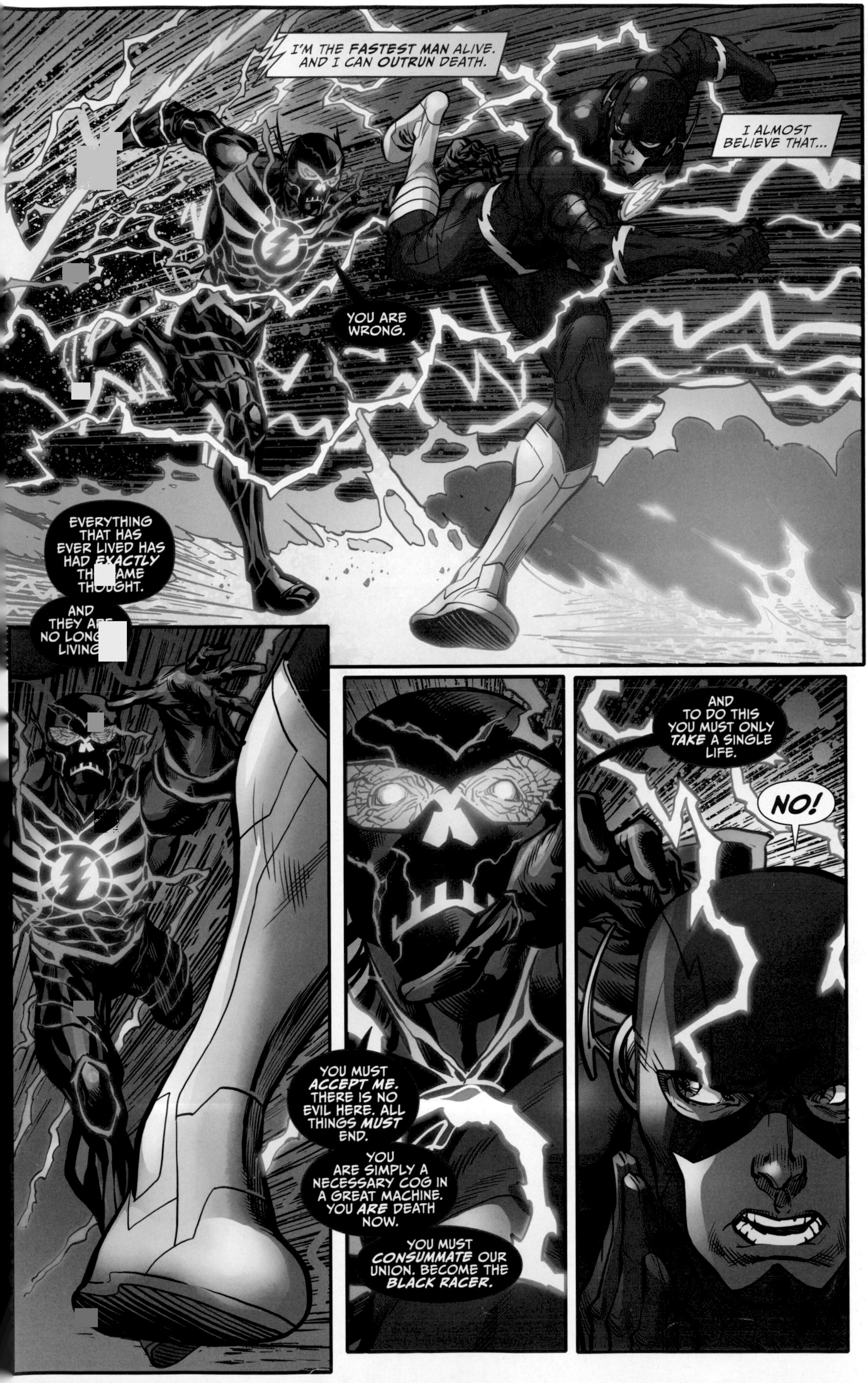

I'M THE FASTEST MAN ALIVE. AND I CAN OUTRUN DEATH.
I ALMOST BELIEVE THAT...
YOU ARE WRONG.
EVERYTHING THAT HAS EVER LIVED HAS HAD EXACTLY TH AME THO GHT.
AND THEY AR NO LONG LIVING
AND TO DO THIS YOU MUST ONLY TAKE A SINGLE LIFE.
NO!
YOU MUST ACCEPT ME. THERE IS NO EVIL HERE. ALL THINGS MUST END.
YOU ARE SIMPLY A NECESSARY COG IN A GREAT MACHINE. YOU ARE DEATH NOW.
YOU MUST CONSUMMATE OUR UNION. BECOME THE BLACK RACER.

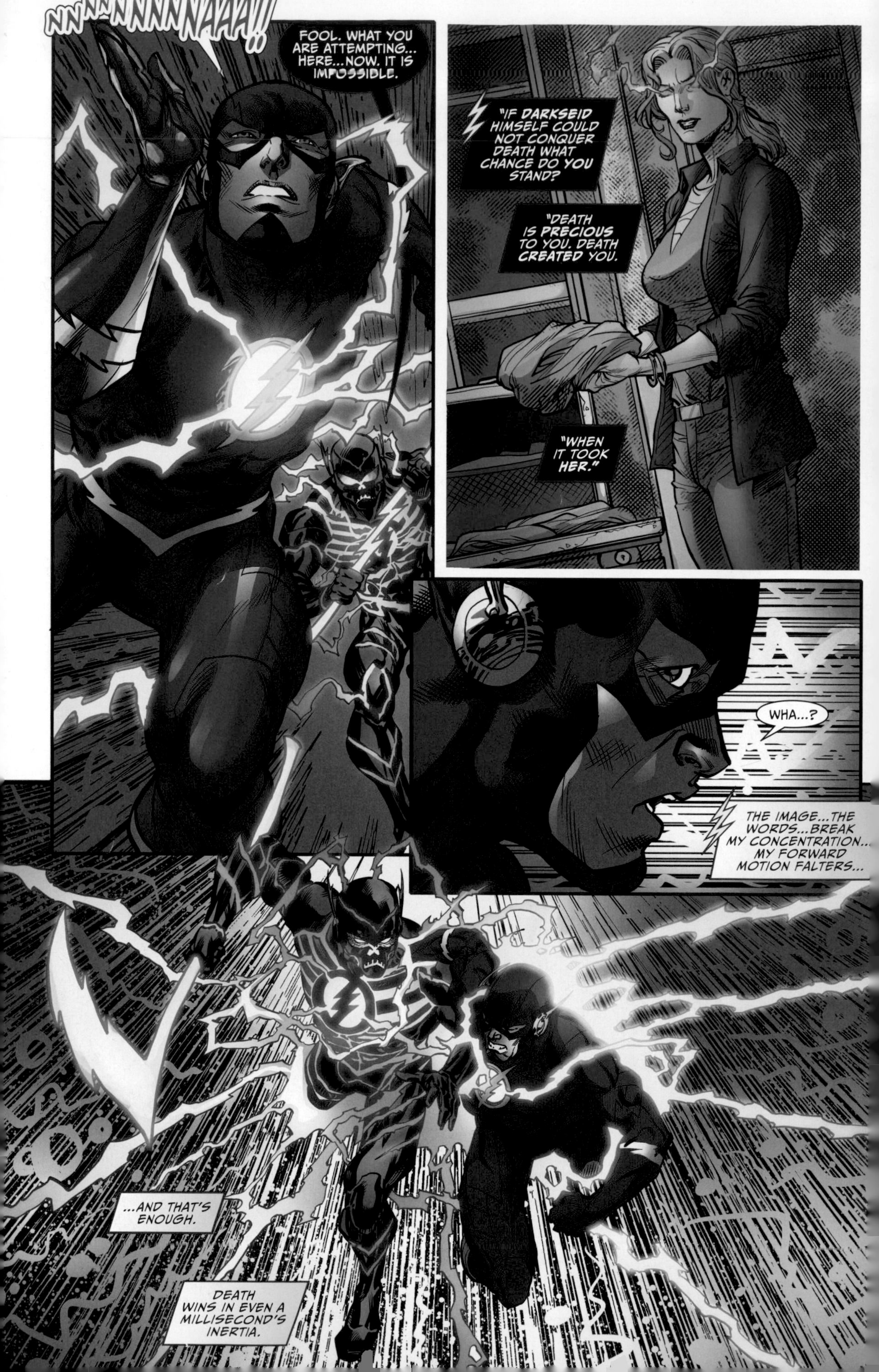

NNNNNNNNNNAAA!!
FOOL. WHAT YOU ARE ATTEMPTING... HERE...NOW. IT IS IMPOSSIBLE.
"IF DARKSEID HIMSELF COULD NOT CONQUER DEATH WHAT CHANCE DO YOU STAND?
"DEATH IS PRECIOUS TO YOU. DEATH CREATED YOU.
"WHEN IT TOOK HER."
WHA...?
THE IMAGE...THE WORDS...BREAK MY CONCENTRATION... MY FORWARD MOTION FALTERS...
...AND THAT'S ENOUGH.
DEATH WINS IN EVEN A MILLISECOND'S INERTIA.

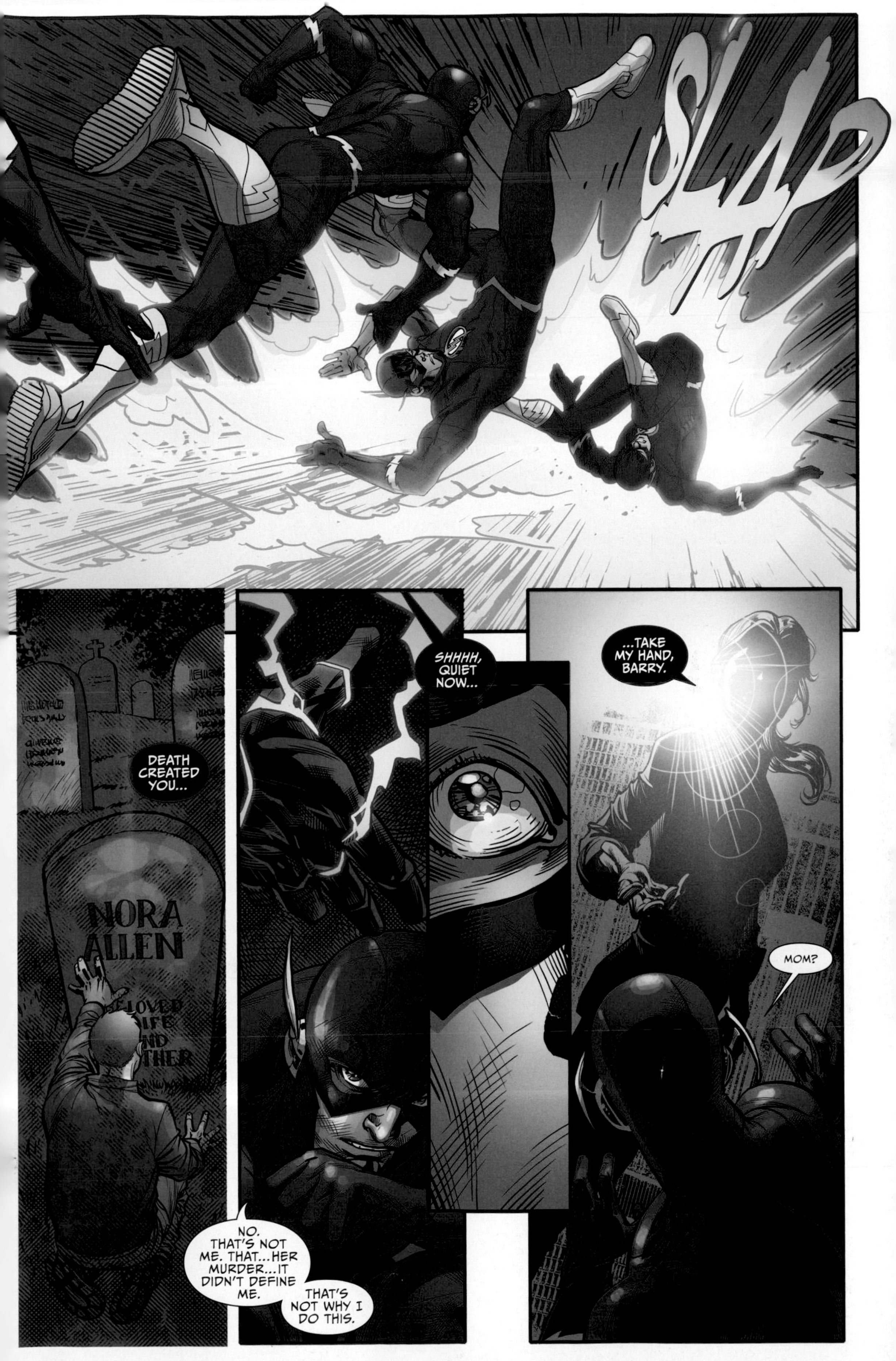
SLAP
DEATH CREATED YOU...
NO. THAT'S NOT ME. THAT...HER MURDER...IT DIDN'T DEFINE ME.
THAT'S NOT WHY I DO THIS.
NORA ALLEN
SHHHH, QUIET NOW...
...TAKE MY HAND, BARRY.
MOM?

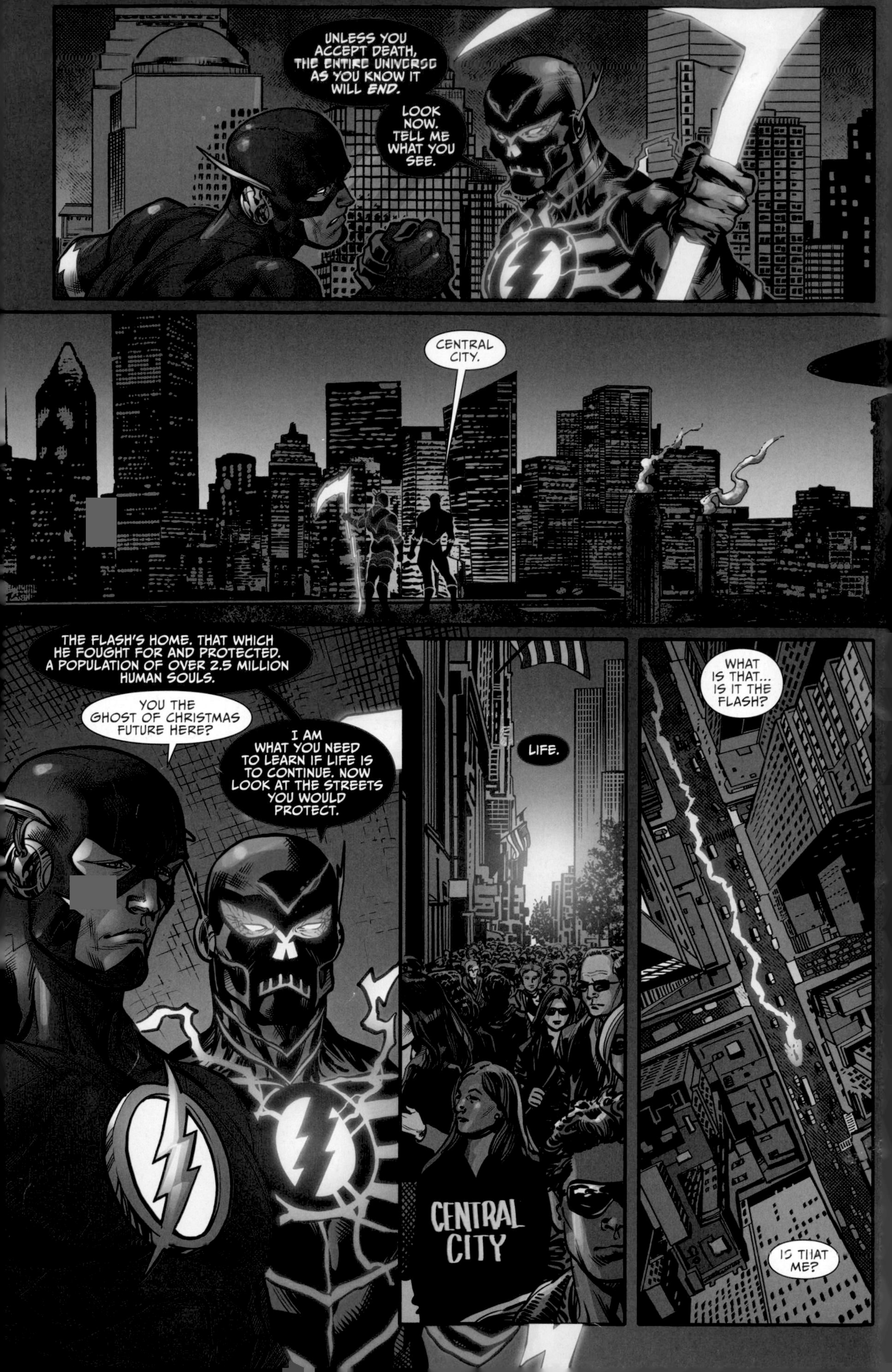
UNLESS YOU ACCEPT DEATH, THE ENTIRE UNIVERSE AS YOU KNOW IT WILL END.
LOOK NOW. TELL ME WHAT YOU SEE.
CENTRAL CITY.
THE FLASH'S HOME. THAT WHICH HE FOUGHT FOR AND PROTECTED. A POPULATION OF OVER 2.5 MILLION HUMAN SOULS.
YOU THE GHOST OF CHRISTMAS FUTURE HERE?
I AM WHAT YOU NEED TO LEARN IF LIFE IS TO CONTINUE. NOW LOOK AT THE STREETS YOU WOULD PROTECT.
LIFE.
CENTRAL CITY
WHAT IS THAT... IS IT THE FLASH?
IS THAT ME?

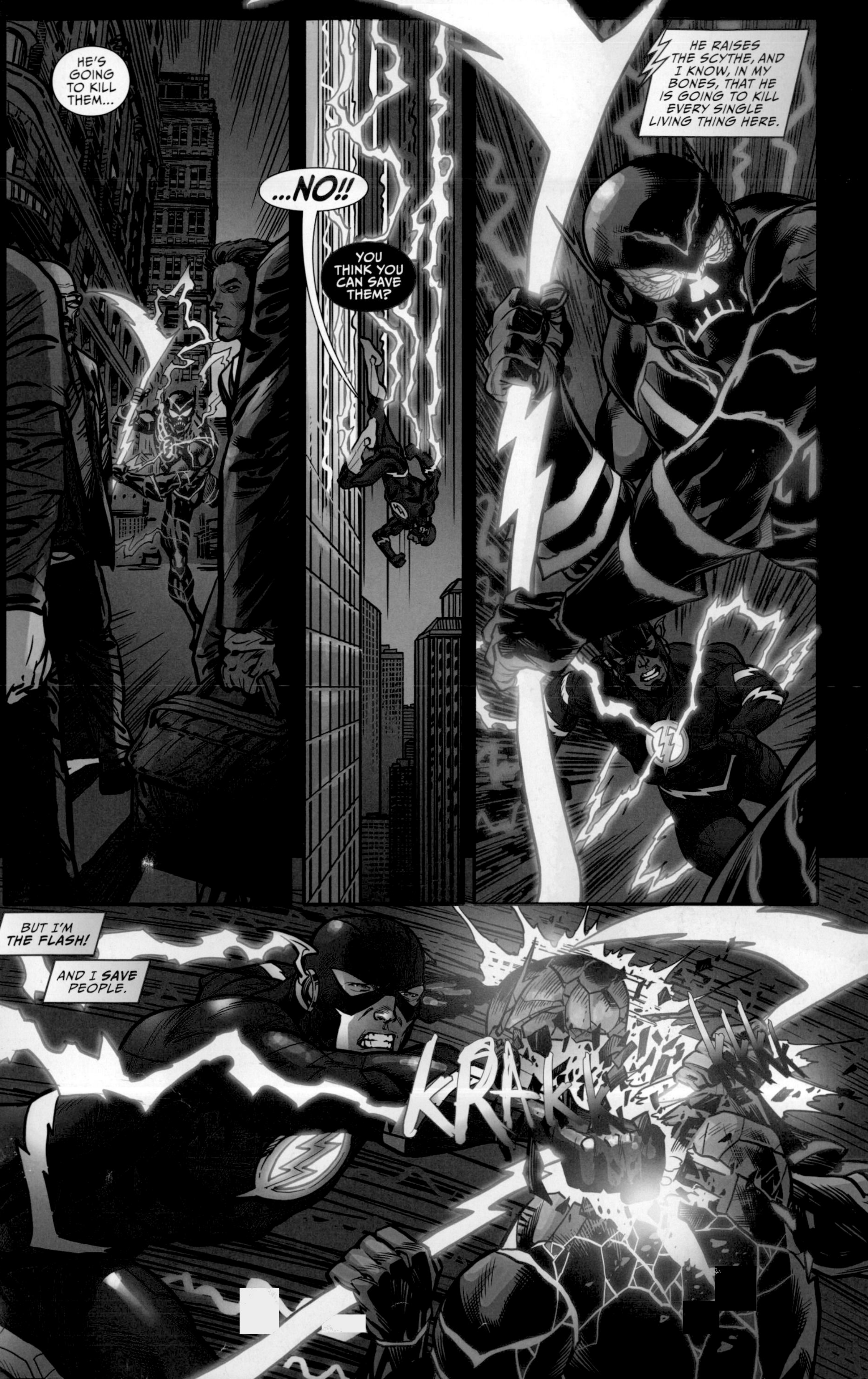
HE'S GOING TO KILL THEM...
...NO!!
YOU THINK YOU CAN SAVE THEM?
HE RAISES THE SCYTHE, AND I KNOW, IN MY BONES, THAT HE IS GOING TO KILL EVERY SINGLE LIVING THING HERE.
BUT I'M THE FLASH!
AND I SAVE PEOPLE.
KRAKK

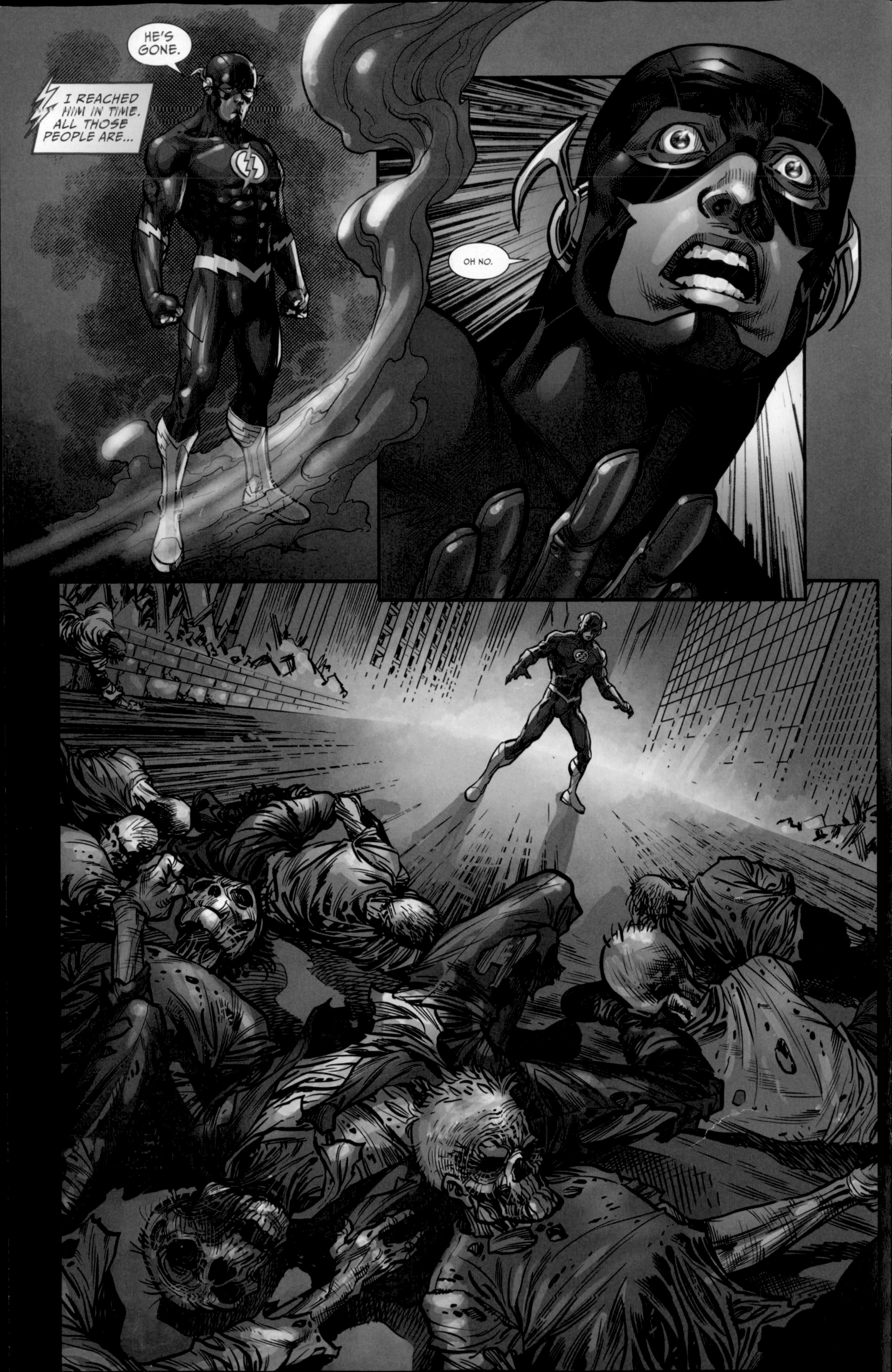
HE'S GONE.
I REACHED HIM IN TIME. ALL THOSE PEOPLE ARE...
OH NO.

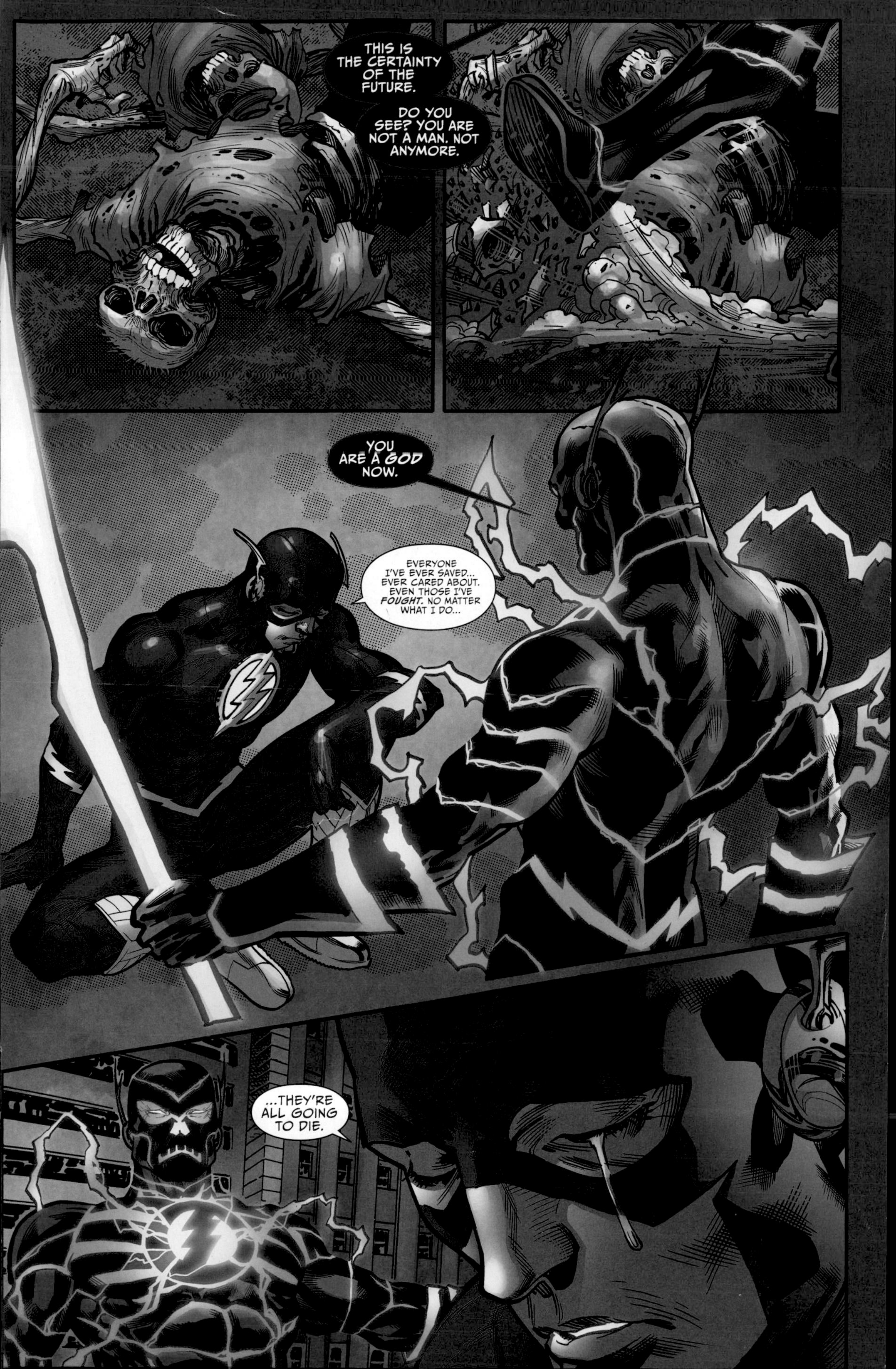
THIS IS THE CERTAINTY OF THE FUTURE.
DO YOU SEE? YOU ARE NOT A MAN. NOT ANYMORE.
YOU ARE A GOD NOW.
EVERYONE I'VE EVER SAVED... EVER CARED ABOUT. EVEN THOSE I'VE FOUGHT. NO MATTER WHAT I DO...
...THEY'RE ALL GOING TO DIE.

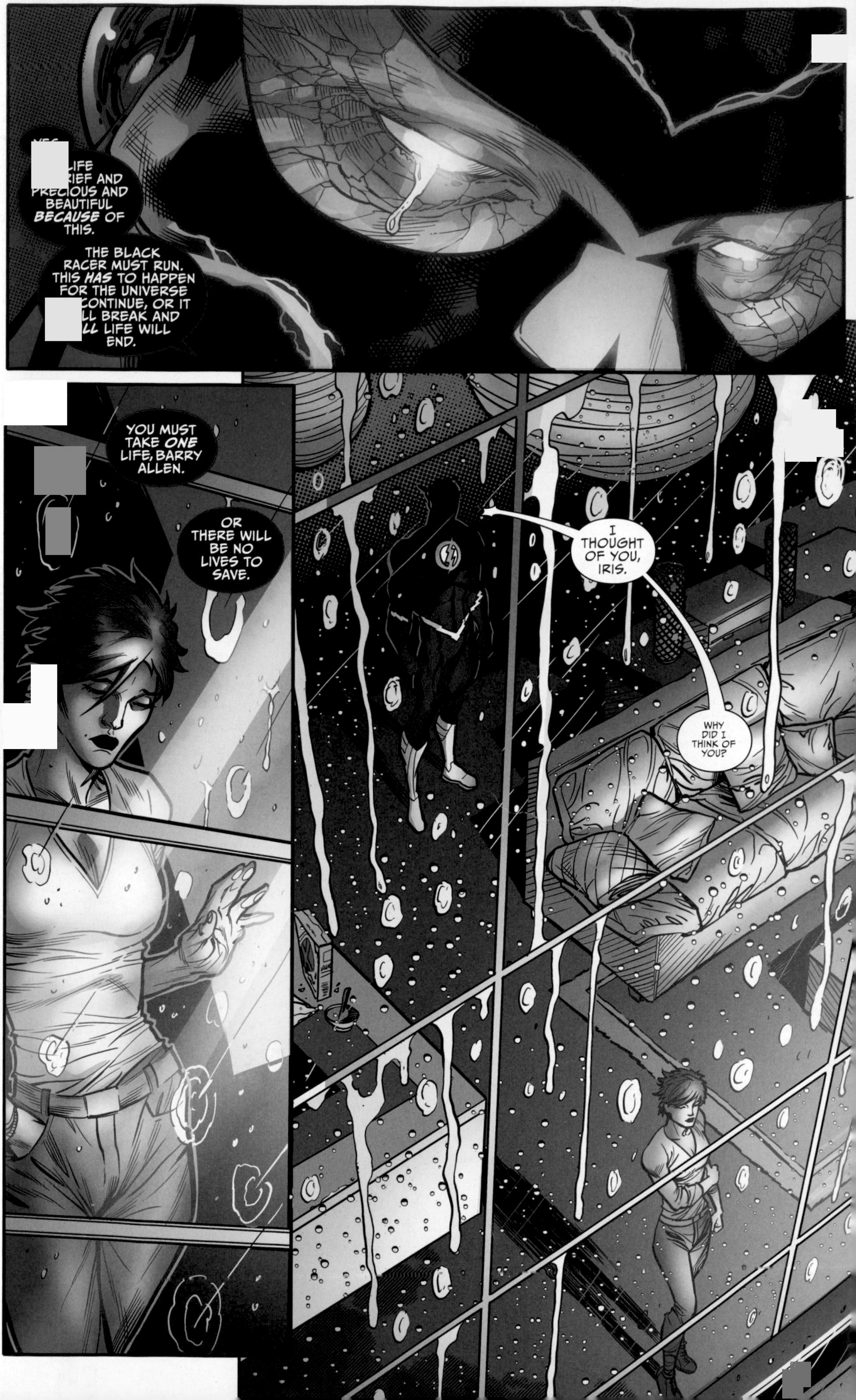
LIFE RIEF AND PRECIOUS AND BEAUTIFUL *BECAUSE* OF THIS.
THE BLACK RACER MUST RUN. THIS *HAS* TO HAPPEN FOR THE UNIVERSE CONTINUE, OR IT LL BREAK AND LL LIFE WILL END.
YOU MUST TAKE *ONE* LIFE, BARRY ALLEN.
OR THERE WILL BE NO LIVES TO SAVE.
I THOUGHT OF YOU, IRIS.
WHY DID I THINK OF YOU?

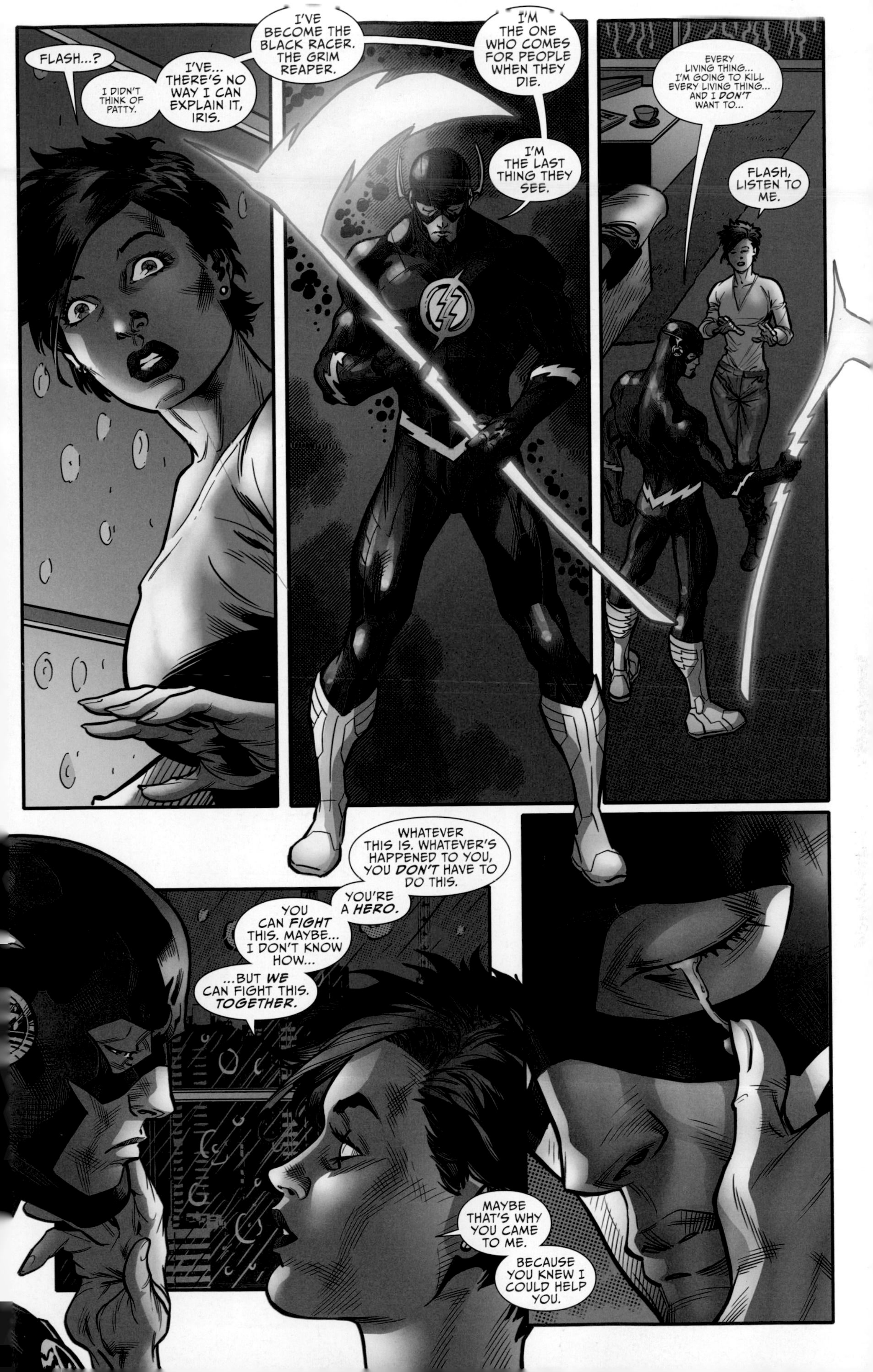
FLASH...?
I DIDN'T THINK OF PATTY.
I'VE... THERE'S NO WAY I CAN EXPLAIN IT, IRIS.
I'VE BECOME THE BLACK RACER. THE GRIM REAPER.
I'M THE ONE WHO COMES FOR PEOPLE WHEN THEY DIE.
I'M THE LAST THING THEY SEE.
EVERY LIVING THING... I'M GOING TO KILL EVERY LIVING THING... AND I DON'T WANT TO...
FLASH, LISTEN TO ME.
WHATEVER THIS IS. WHATEVER'S HAPPENED TO YOU, YOU DON'T HAVE TO DO THIS.
YOU'RE A HERO.
YOU CAN FIGHT THIS. MAYBE... I DON'T KNOW HOW...
...BUT WE CAN FIGHT THIS. TOGETHER.
MAYBE THAT'S WHY YOU CAME TO ME.
BECAUSE YOU KNEW I COULD HELP YOU.

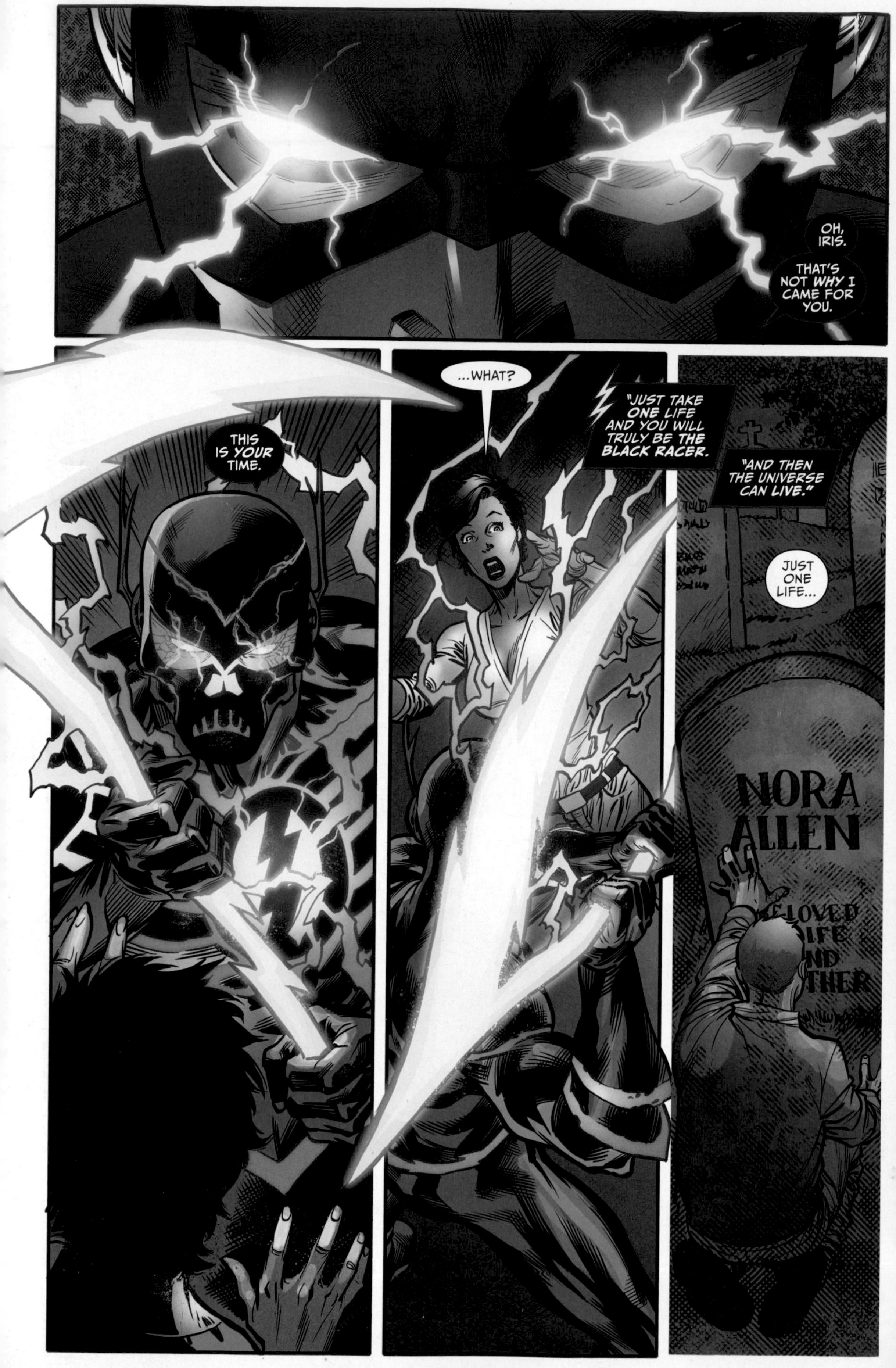
OH, IRIS.
THAT'S NOT WHY I CAME FOR YOU.
THIS IS YOUR TIME.
...WHAT?
"JUST TAKE ONE LIFE AND YOU WILL TRULY BE THE BLACK RACER.
"AND THEN THE UNIVERSE CAN LIVE."
JUST ONE LIFE...
NORA ALLEN

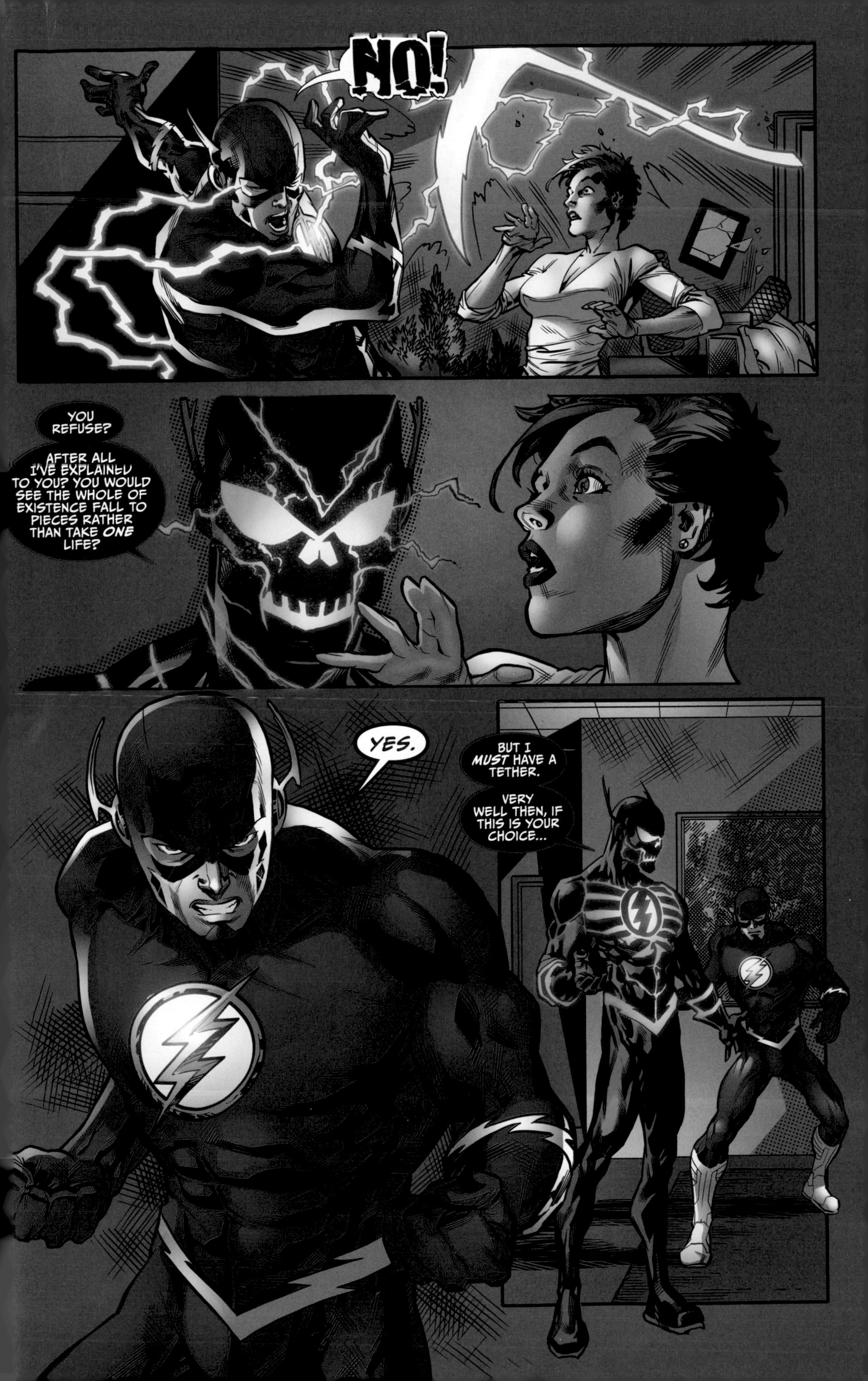
NO!
YOU REFUSE?
AFTER ALL I'VE EXPLAINED TO YOU? YOU WOULD SEE THE WHOLE OF EXISTENCE FALL TO PIECES RATHER THAN TAKE *ONE* LIFE?
YES.
BUT I *MUST* HAVE A TETHER.
VERY WELL THEN, IF THIS IS YOUR CHOICE...

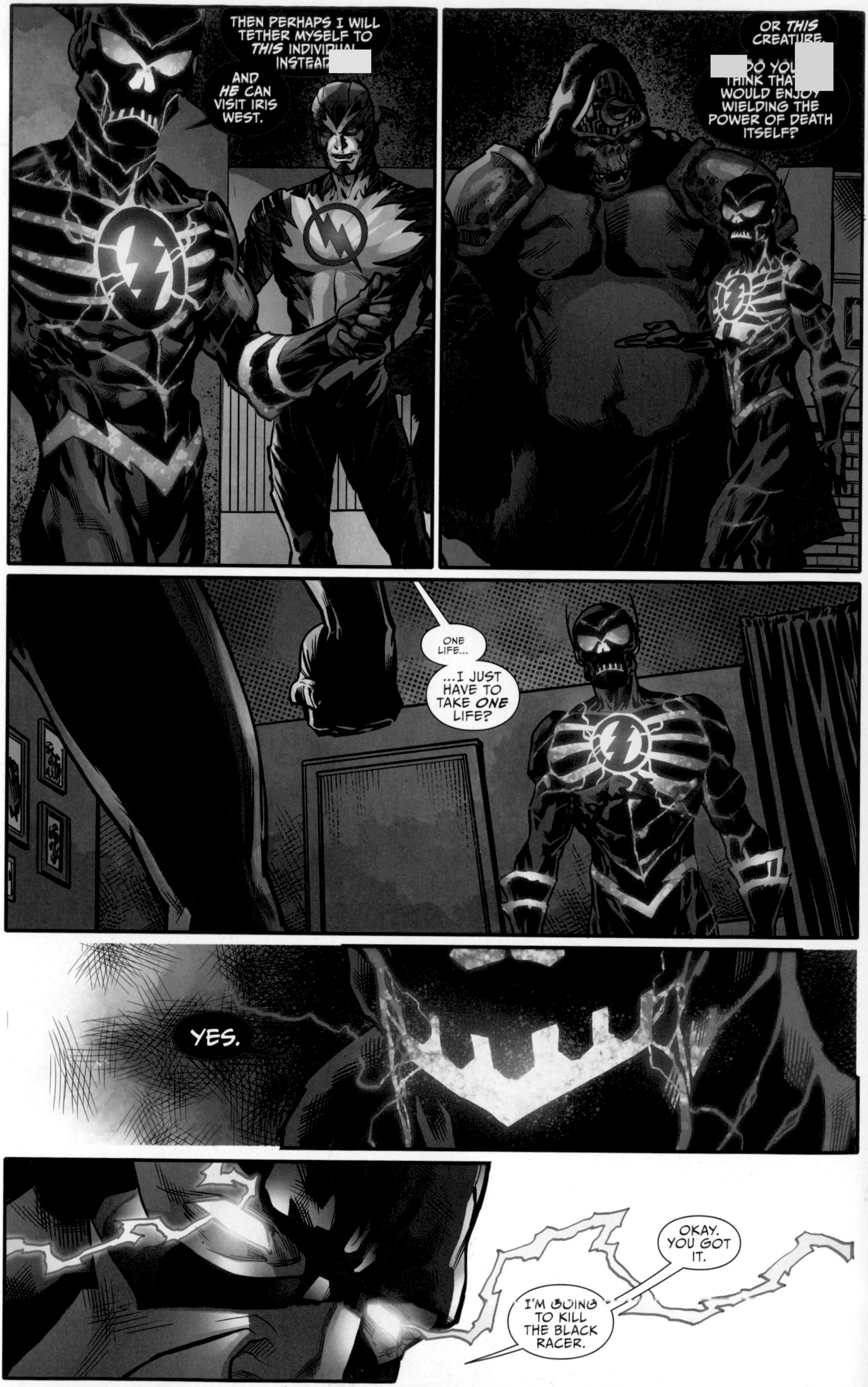
THEN PERHAPS I WILL TETHER MYSELF TO *THIS* INDIVIDUAL INSTEAD.
AND *HE* CAN VISIT IRIS WEST.
OR *THIS* CREATURE.
DO YOU THINK THAT WOULD ENJOY WIELDING THE POWER OF DEATH ITSELF?
ONE LIFE...
...I JUST HAVE TO TAKE *ONE* LIFE?
YES.
OKAY. YOU GOT IT.
I'M GOING TO KILL THE BLACK RACER.

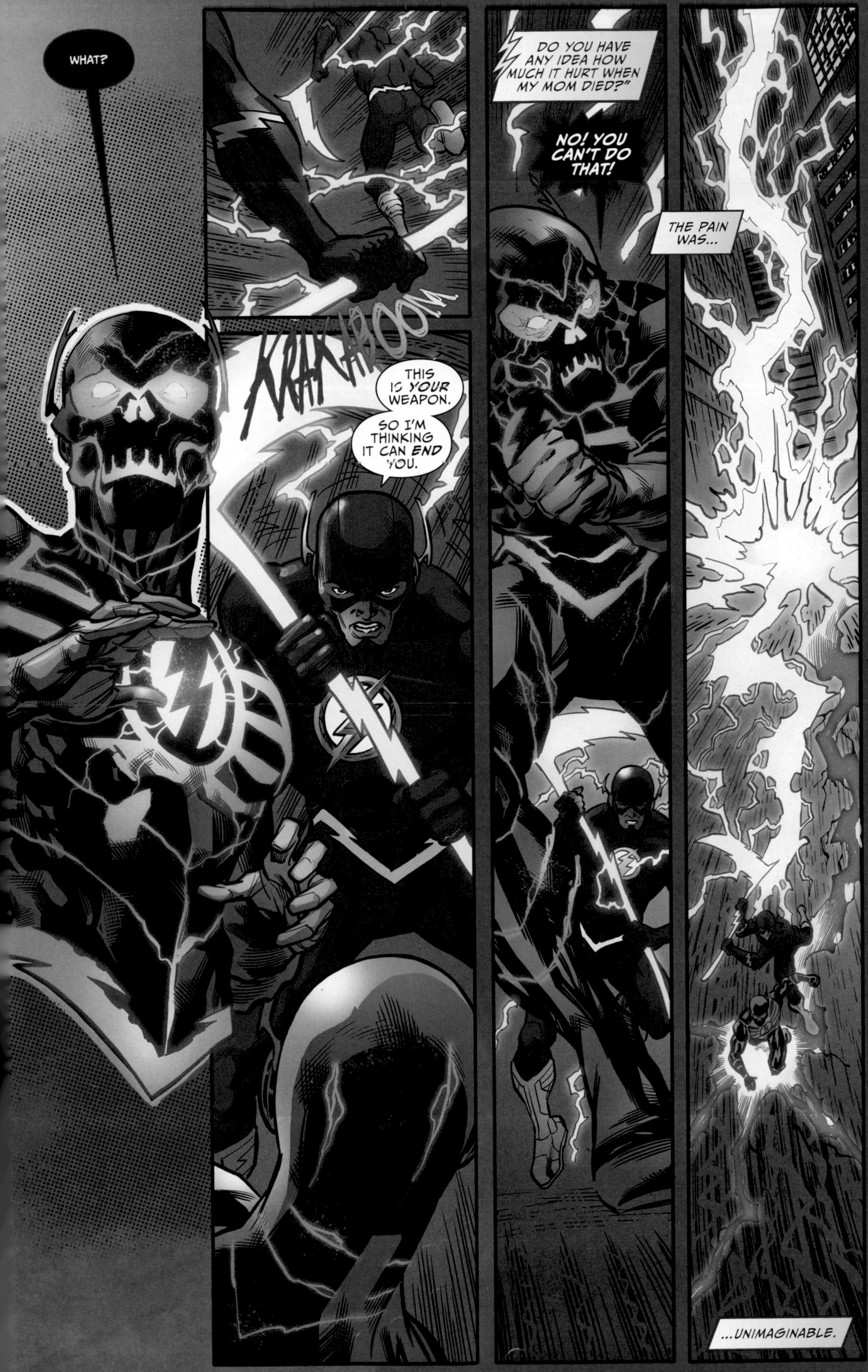
WHAT?
DO YOU HAVE ANY IDEA HOW MUCH IT HURT WHEN MY MOM DIED?"
NO! YOU CAN'T DO THAT!
THE PAIN WAS...
KRAKABOOM
THIS IS YOUR WEAPON.
SO I'M THINKING IT CAN END YOU.
...UNIMAGINABLE.

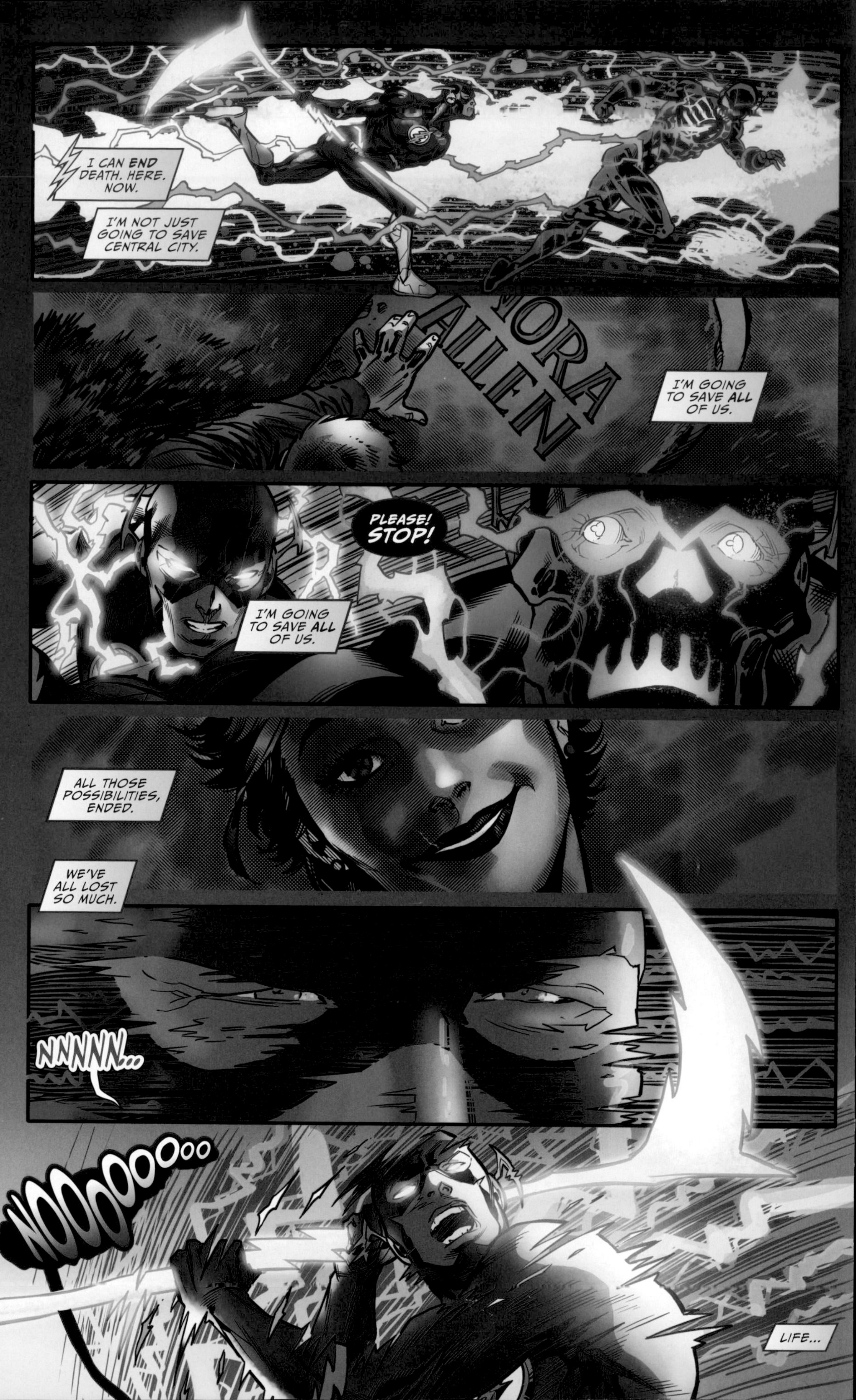

I CAN END DEATH. HERE. NOW.
I'M NOT JUST GOING TO SAVE CENTRAL CITY.
NORA ALLEN
I'M GOING TO SAVE ALL OF US.
PLEASE! STOP!
I'M GOING TO SAVE ALL OF US.
ALL THOSE POSSIBILITIES, ENDED.
WE'VE ALL LOST SO MUCH.
NNNNN...
NOOOOOOoo
LIFE...

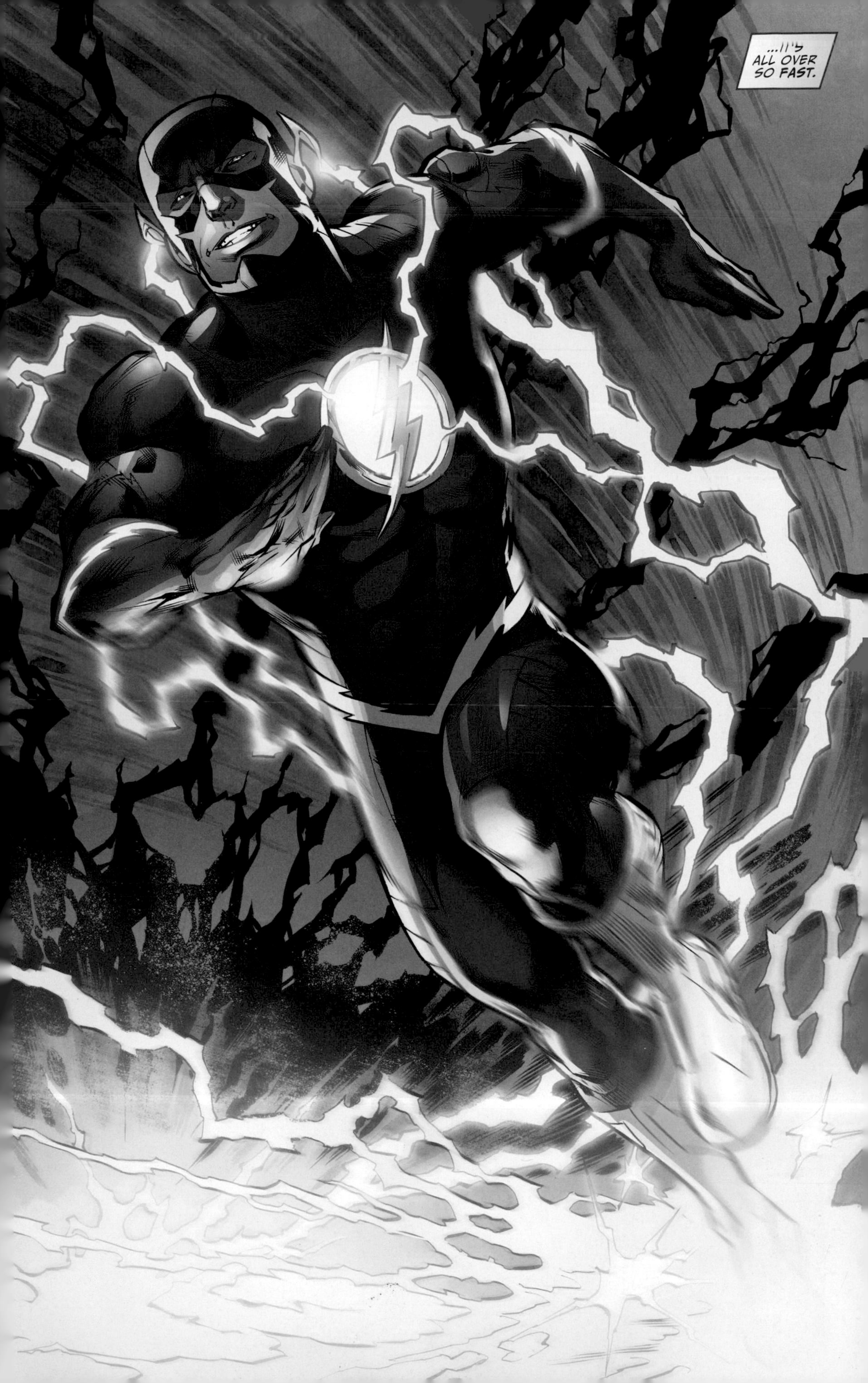
...IT'S ALL OVER SO FAST.

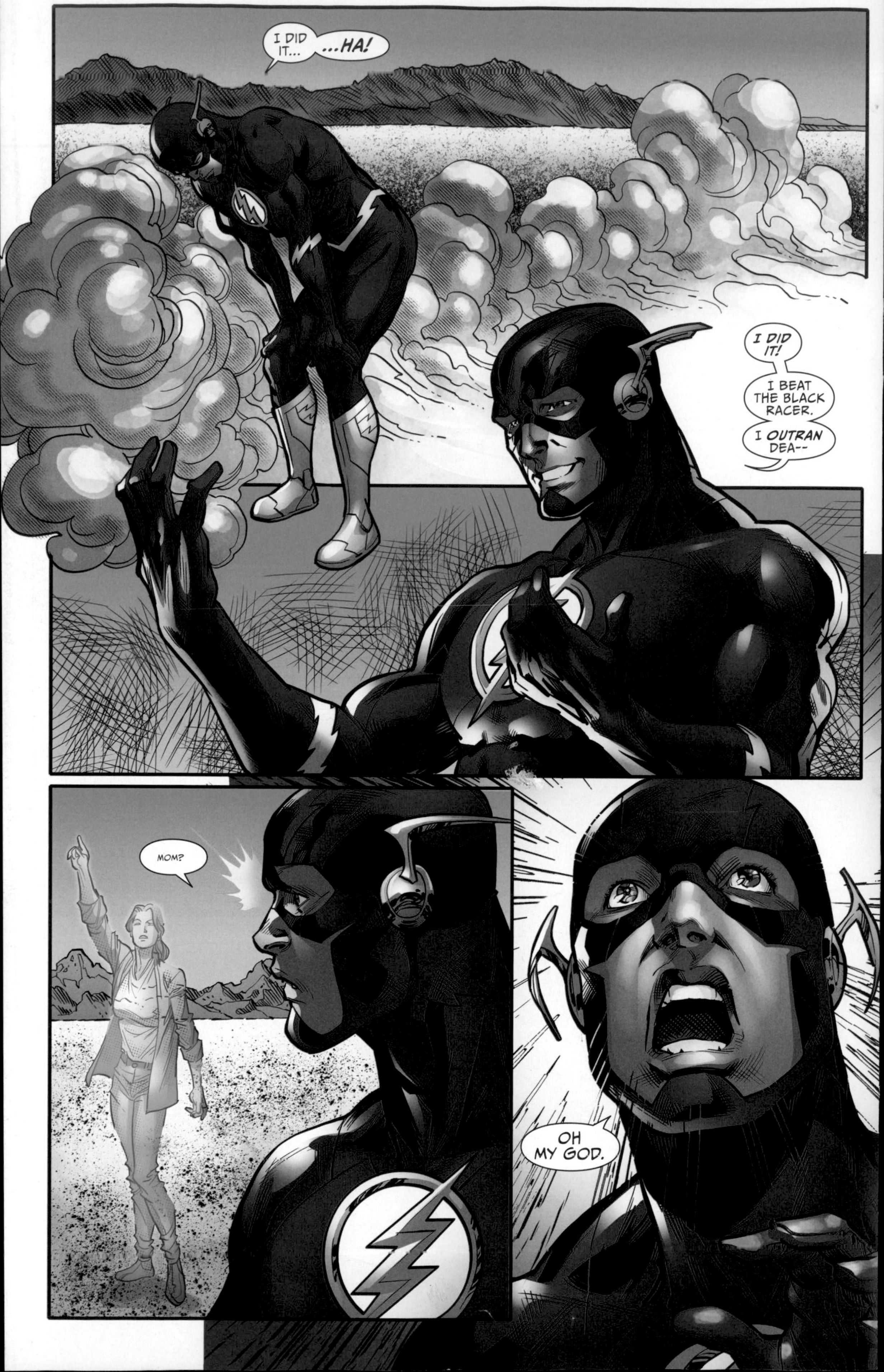
I DID IT...
...HA!
I DID IT!
I BEAT THE BLACK RACER.
I OUTRAN DEA--
MOM?
OH MY GOD.

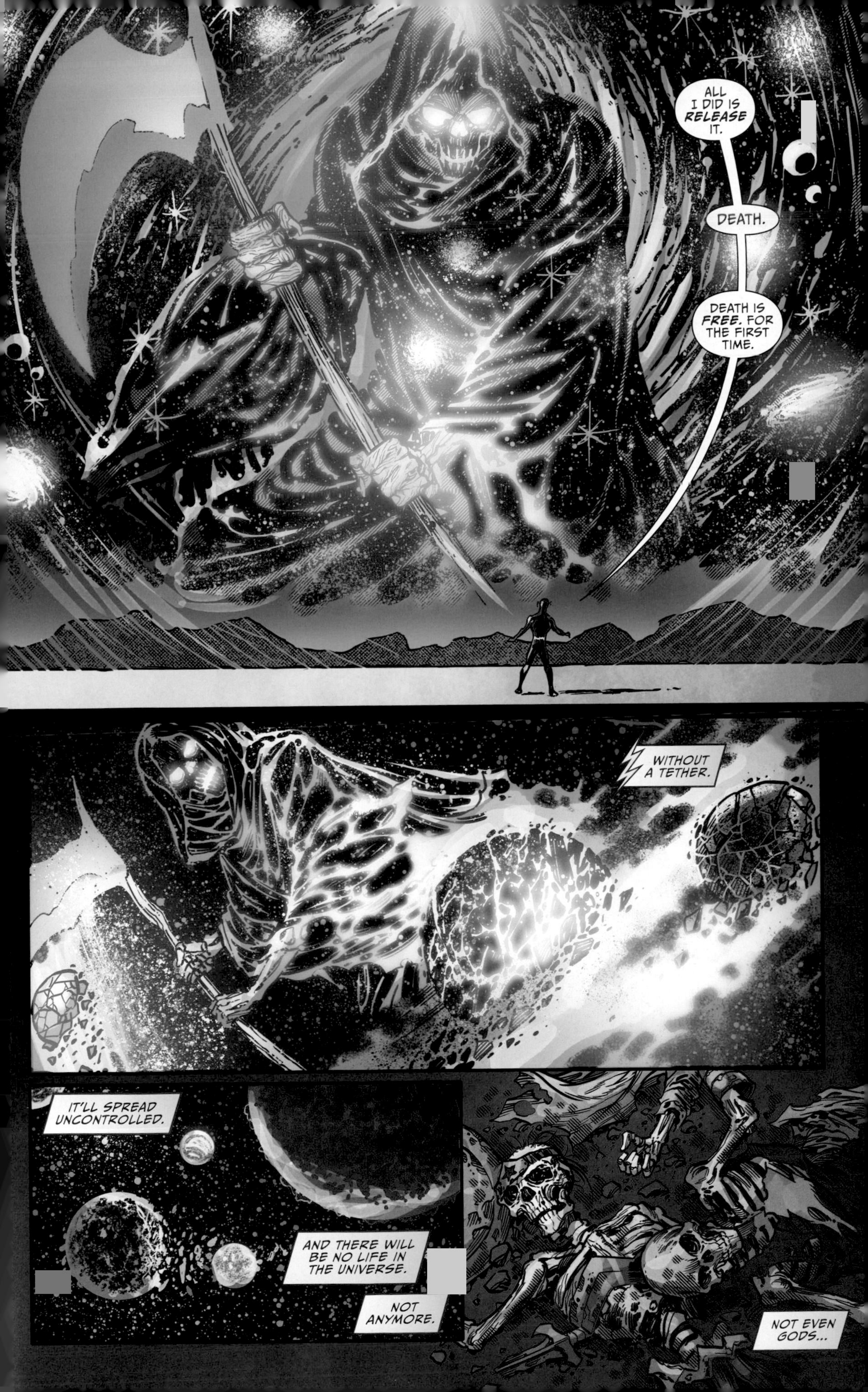
ALL I DID IS RELEASE IT.
DEATH.
DEATH IS FREE. FOR THE FIRST TIME.
WITHOUT A TETHER.
IT'LL SPREAD UNCONTROLLED.
AND THERE WILL BE NO LIFE IN THE UNIVERSE.
NOT ANYMORE.
NOT EVEN GODS...

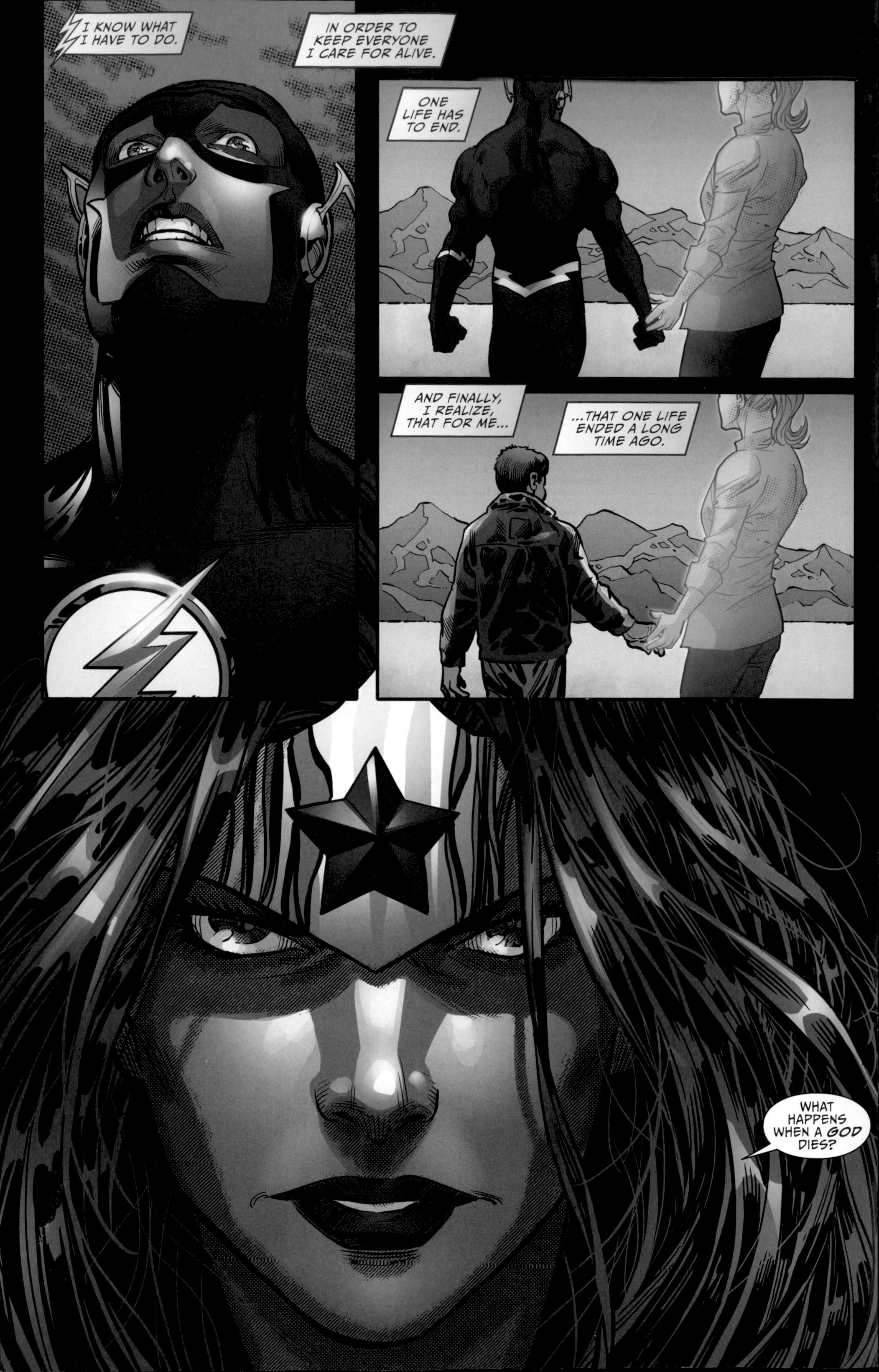
I KNOW WHAT I HAVE TO DO.
IN ORDER TO KEEP EVERYONE I CARE FOR ALIVE.
ONE LIFE HAS TO END.
AND FINALLY, I REALIZE, THAT FOR ME...
...THAT ONE LIFE ENDED A LONG TIME AGO.
WHAT HAPPENS WHEN A GOD DIES?

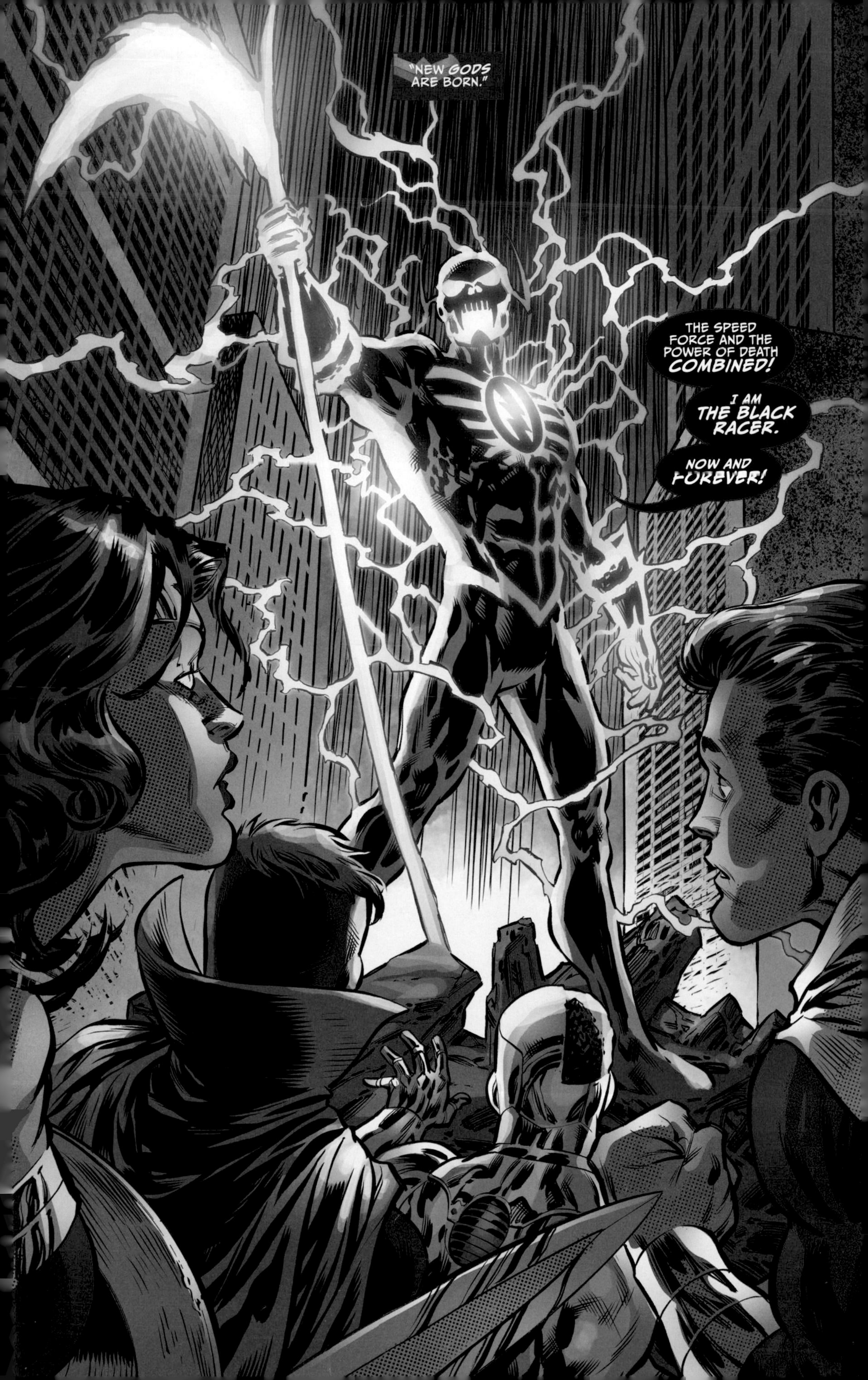
"NEW GODS ARE BORN."
THE SPEED FORCE AND THE POWER OF DEATH COMBINED!
I AM THE BLACK RACER.
NOW AND FOREVER!

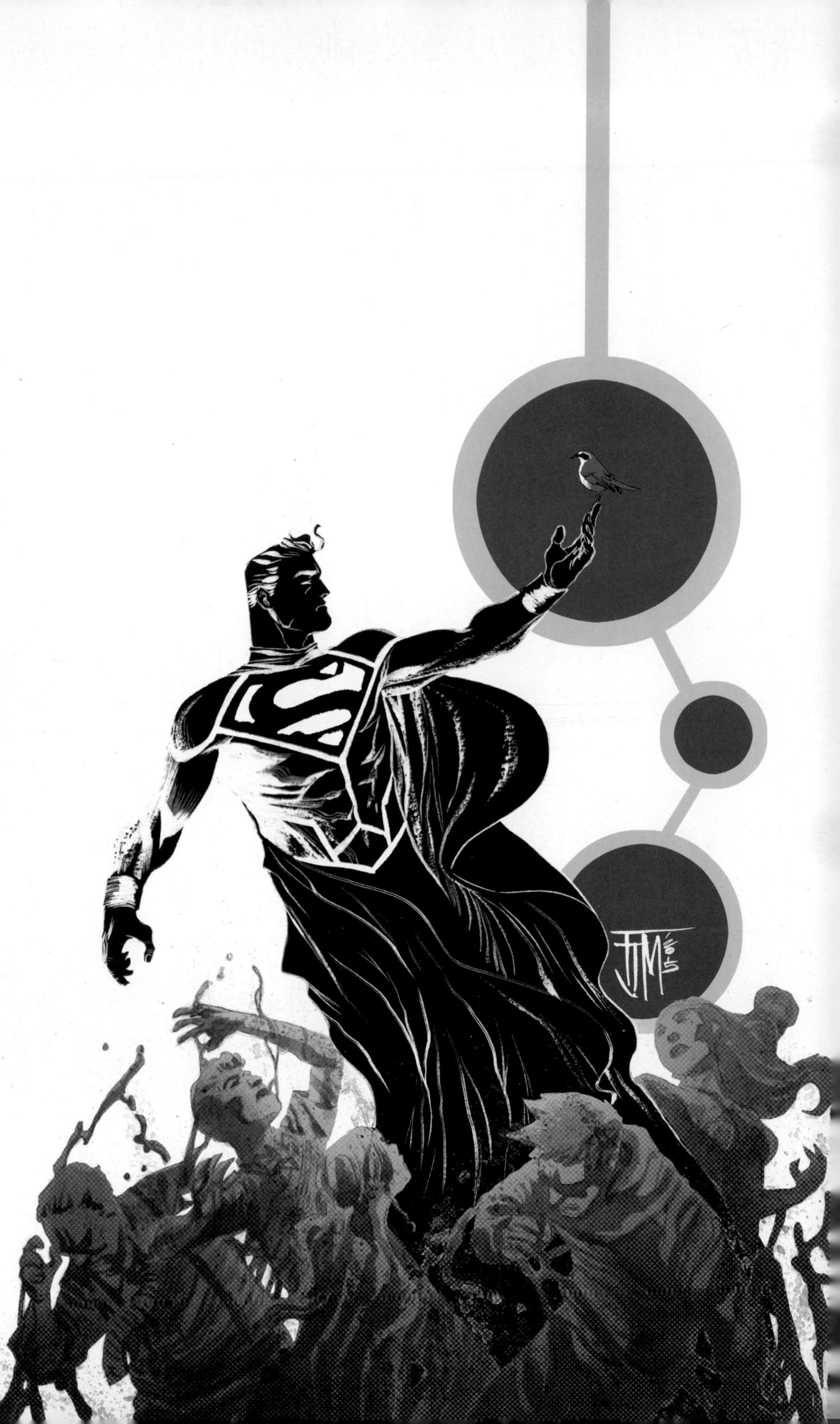

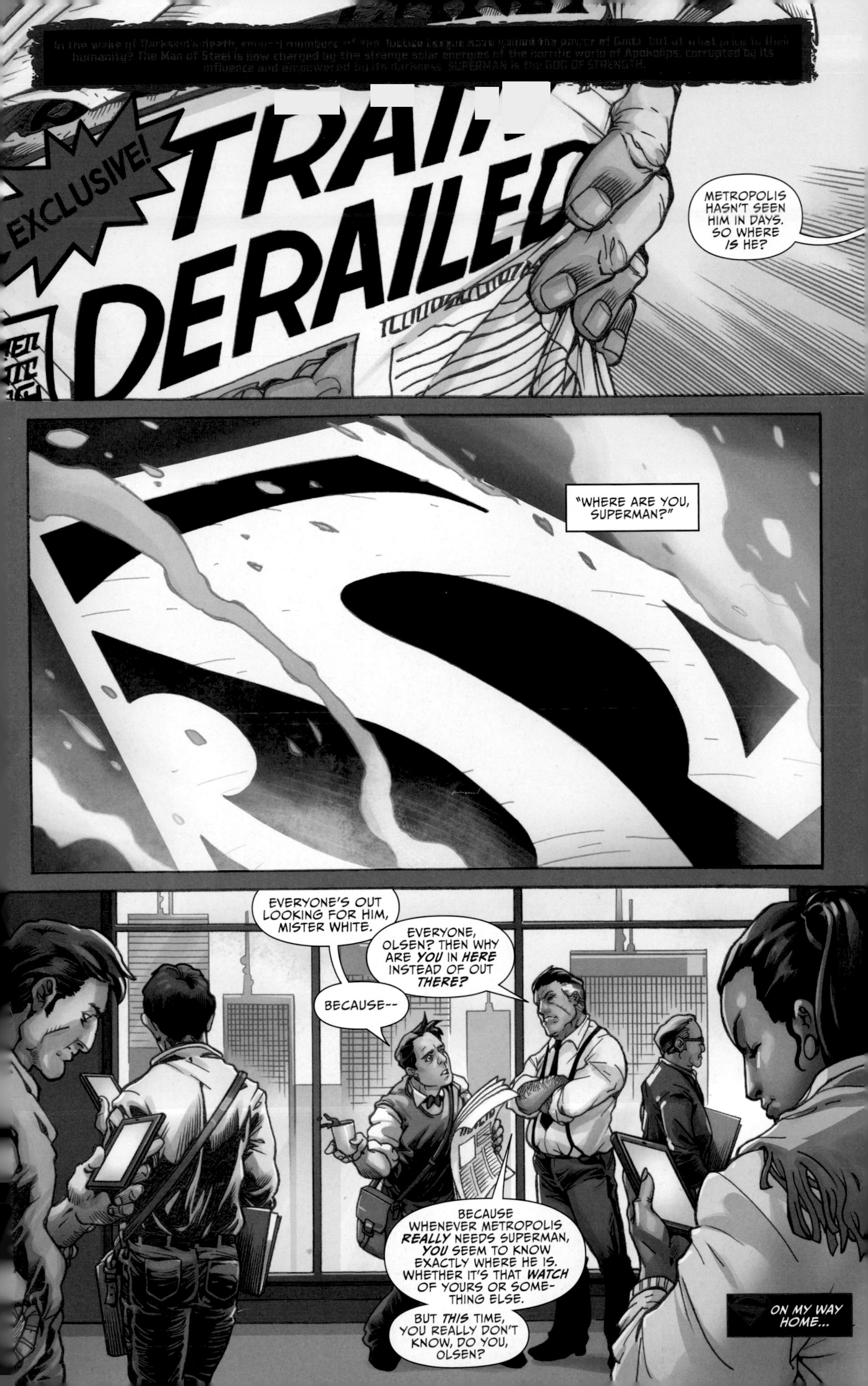
[redacted]
EXCLUSIVE!
TRAI
DERAILED
METROPOLIS HASN'T SEEN HIM IN DAYS. SO WHERE *IS* HE?
"WHERE ARE YOU, SUPERMAN?"
EVERYONE'S OUT LOOKING FOR HIM, MISTER WHITE.
EVERYONE, OLSEN? THEN WHY ARE *YOU* IN *HERE* INSTEAD OF OUT *THERE?*
BECAUSE--
BECAUSE WHENEVER METROPOLIS *REALLY* NEEDS SUPERMAN, *YOU* SEEM TO KNOW EXACTLY WHERE HE IS. WHETHER IT'S THAT *WATCH* OF YOURS OR SOME-THING ELSE.
BUT *THIS* TIME, YOU REALLY DON'T KNOW, DO YOU, OLSEN?
ON MY WAY HOME...

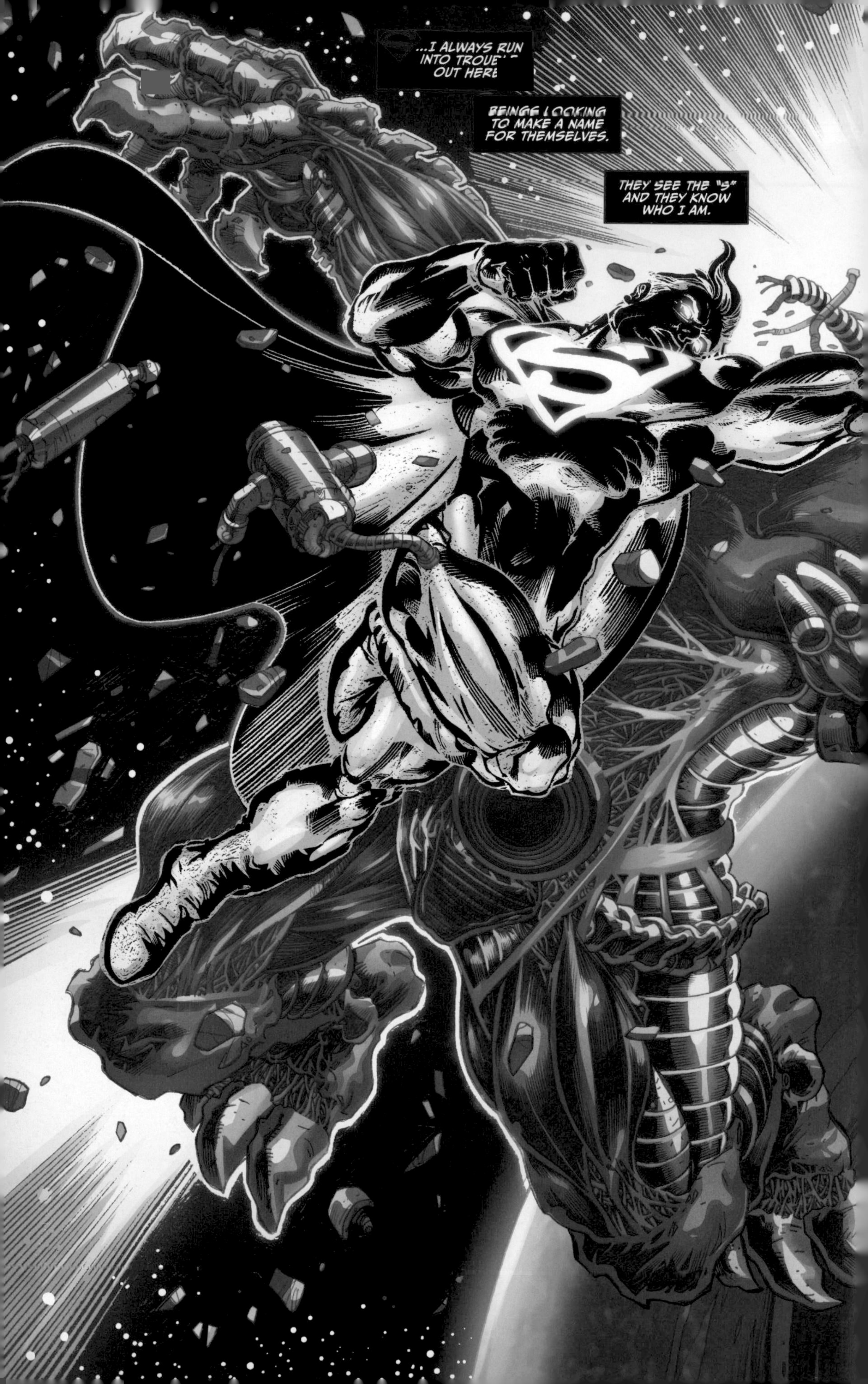
...I ALWAYS RUN INTO TROUE[redacted] OUT HERE[redacted]
BEINGS LOOKING TO MAKE A NAME FOR THEMSELVES.
THEY SEE THE "S" AND THEY KNOW WHO I AM.

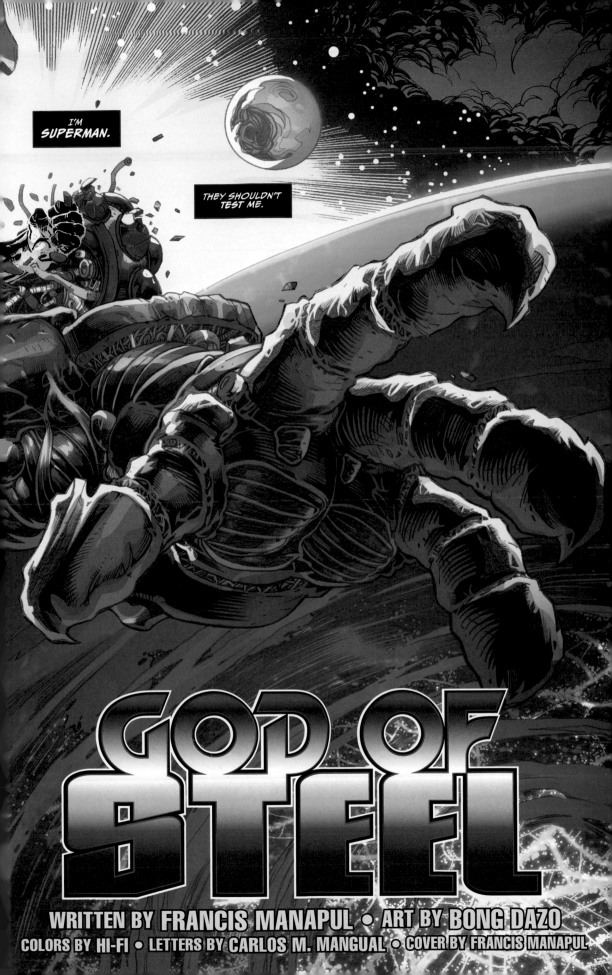

I'M SUPERMAN.

THEY SHOULDN'T TEST ME.

GOD OF STEEL

WRITTEN BY FRANCIS MANAPUL • ART BY BONG DAZO
COLORS BY HI-FI • LETTERS BY CARLOS M. MANGUAL • COVER BY FRANCIS MANAPUL

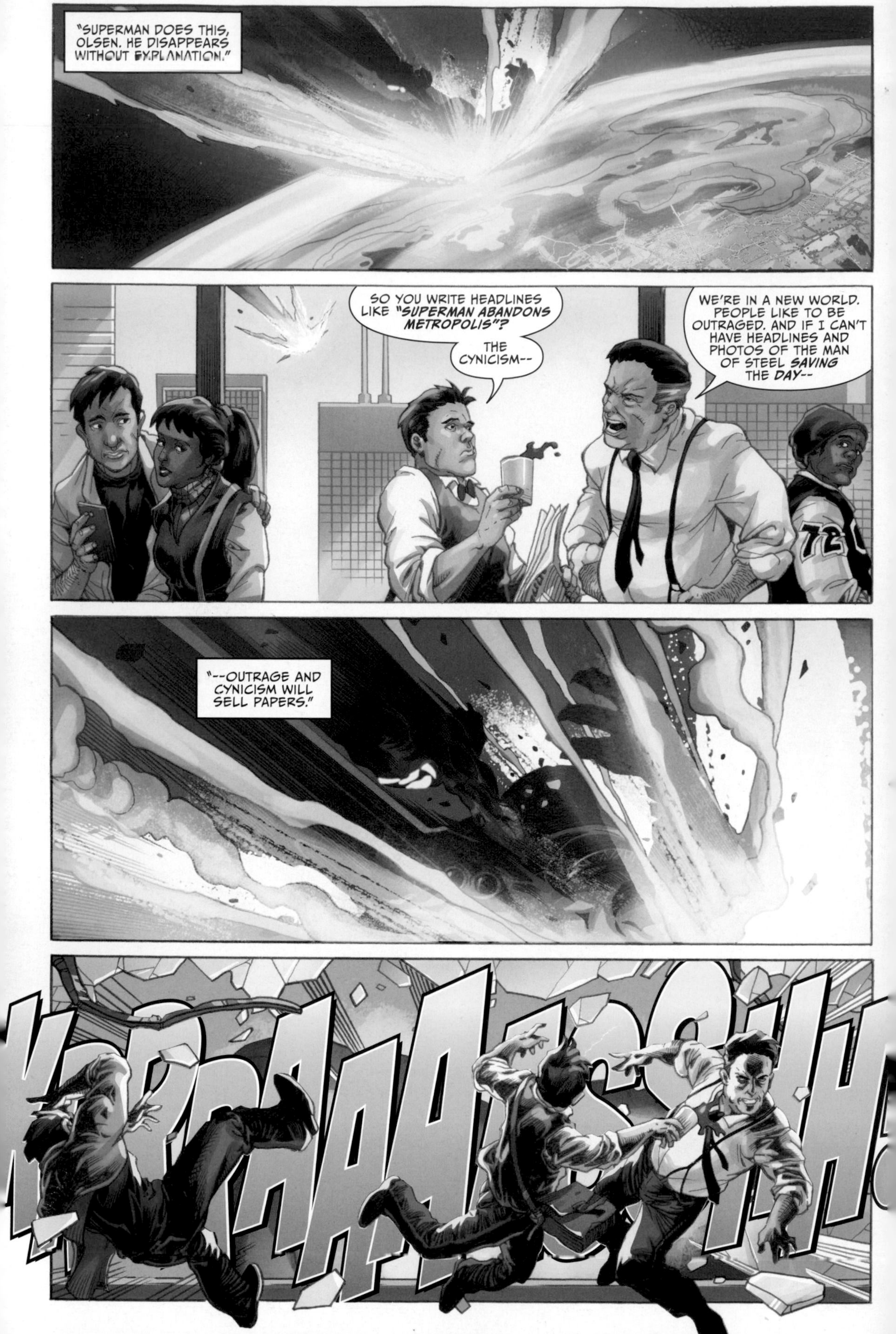
"SUPERMAN DOES THIS, OLSEN. HE DISAPPEARS WITHOUT EXPLANATION."
SO YOU WRITE HEADLINES LIKE "SUPERMAN ABANDONS METROPOLIS"?
THE CYNICISM--
WE'RE IN A NEW WORLD. PEOPLE LIKE TO BE OUTRAGED. AND IF I CAN'T HAVE HEADLINES AND PHOTOS OF THE MAN OF STEEL SAVING THE DAY--
"--OUTRAGE AND CYNICISM WILL SELL PAPERS."

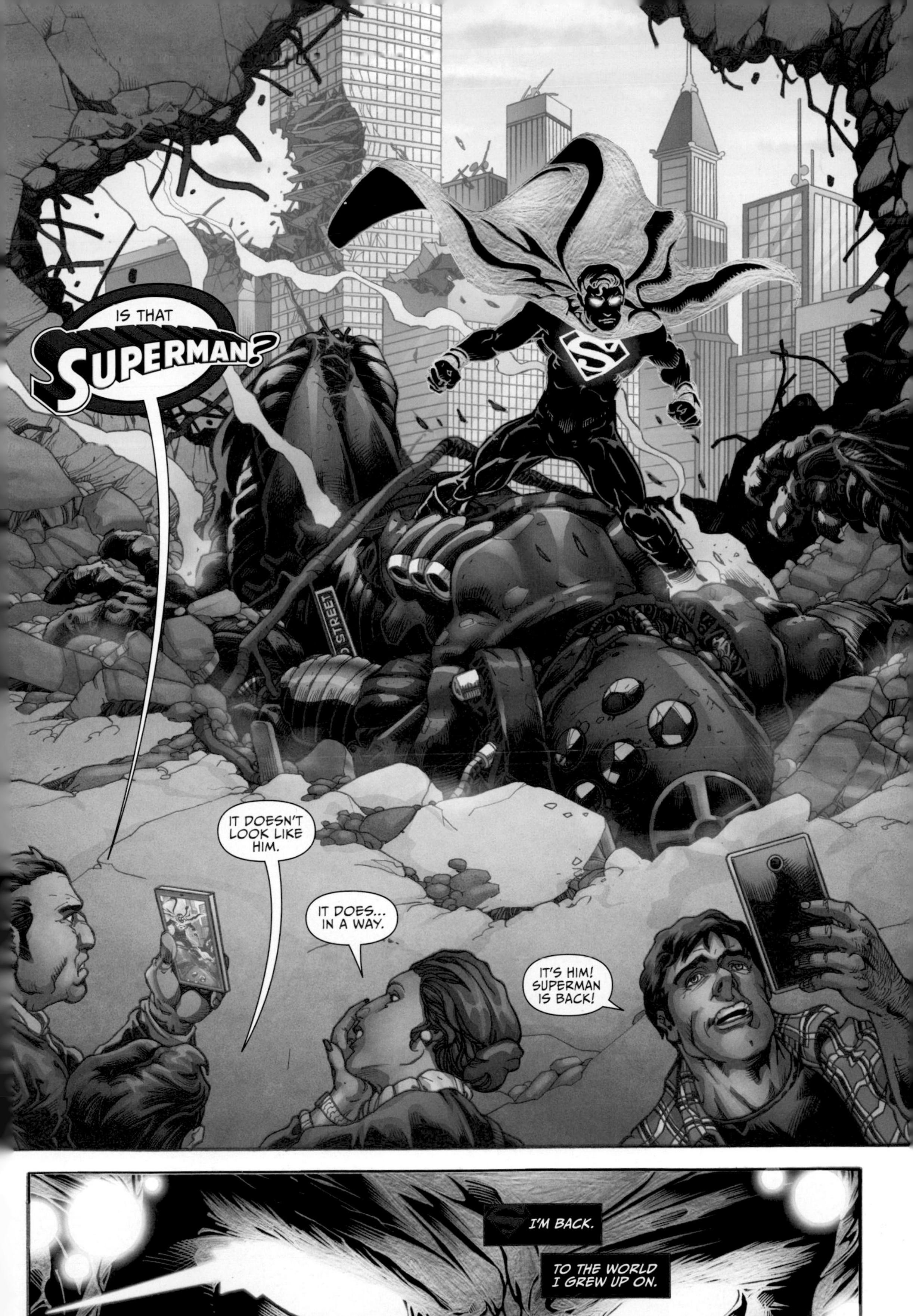
IS THAT SUPERMAN?
STREET
IT DOESN'T LOOK LIKE HIM.
IT DOES... IN A WAY.
IT'S HIM! SUPERMAN IS BACK!

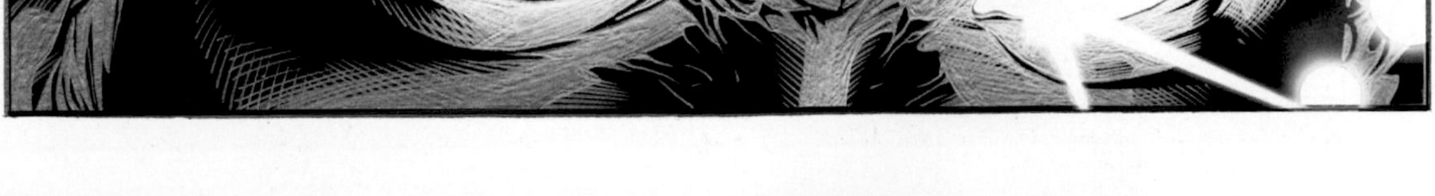
I'M BACK.
TO THE WORLD I GREW UP ON.

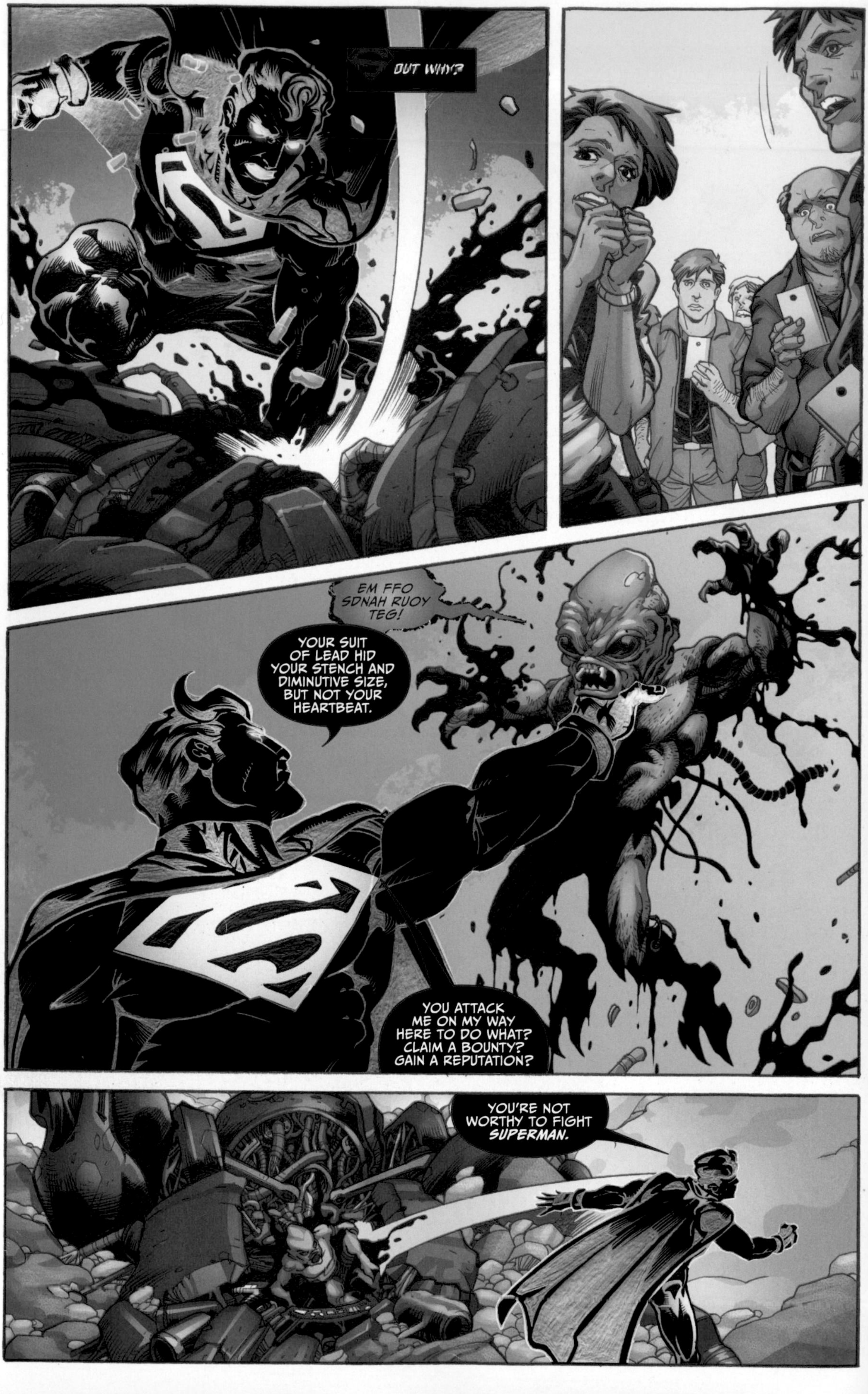
BUT WHY?
EM FFO SDNAH RUOY TEG!
YOUR SUIT OF LEAD HID YOUR STENCH AND DIMINUTIVE SIZE, BUT NOT YOUR HEARTBEAT.
YOU ATTACK ME ON MY WAY HERE TO DO WHAT? CLAIM A BOUNTY? GAIN A REPUTATION?
YOU'RE NOT WORTHY TO FIGHT *SUPERMAN.*

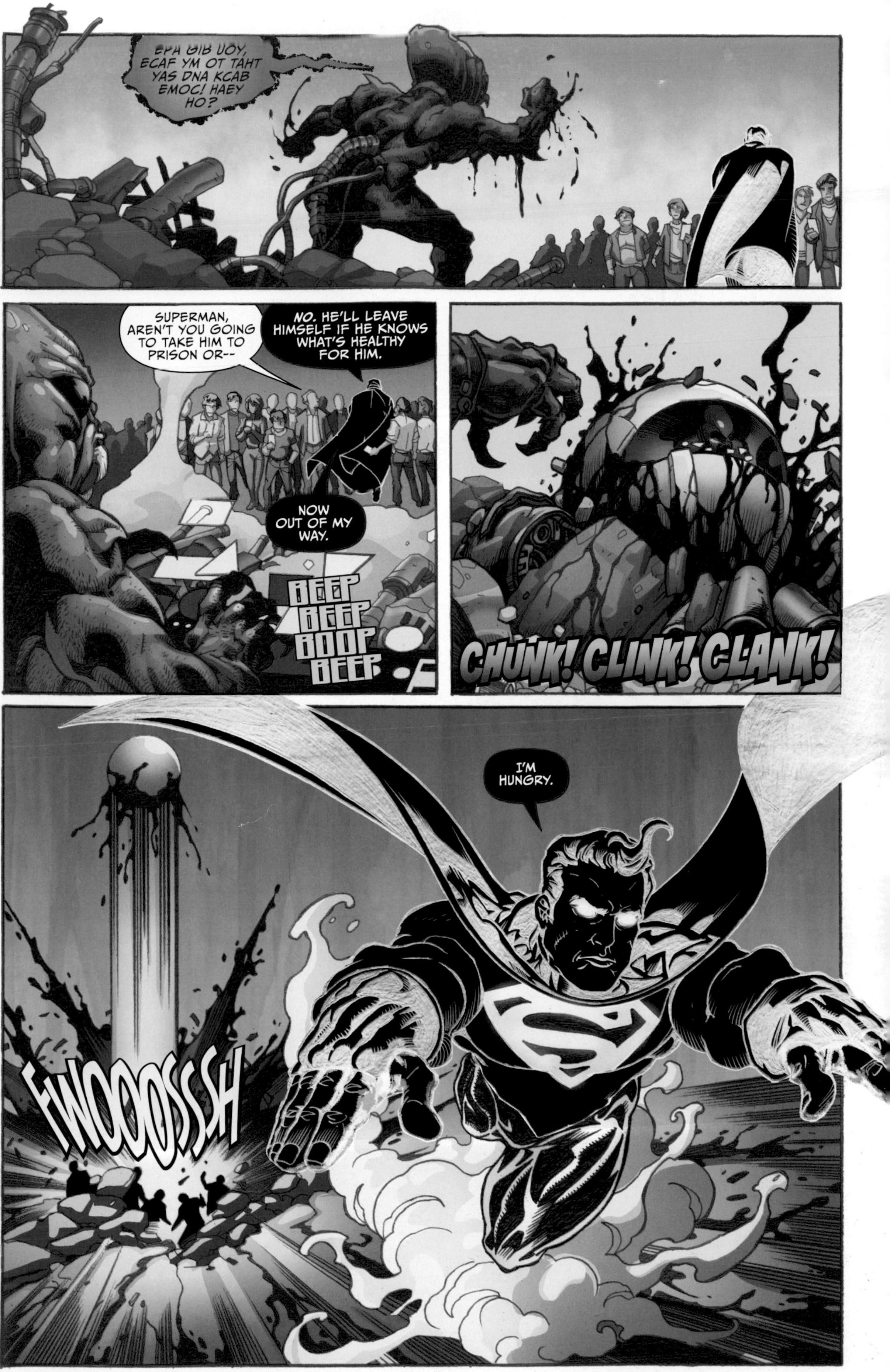
EPA GIB UOY, ECAF YM OT TAHT YAS DNA KCAB EMOC! HAEY HO?
SUPERMAN, AREN'T YOU GOING TO TAKE HIM TO PRISON OR--
NO. HE'LL LEAVE HIMSELF IF HE KNOWS WHAT'S HEALTHY FOR HIM.
NOW OUT OF MY WAY.
BEEP BEEP BOOP BEEP
CHUNK! CLINK! CLANK!
I'M HUNGRY.
FWOOOSSSH

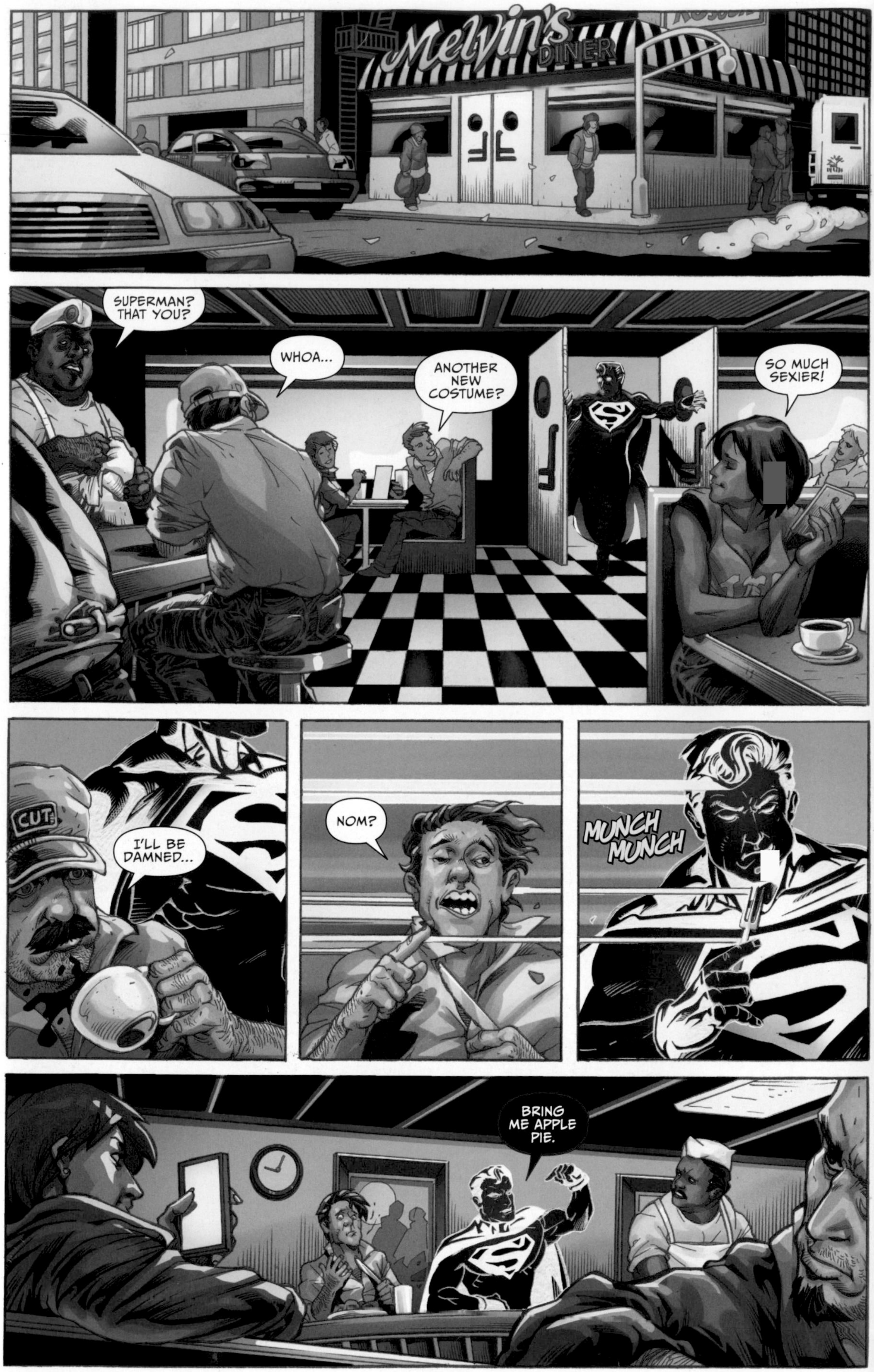
Melvin's DINER
SUPERMAN? THAT YOU?
WHOA...
ANOTHER NEW COSTUME?
SO MUCH SEXIER!
CUT
I'LL BE DAMNED...
NOM?
MUNCH MUNCH
BRING ME APPLE PIE.

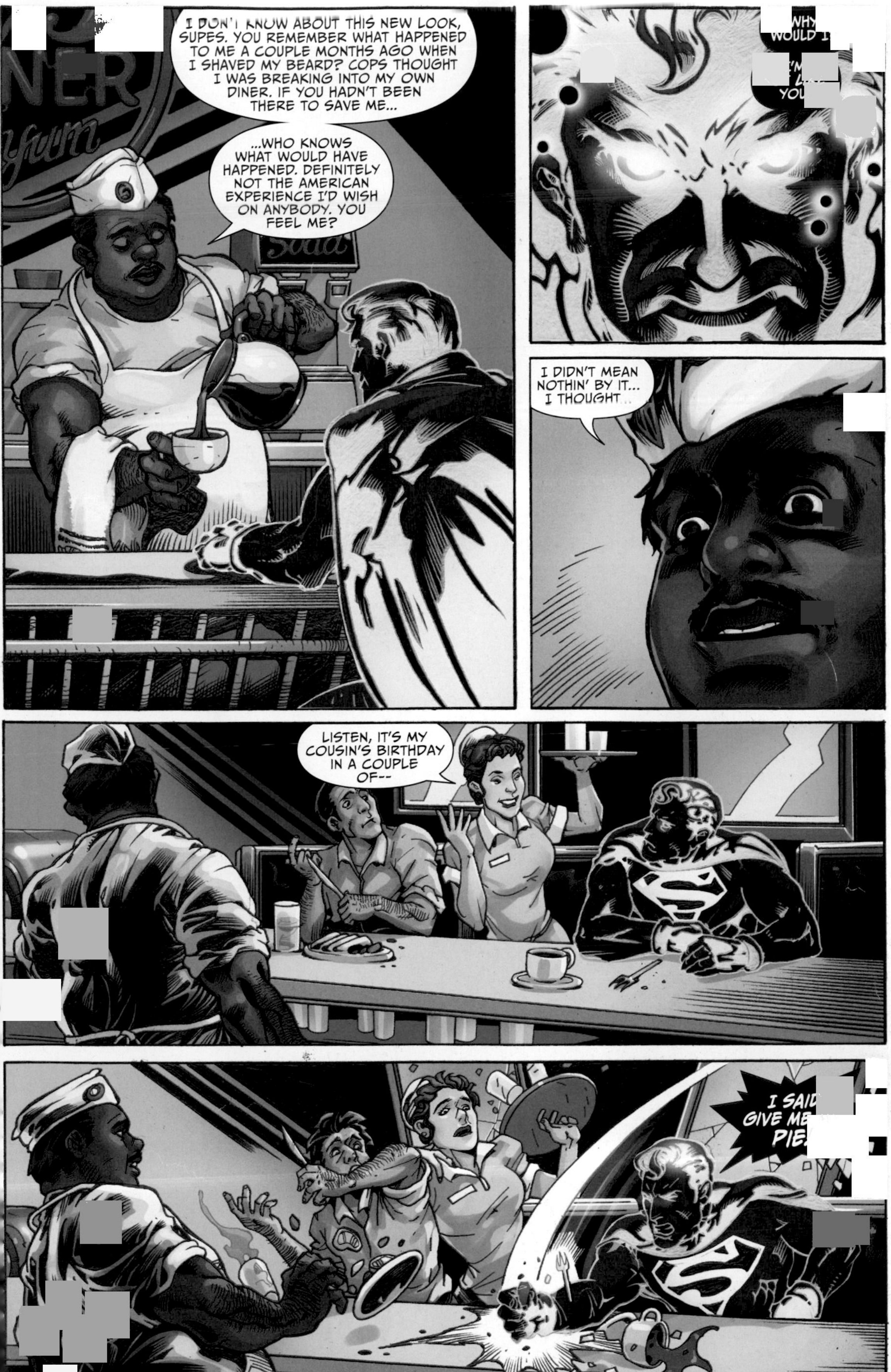
I DON'T KNOW ABOUT THIS NEW LOOK, SUPES. YOU REMEMBER WHAT HAPPENED TO ME A COUPLE MONTHS AGO WHEN I SHAVED MY BEARD? COPS THOUGHT I WAS BREAKING INTO MY OWN DINER. IF YOU HADN'T BEEN THERE TO SAVE ME...
...WHO KNOWS WHAT WOULD HAVE HAPPENED. DEFINITELY NOT THE AMERICAN EXPERIENCE I'D WISH ON ANYBODY. YOU FEEL ME?
WOULD I
I DIDN'T MEAN NOTHIN' BY IT... I THOUGHT...
LISTEN, IT'S MY COUSIN'S BIRTHDAY IN A COUPLE OF--
GIVE ME

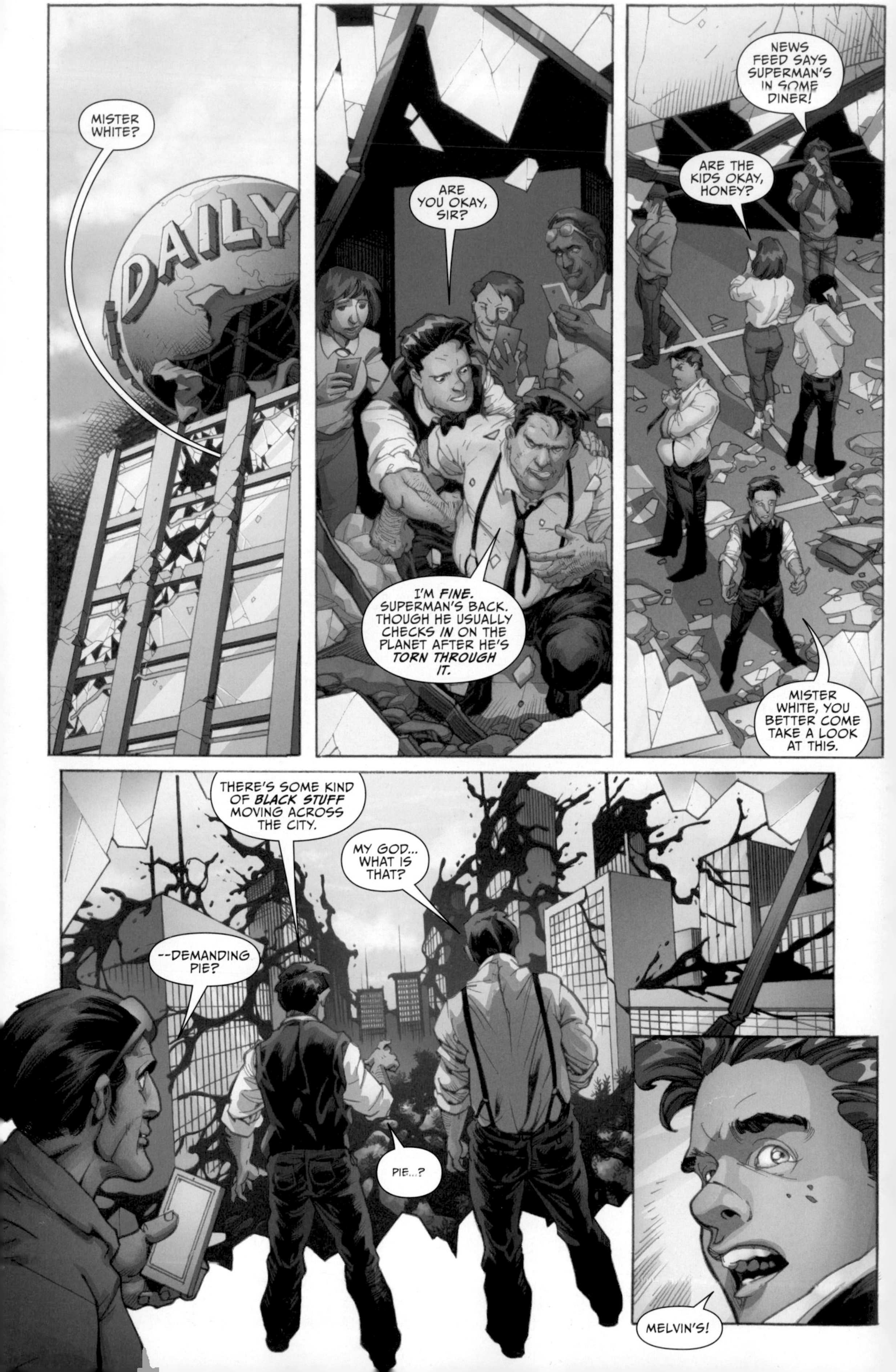
MISTER WHITE?
ARE YOU OKAY, SIR?
I'M *FINE.* SUPERMAN'S BACK. THOUGH HE USUALLY CHECKS *IN* ON THE PLANET AFTER HE'S *TORN THROUGH IT.*
NEWS FEED SAYS SUPERMAN'S IN *SOME* DINER!
ARE THE KIDS OKAY, HONEY?
MISTER WHITE, YOU BETTER COME TAKE A LOOK AT THIS.
THERE'S SOME KIND OF *BLACK STUFF* MOVING ACROSS THE CITY.
MY GOD... WHAT IS THAT?
--DEMANDING PIE?
PIE...?
MELVIN'S!

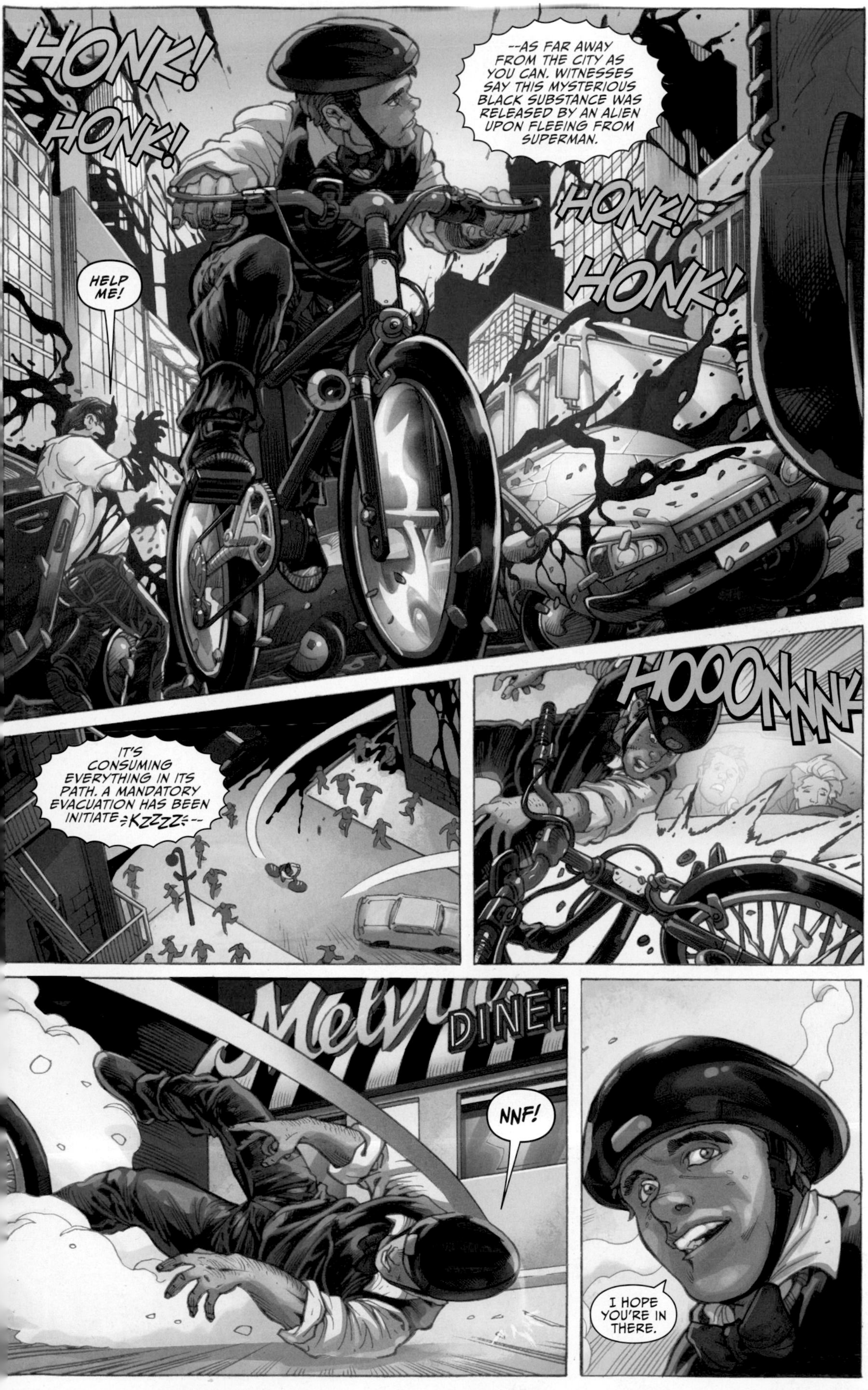
HONK!
HONK!
--AS FAR AWAY FROM THE CITY AS YOU CAN. WITNESSES SAY THIS MYSTERIOUS BLACK SUBSTANCE WAS RELEASED BY AN ALIEN UPON FLEEING FROM SUPERMAN.
HONK!
HONK!
HELP ME!
IT'S CONSUMING EVERYTHING IN ITS PATH. A MANDATORY EVACUATION HAS BEEN INITIATE=KZZZZ=--
HOOONNNK
Melvi
DINER
NNF!
I HOPE YOU'RE IN THERE.

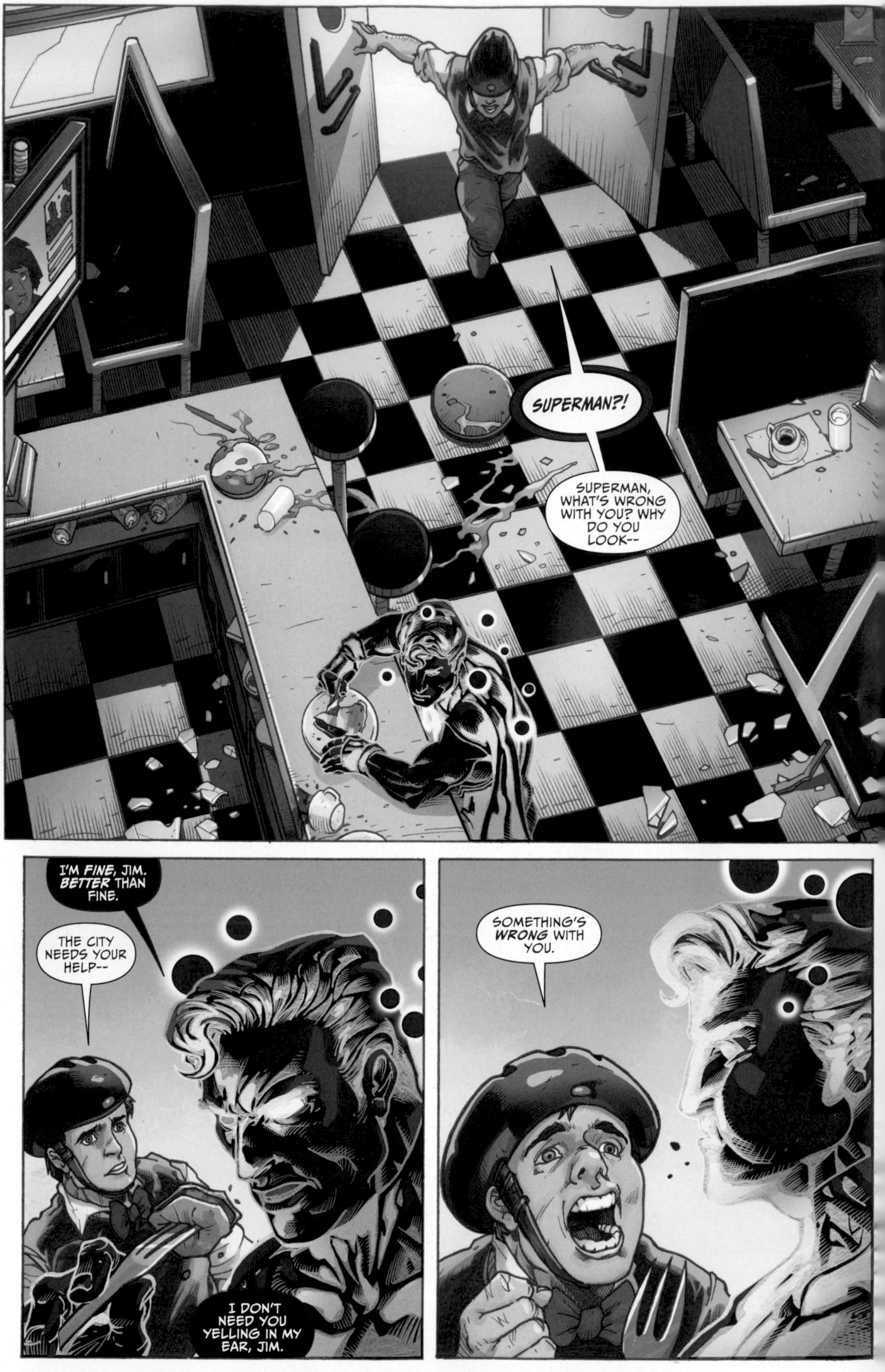
SUPERMAN?!
SUPERMAN, WHAT'S WRONG WITH YOU? WHY DO YOU LOOK--
I'M *FINE*, JIM. *BETTER* THAN FINE.
THE CITY NEEDS YOUR HELP--
I DON'T NEED YOU YELLING IN MY EAR, JIM.
SOMETHING'S *WRONG* WITH YOU.

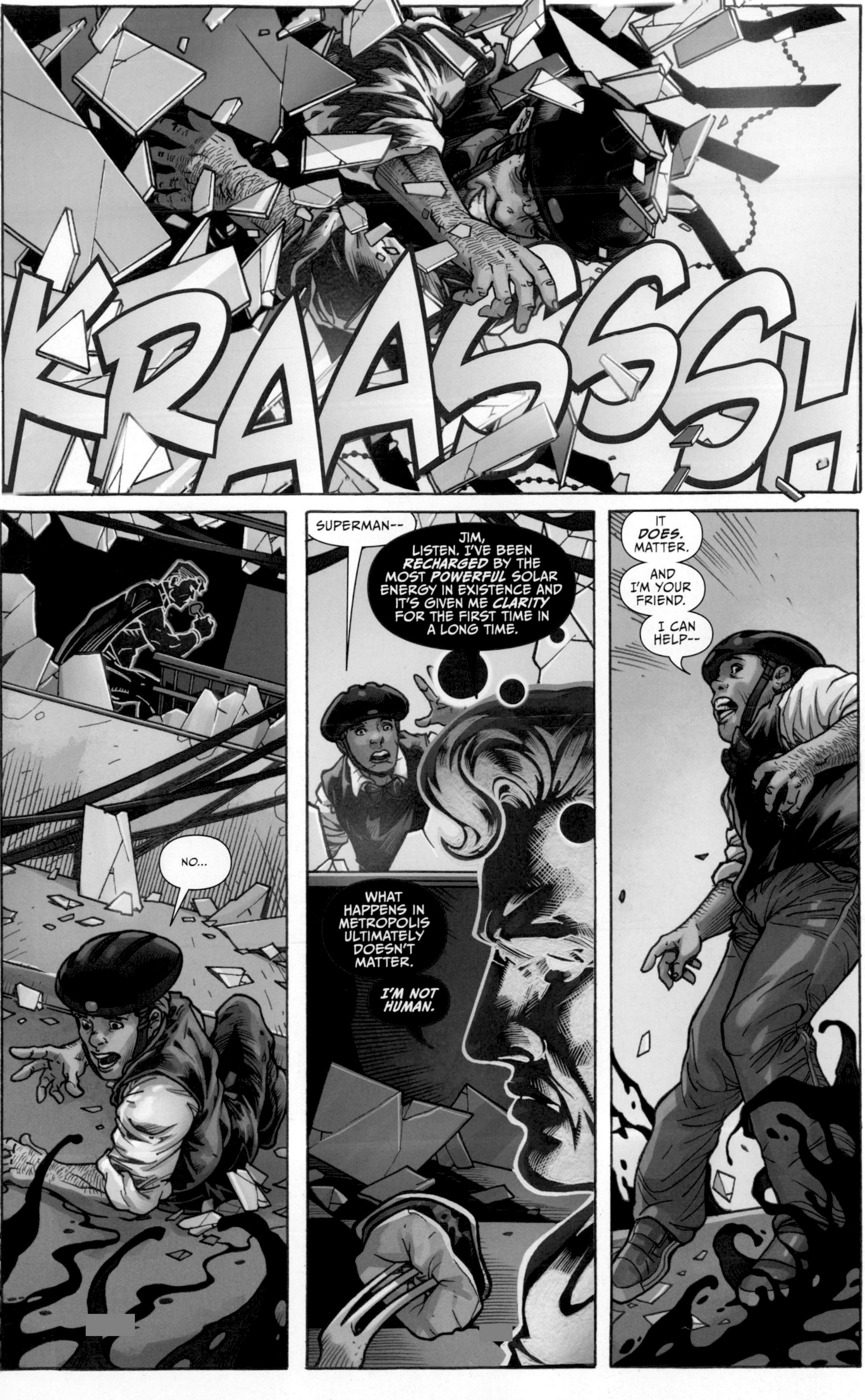
KRAASSH!
NO...
SUPERMAN--
JIM, LISTEN. I'VE BEEN RECHARGED BY THE MOST POWERFUL SOLAR ENERGY IN EXISTENCE AND IT'S GIVEN ME CLARITY FOR THE FIRST TIME IN A LONG TIME.
WHAT HAPPENS IN METROPOLIS ULTIMATELY DOESN'T MATTER.
I'M NOT HUMAN.
IT DOES. MATTER.
AND I'M YOUR FRIEND.
I CAN HELP--

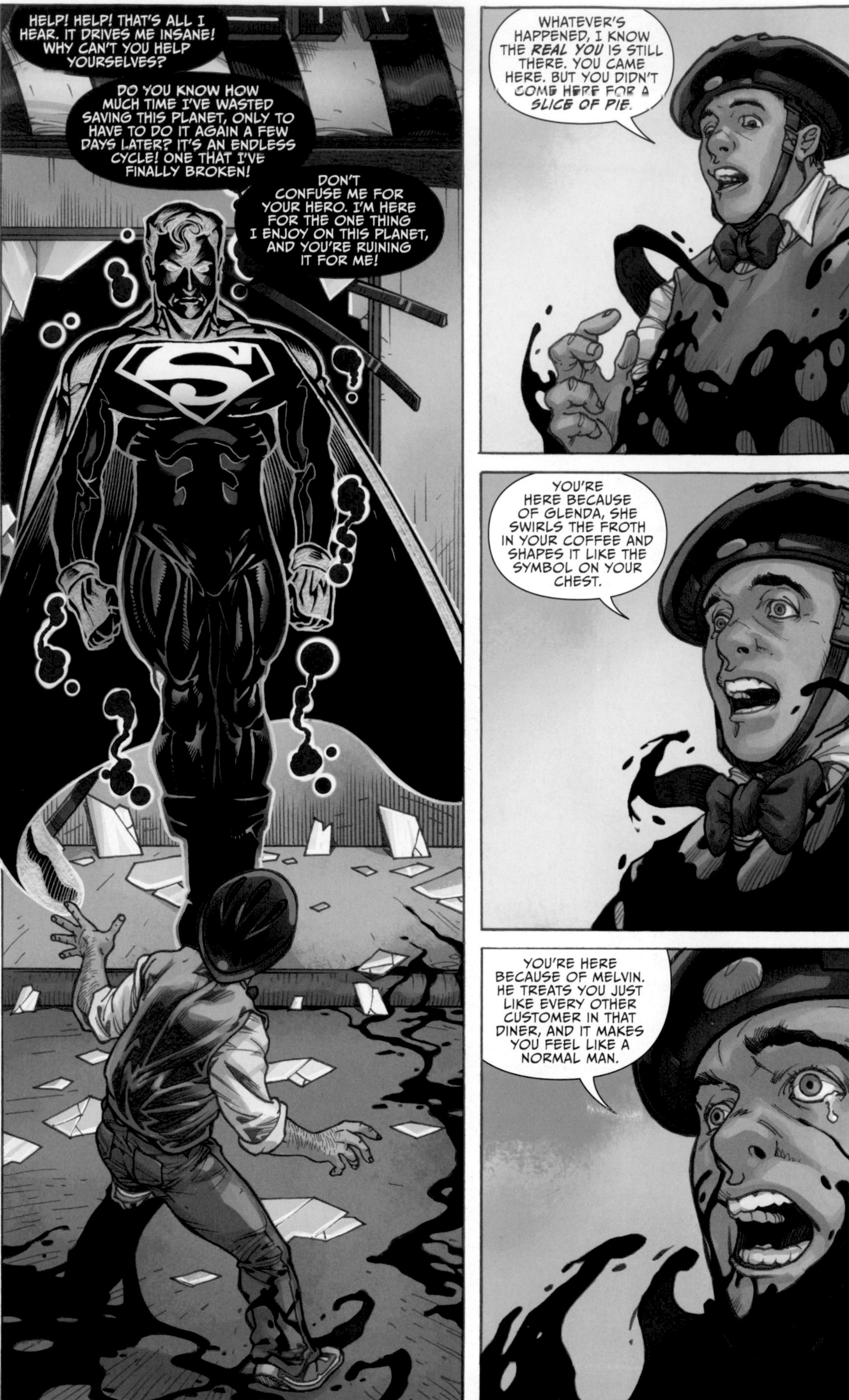
HELP! HELP! THAT'S ALL I HEAR. IT DRIVES ME INSANE! WHY CAN'T YOU HELP YOURSELVES?
DO YOU KNOW HOW MUCH TIME I'VE WASTED SAVING THIS PLANET, ONLY TO HAVE TO DO IT AGAIN A FEW DAYS LATER? IT'S AN ENDLESS CYCLE! ONE THAT I'VE FINALLY BROKEN!
DON'T CONFUSE ME FOR YOUR HERO. I'M HERE FOR THE ONE THING I ENJOY ON THIS PLANET, AND YOU'RE RUINING IT FOR ME!
WHATEVER'S HAPPENED, I KNOW THE REAL YOU IS STILL THERE. BUT YOU CAME HERE. BUT YOU DIDN'T COME HERE FOR A SLICE OF PIE.
YOU'RE HERE BECAUSE OF GLENDA, SHE SWIRLS THE FROTH IN YOUR COFFEE AND SHAPES IT LIKE THE SYMBOL ON YOUR CHEST.
YOU'RE HERE BECAUSE OF MELVIN. HE TREATS YOU JUST LIKE EVERY OTHER CUSTOMER IN THAT DINER, AND IT MAKES YOU FEEL LIKE A NORMAL MAN.

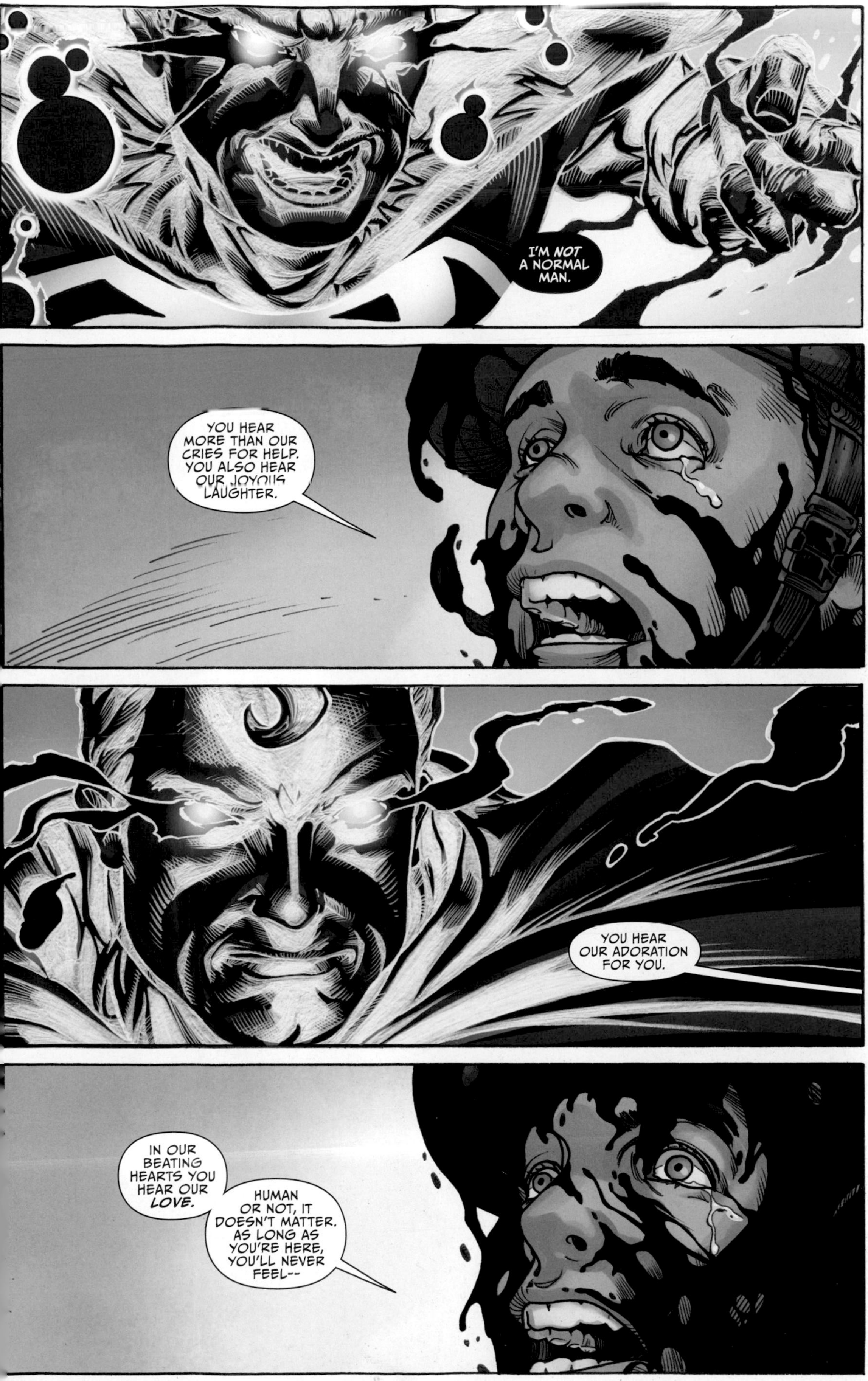
I'M *NOT* A NORMAL MAN.
YOU HEAR MORE THAN OUR CRIES FOR HELP. YOU ALSO HEAR OUR JOYOUS LAUGHTER.
YOU HEAR OUR ADORATION FOR YOU.
IN OUR BEATING HEARTS YOU HEAR OUR ***LOVE.***
HUMAN OR NOT, IT DOESN'T MATTER. AS LONG AS YOU'RE HERE, YOU'LL NEVER FEEL--

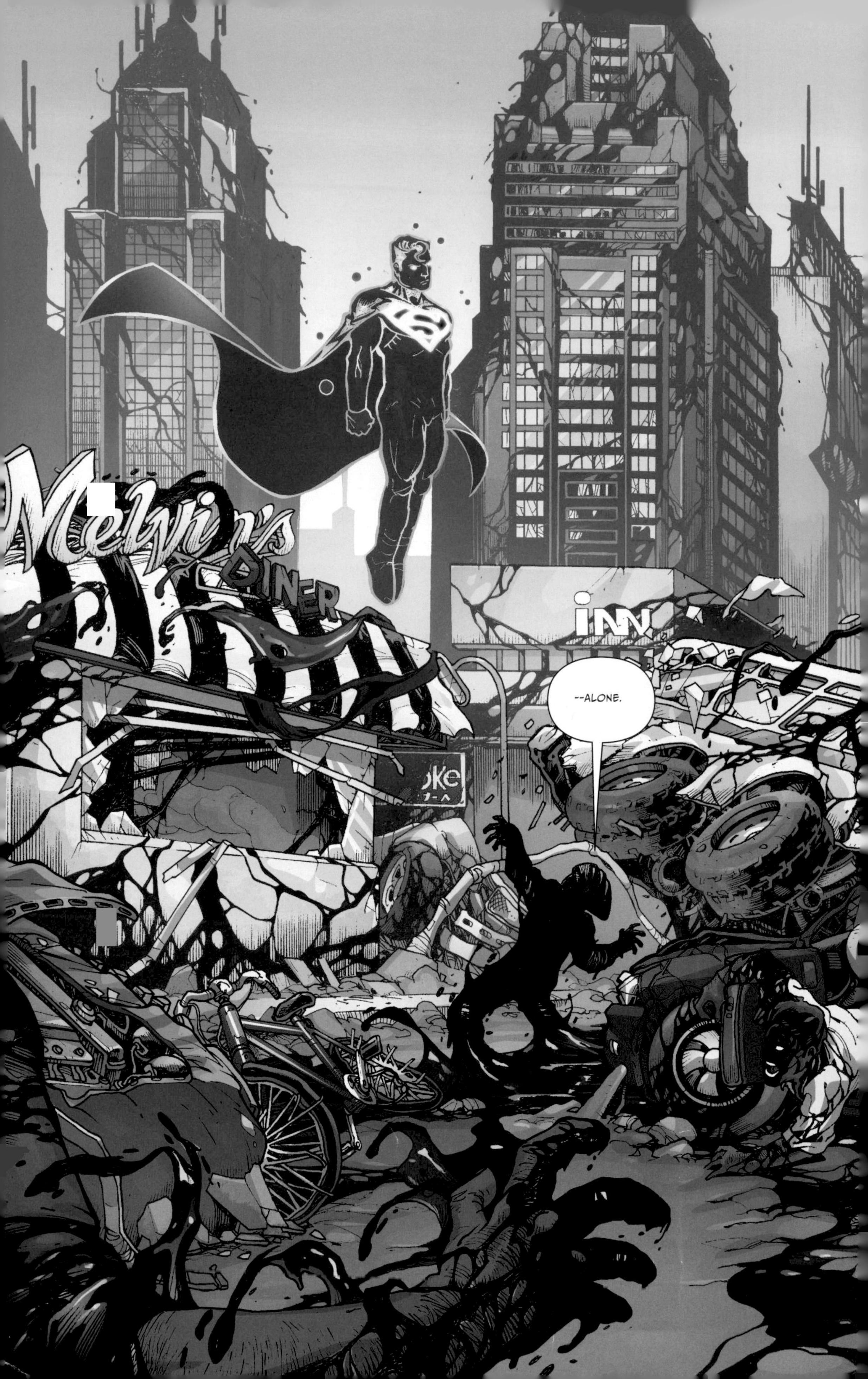

Melvin's
DINER
INN
--ALONE.

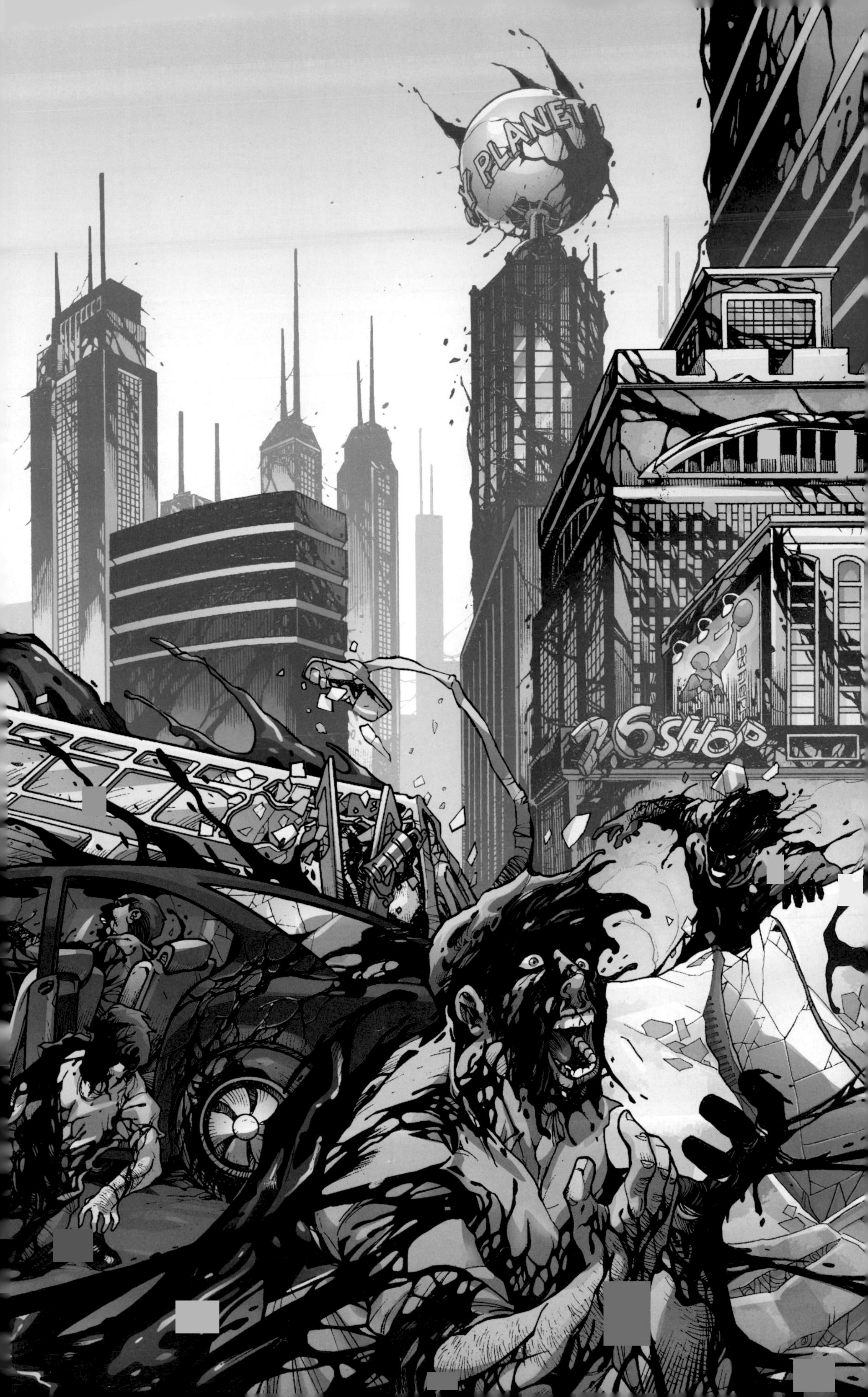
PLANET
26SHOP

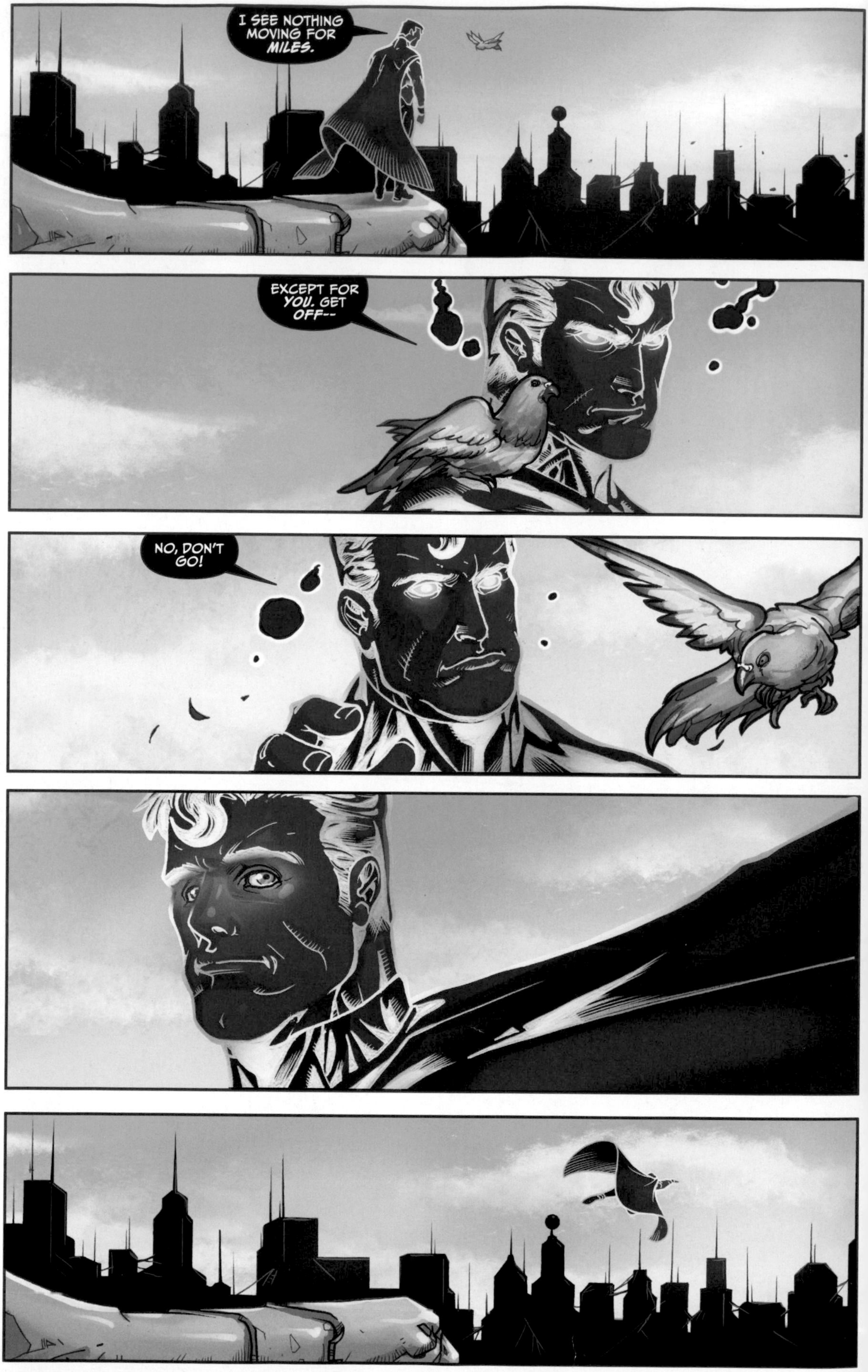
I SEE NOTHING MOVING FOR MILES.
EXCEPT FOR YOU. GET OFF--
NO, DON'T GO!

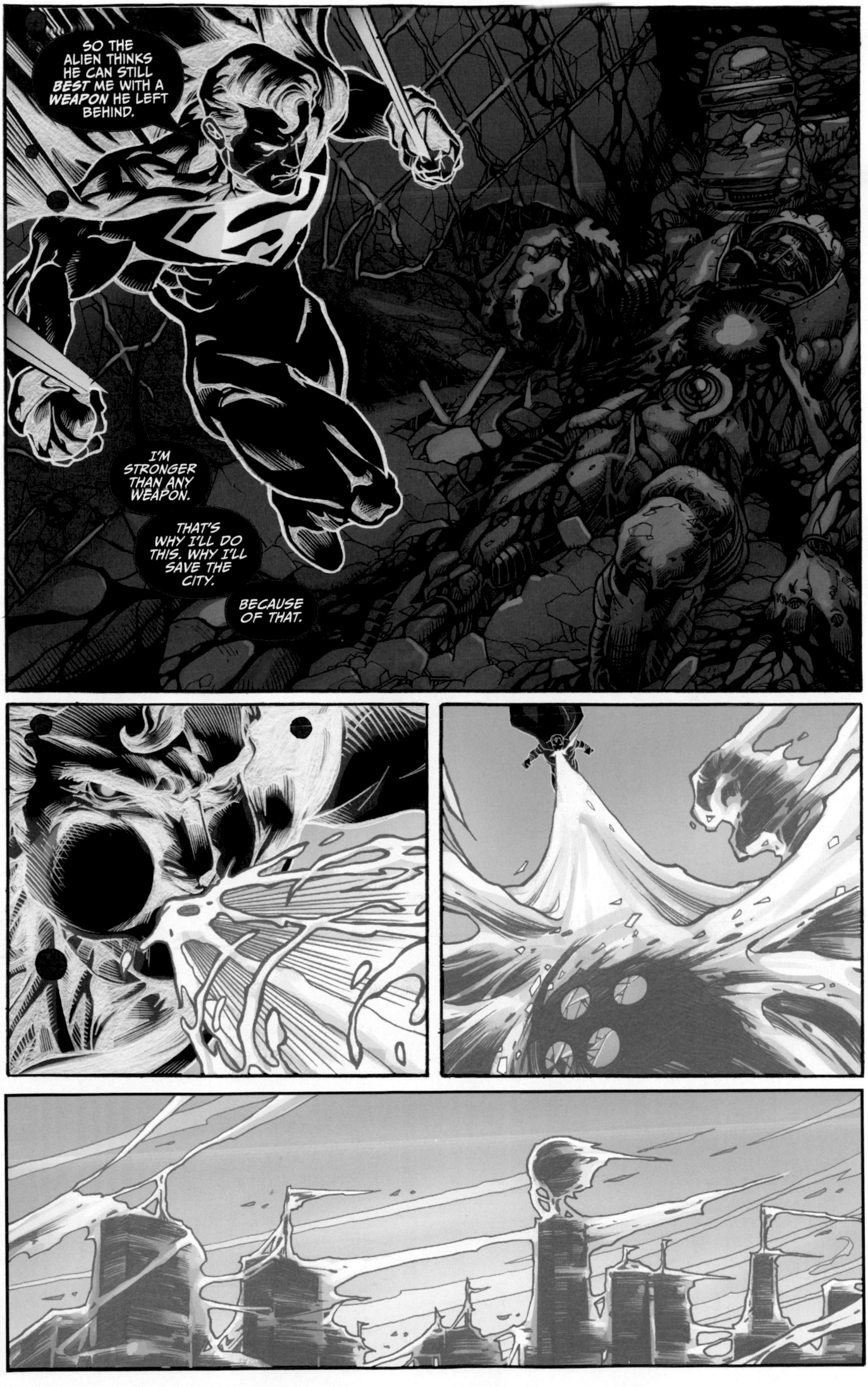
SO THE ALIEN THINKS HE CAN STILL BEST ME WITH A WEAPON HE LEFT BEHIND.
I'M STRONGER THAN ANY WEAPON.
THAT'S WHY I'LL DO THIS. WHY I'LL SAVE THE CITY.
BECAUSE OF THAT.

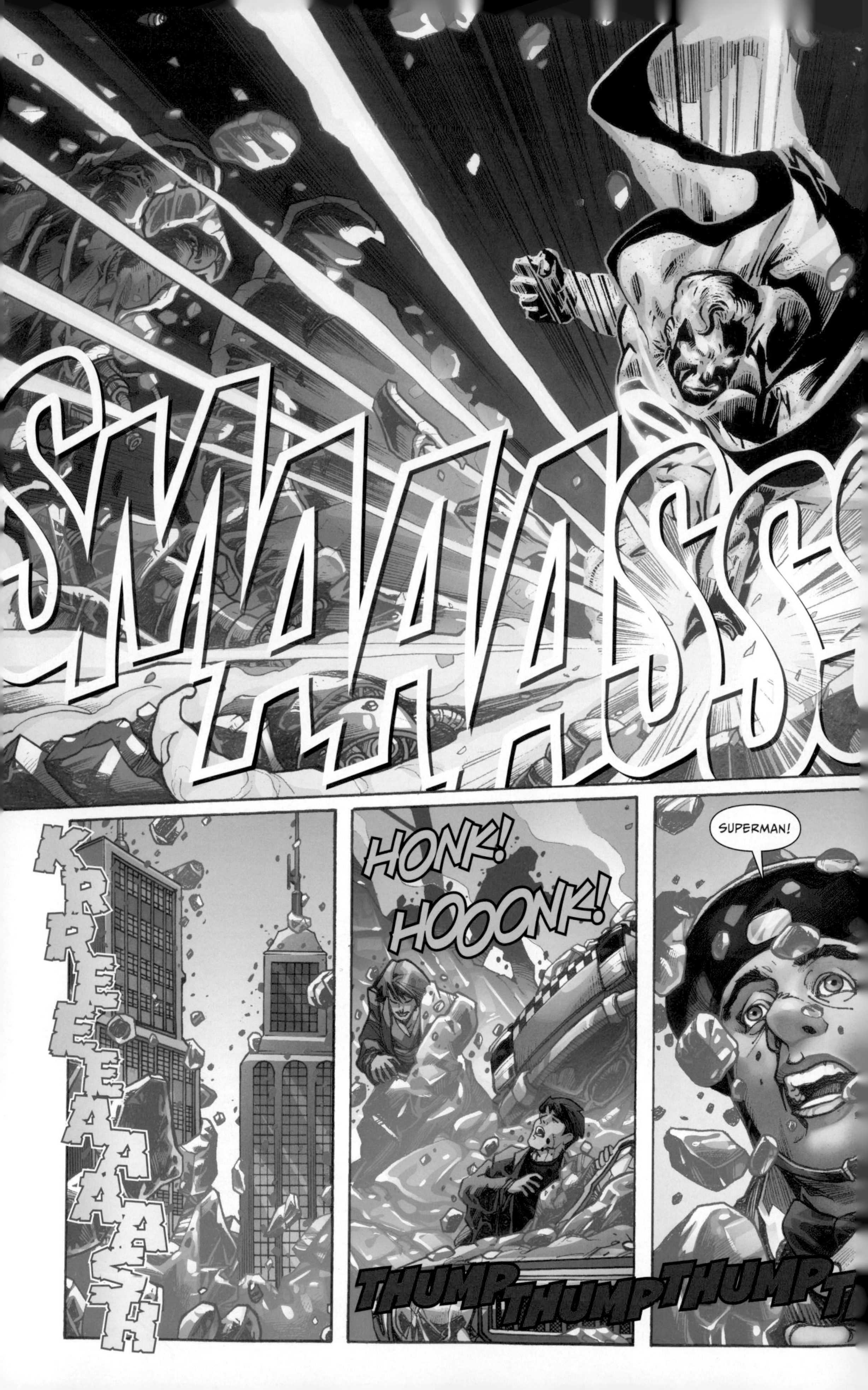
SMASSS
KREEEAAASH
HONK!
HOOONK!
SUPERMAN!
THUMP THUMP THUMP

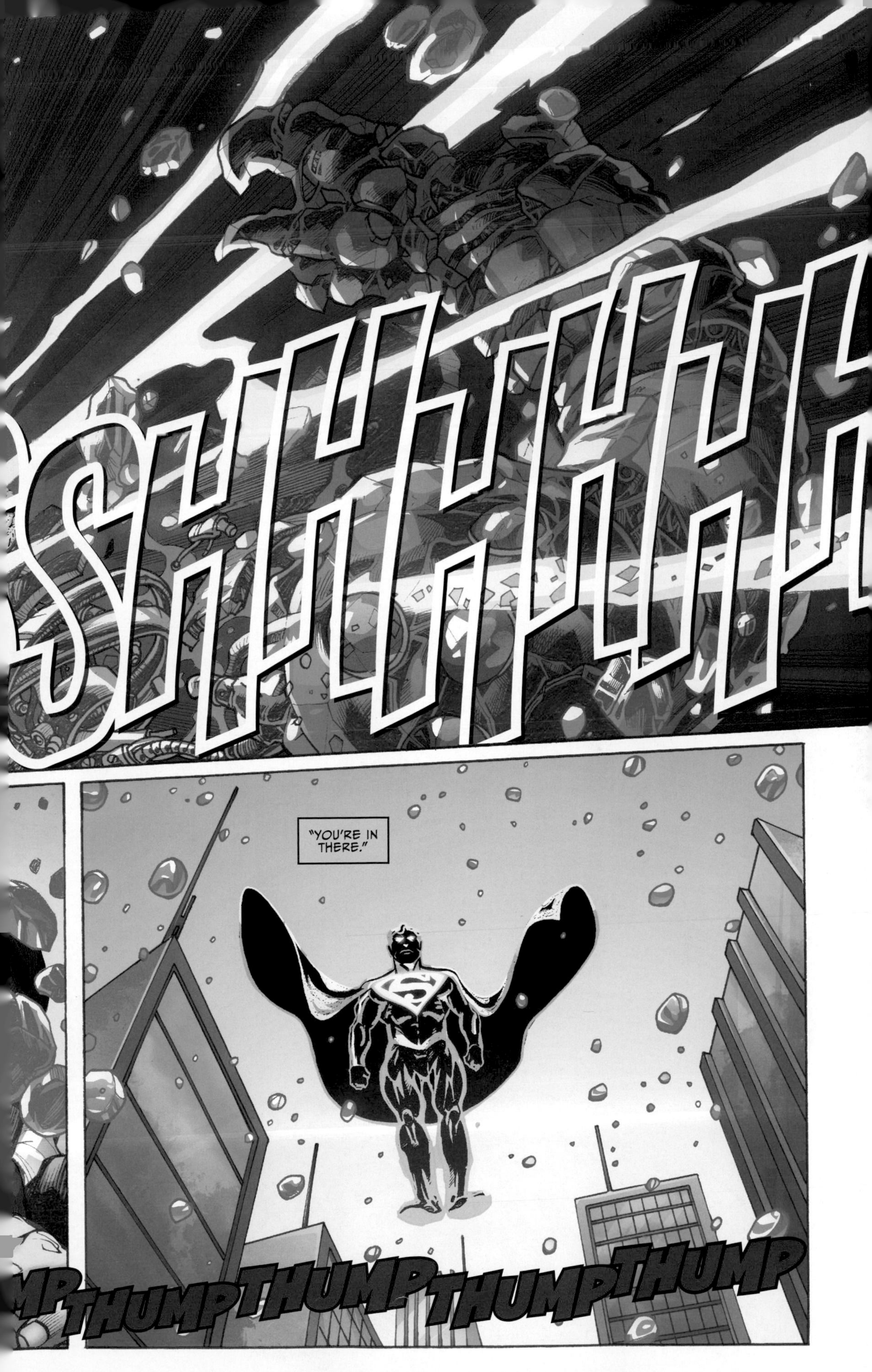
SHHHHHH
"YOU'RE IN THERE."
MP THUMP THUMP THUMP THUMP

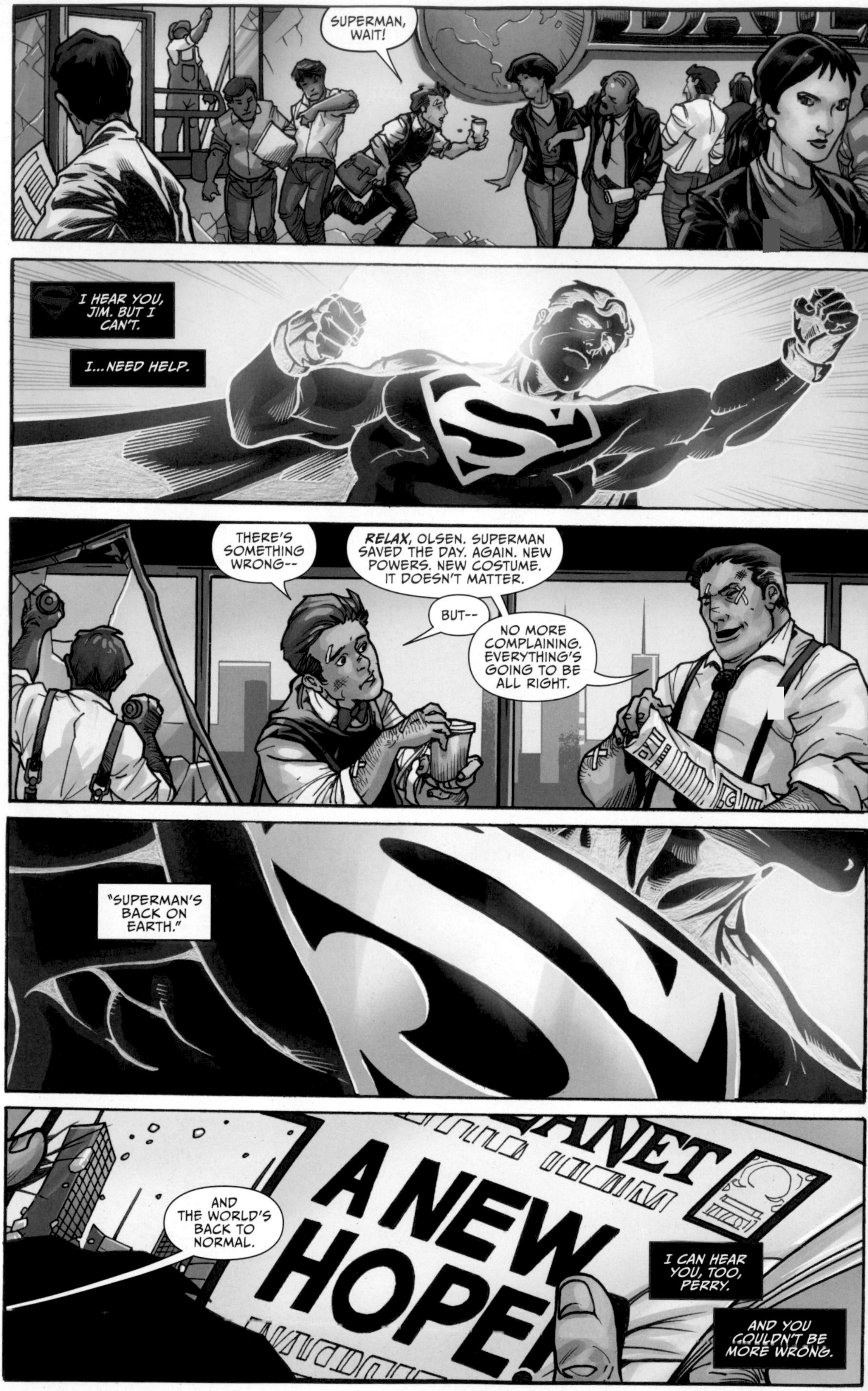
SUPERMAN, WAIT!
I HEAR YOU, JIM. BUT I CAN'T.
I...NEED HELP.
THERE'S SOMETHING WRONG--
RELAX, OLSEN. SUPERMAN SAVED THE DAY. AGAIN. NEW POWERS. NEW COSTUME. IT DOESN'T MATTER.
BUT--
NO MORE COMPLAINING. EVERYTHING'S GOING TO BE ALL RIGHT.
"SUPERMAN'S BACK ON EARTH."
PLANET
A NEW HOPE!
AND THE WORLD'S BACK TO NORMAL.
I CAN HEAR YOU, TOO, PERRY.
AND YOU COULDN'T BE MORE WRONG.

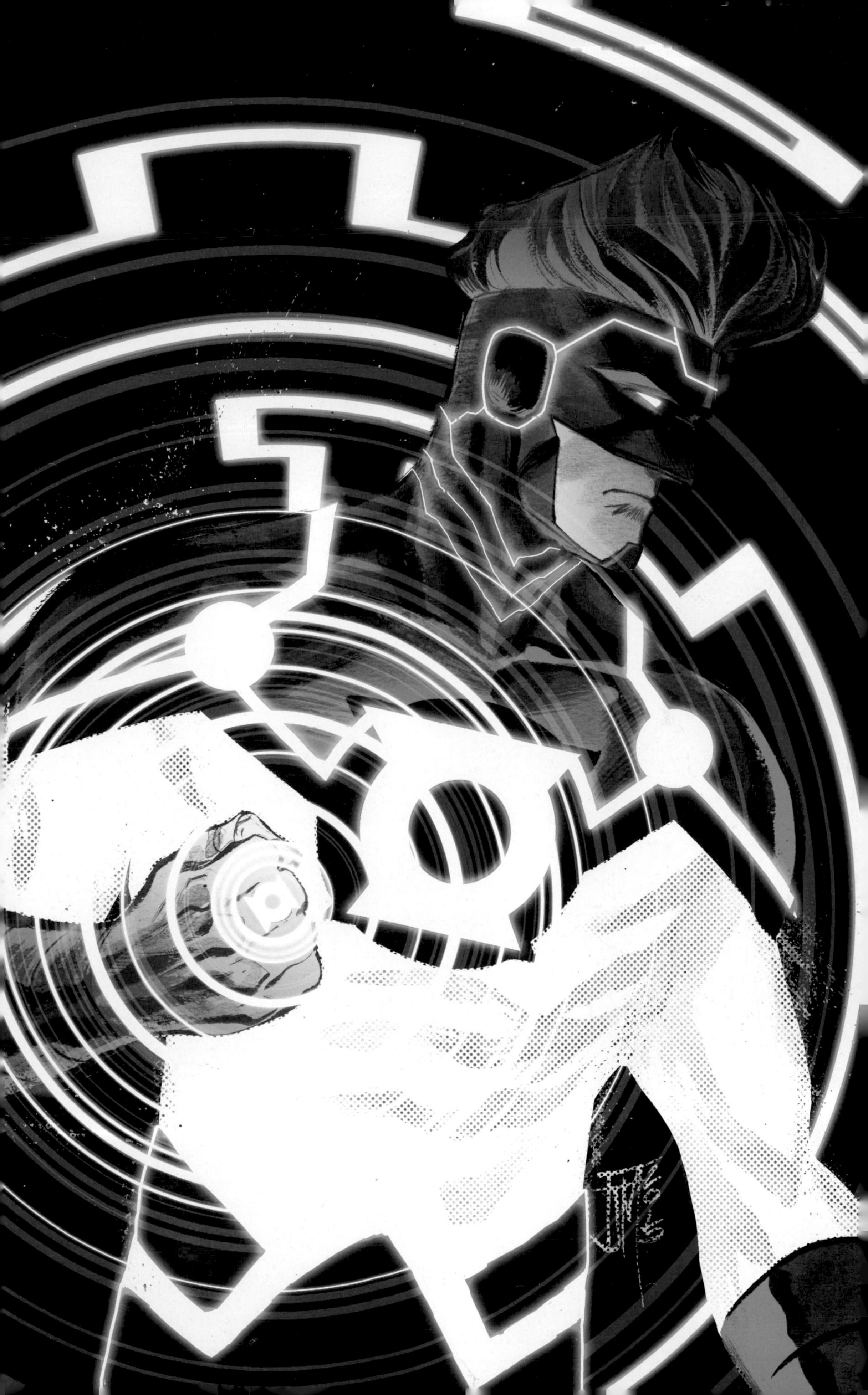

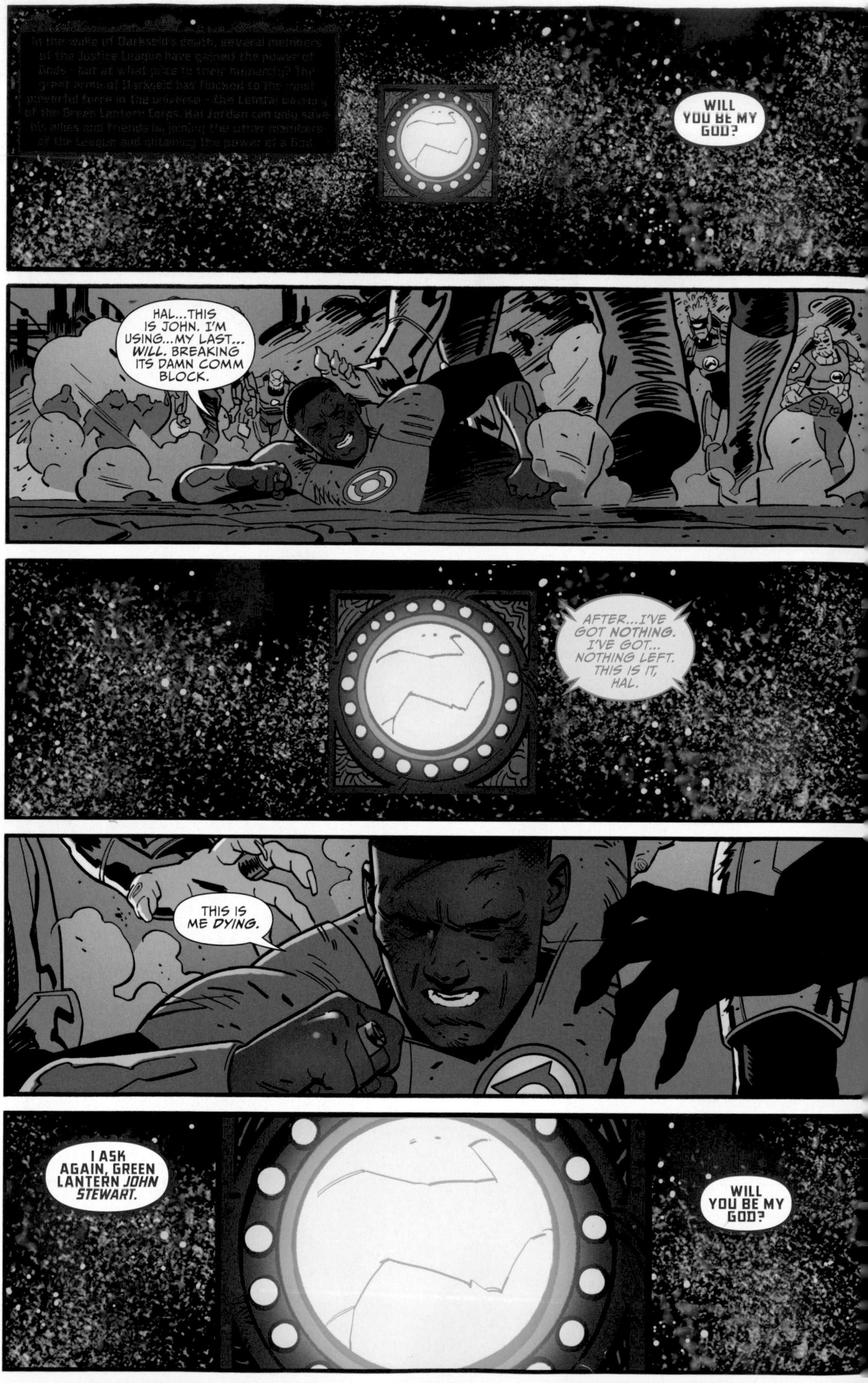
In the wake of Darkseid's death, several members of the Justice League have gained the power of Gods - but at what price to their humanity? The great army of Darkseid has flocked to the most powerful force in the universe - the Lantern battery of the Green Lantern Corps. Hal Jordan can only save his allies and friends by joining the other members of the League and obtaining the power of a God.
WILL YOU BE MY GOD?
HAL...THIS IS JOHN. I'M USING...MY LAST... WILL. BREAKING ITS DAMN COMM BLOCK.
AFTER...I'VE GOT NOTHING. I'VE GOT... NOTHING LEFT. THIS IS IT, HAL.
THIS IS ME DYING.
I ASK AGAIN, GREEN LANTERN JOHN STEWART.
WILL YOU BE MY GOD?

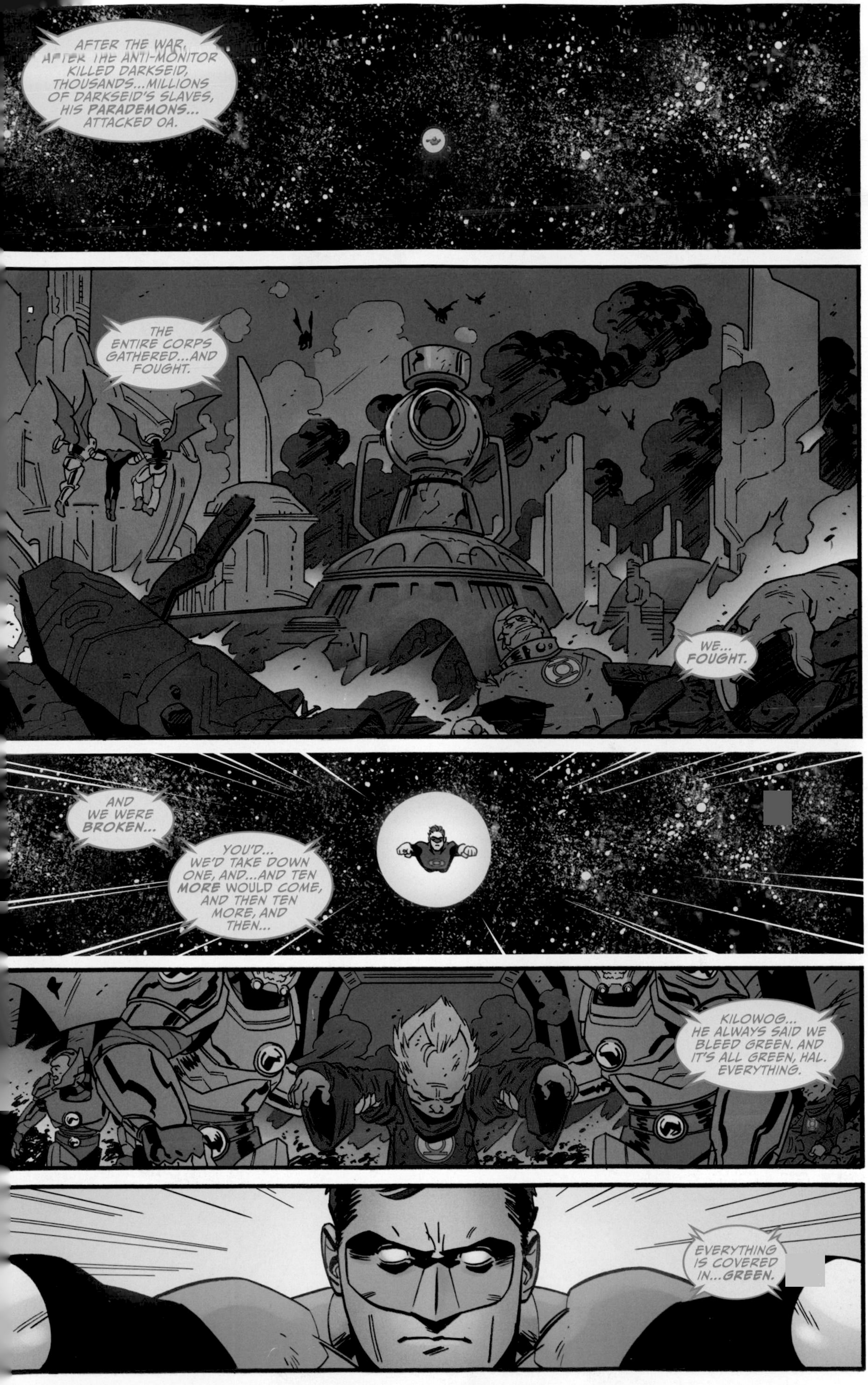
AFTER THE WAR, AFTER THE ANTI-MONITOR KILLED DARKSEID, THOUSANDS...MILLIONS OF DARKSEID'S SLAVES, HIS PARADEMONS... ATTACKED OA.
THE ENTIRE CORPS GATHERED...AND FOUGHT.
WE... FOUGHT.
AND WE WERE BROKEN...
YOU'D... WE'D TAKE DOWN ONE, AND...AND TEN MORE WOULD COME, AND THEN TEN MORE, AND THEN...
KILOWOG... HE ALWAYS SAID WE BLEED GREEN. AND IT'S ALL GREEN, HAL. EVERYTHING.
EVERYTHING IS COVERED IN...GREEN.

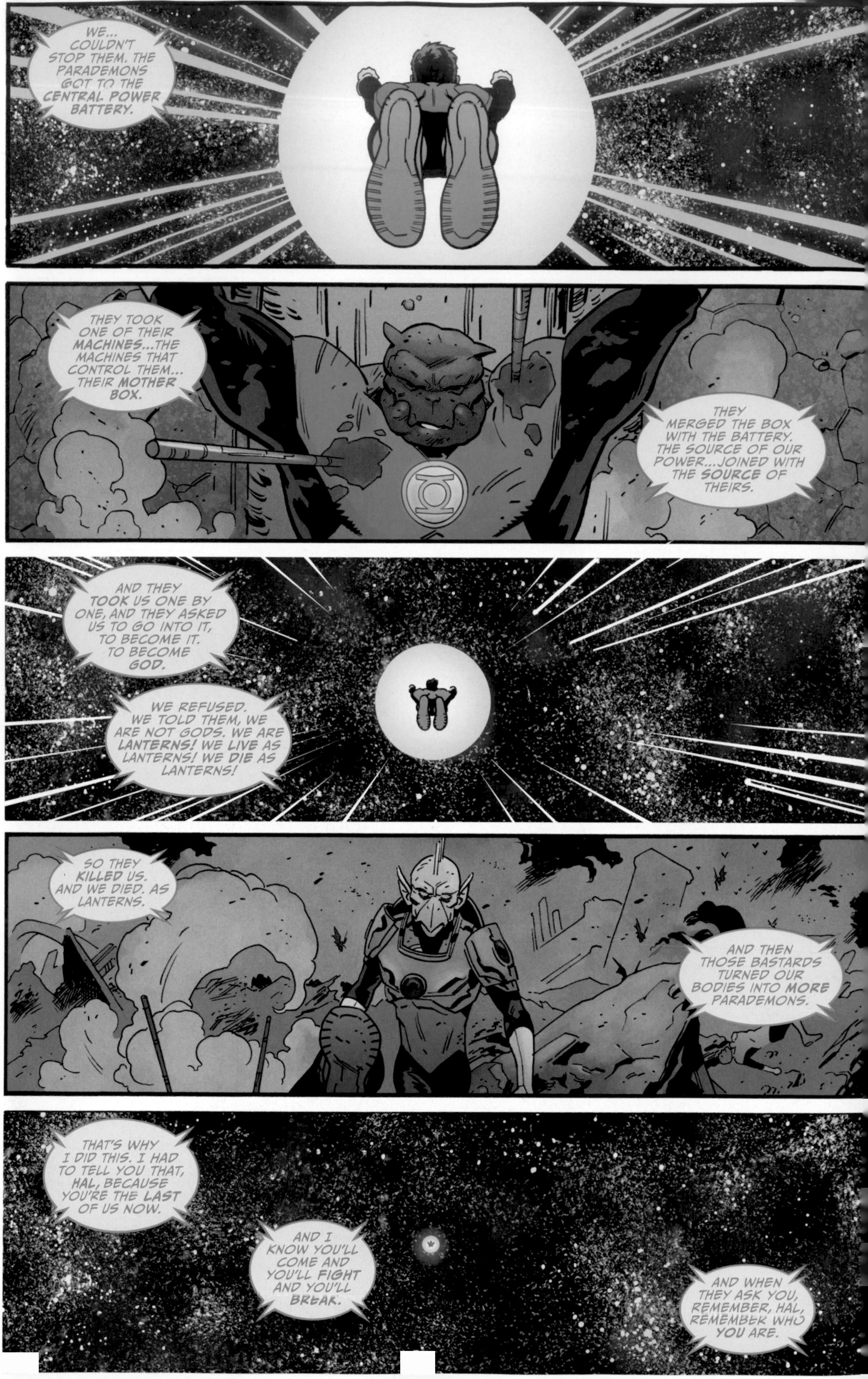
WE... COULDN'T STOP THEM. THE PARADEMONS GOT TO THE CENTRAL POWER BATTERY.
THEY TOOK ONE OF THEIR MACHINES...THE MACHINES THAT CONTROL THEM... THEIR MOTHER BOX.
THEY MERGED THE BOX WITH THE BATTERY. THE SOURCE OF OUR POWER...JOINED WITH THE SOURCE OF THEIRS.
AND THEY TOOK US ONE BY ONE, AND THEY ASKED US TO GO INTO IT, TO BECOME IT. TO BECOME GOD.
WE REFUSED. WE TOLD THEM, WE ARE NOT GODS. WE ARE LANTERNS! WE LIVE AS LANTERNS! WE DIE AS LANTERNS!
SO THEY KILLED US. AND WE DIED. AS LANTERNS.
AND THEN THOSE BASTARDS TURNED OUR BODIES INTO MORE PARADEMONS.
THAT'S WHY I DID THIS. I HAD TO TELL YOU THAT, HAL, BECAUSE YOU'RE THE LAST OF US NOW.
AND I KNOW YOU'LL COME AND YOU'LL FIGHT AND YOU'LL BREAK.
AND WHEN THEY ASK YOU, REMEMBER, HAL, REMEMBER WHO YOU ARE.

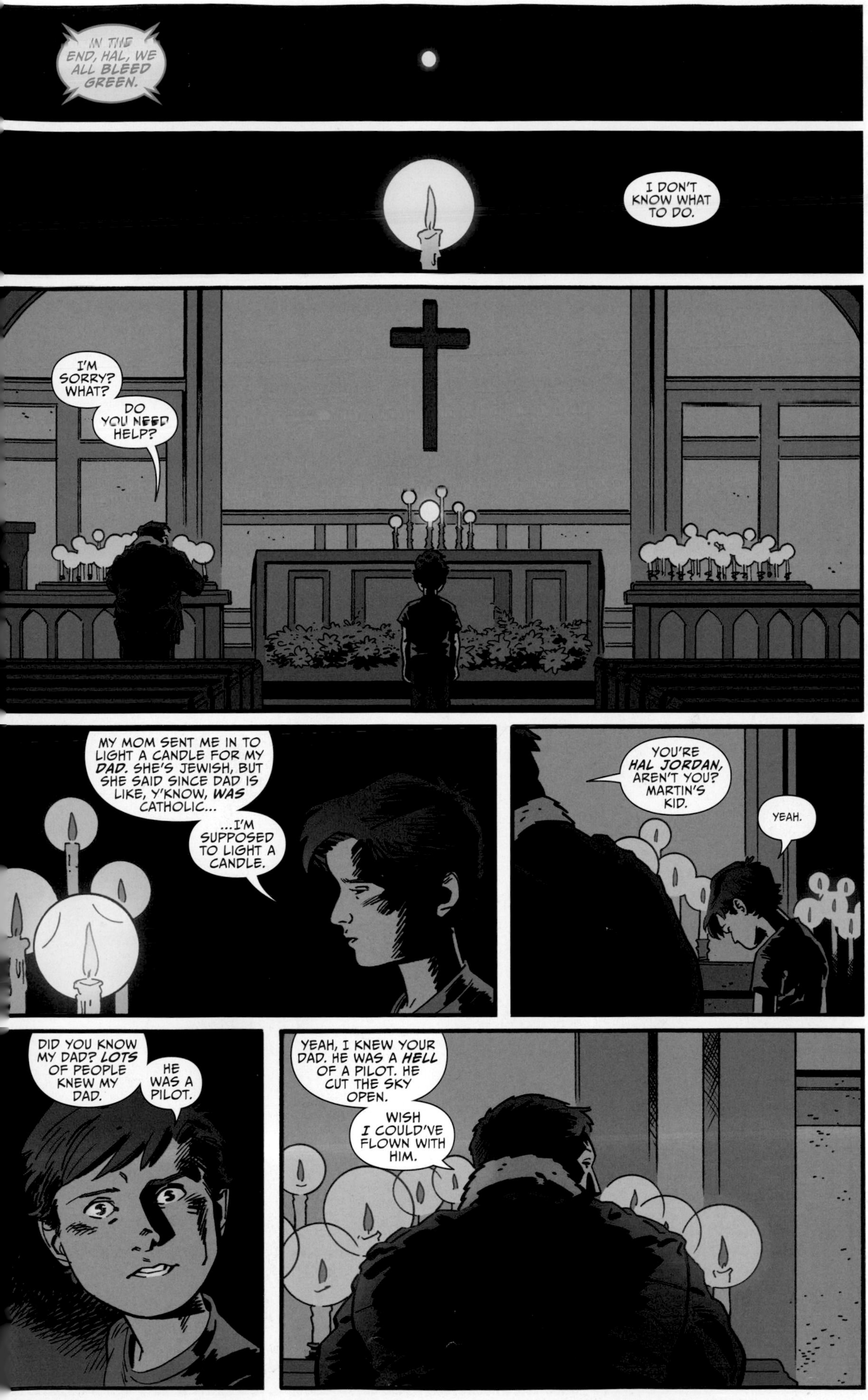
IN THE END, HAL, WE ALL BLEED GREEN.
I DON'T KNOW WHAT TO DO.
I'M SORRY? WHAT?
DO YOU NEED HELP?
MY MOM SENT ME IN TO LIGHT A CANDLE FOR MY DAD. SHE'S JEWISH, BUT SHE SAID SINCE DAD IS LIKE, Y'KNOW, WAS CATHOLIC...
...I'M SUPPOSED TO LIGHT A CANDLE.
YOU'RE HAL JORDAN, AREN'T YOU? MARTIN'S KID.
YEAH.
DID YOU KNOW MY DAD? LOTS OF PEOPLE KNEW MY DAD.
HE WAS A PILOT.
YEAH, I KNEW YOUR DAD. HE WAS A HELL OF A PILOT. HE CUT THE SKY OPEN.
WISH I COULD'VE FLOWN WITH HIM.

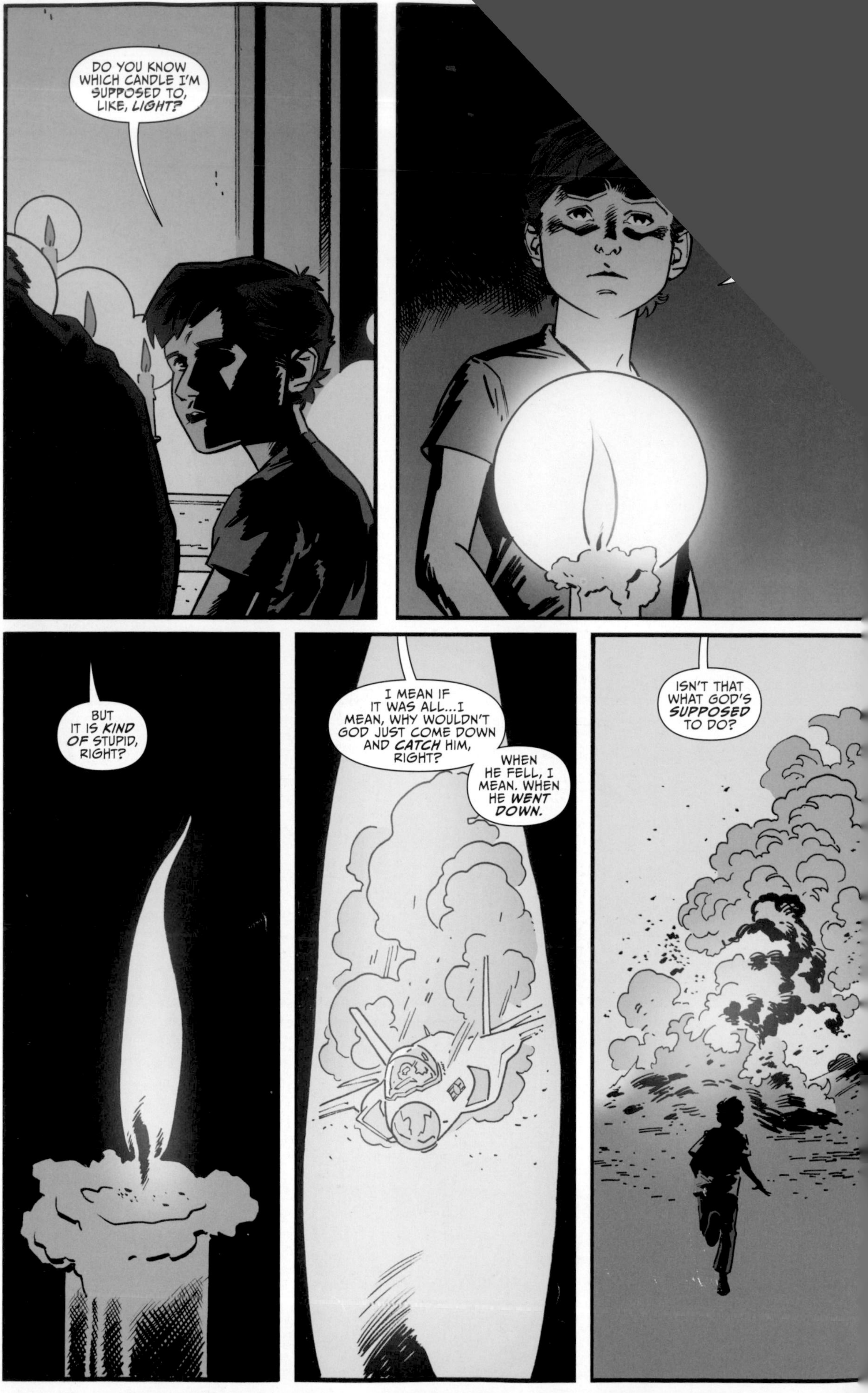
DO YOU KNOW WHICH CANDLE I'M SUPPOSED TO, LIKE, *LIGHT?*
BUT IT IS *KIND OF* STUPID, RIGHT?
I MEAN IF IT WAS ALL... I MEAN, WHY WOULDN'T GOD JUST COME DOWN AND *CATCH* HIM, RIGHT?
WHEN HE FELL, I MEAN. WHEN HE *WENT DOWN.*
ISN'T THAT WHAT GOD'S *SUPPOSED* TO DO?

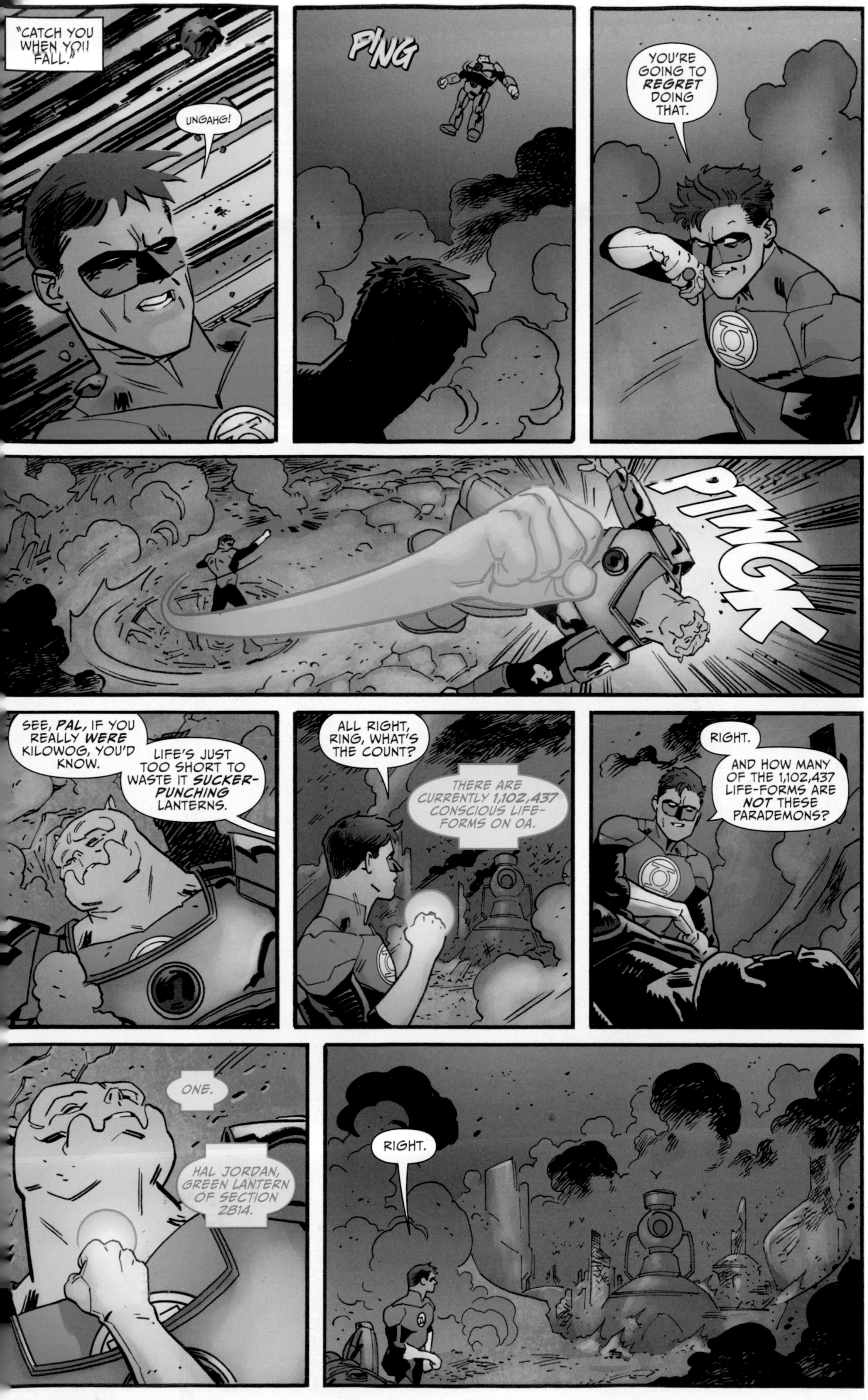
"CATCH YOU WHEN YOU FALL."
UNGAHG!
PING
YOU'RE GOING TO REGRET DOING THAT.
PTINGK
SEE, PAL, IF YOU REALLY WERE KILOWOG, YOU'D KNOW.
LIFE'S JUST TOO SHORT TO WASTE IT SUCKER-PUNCHING LANTERNS.
ALL RIGHT, RING, WHAT'S THE COUNT?
THERE ARE CURRENTLY 1,102,437 CONSCIOUS LIFE-FORMS ON OA.
RIGHT.
AND HOW MANY OF THE 1,102,437 LIFE-FORMS ARE NOT THESE PARADEMONS?
ONE.
HAL JORDAN, GREEN LANTERN OF SECTION 2814.
RIGHT.

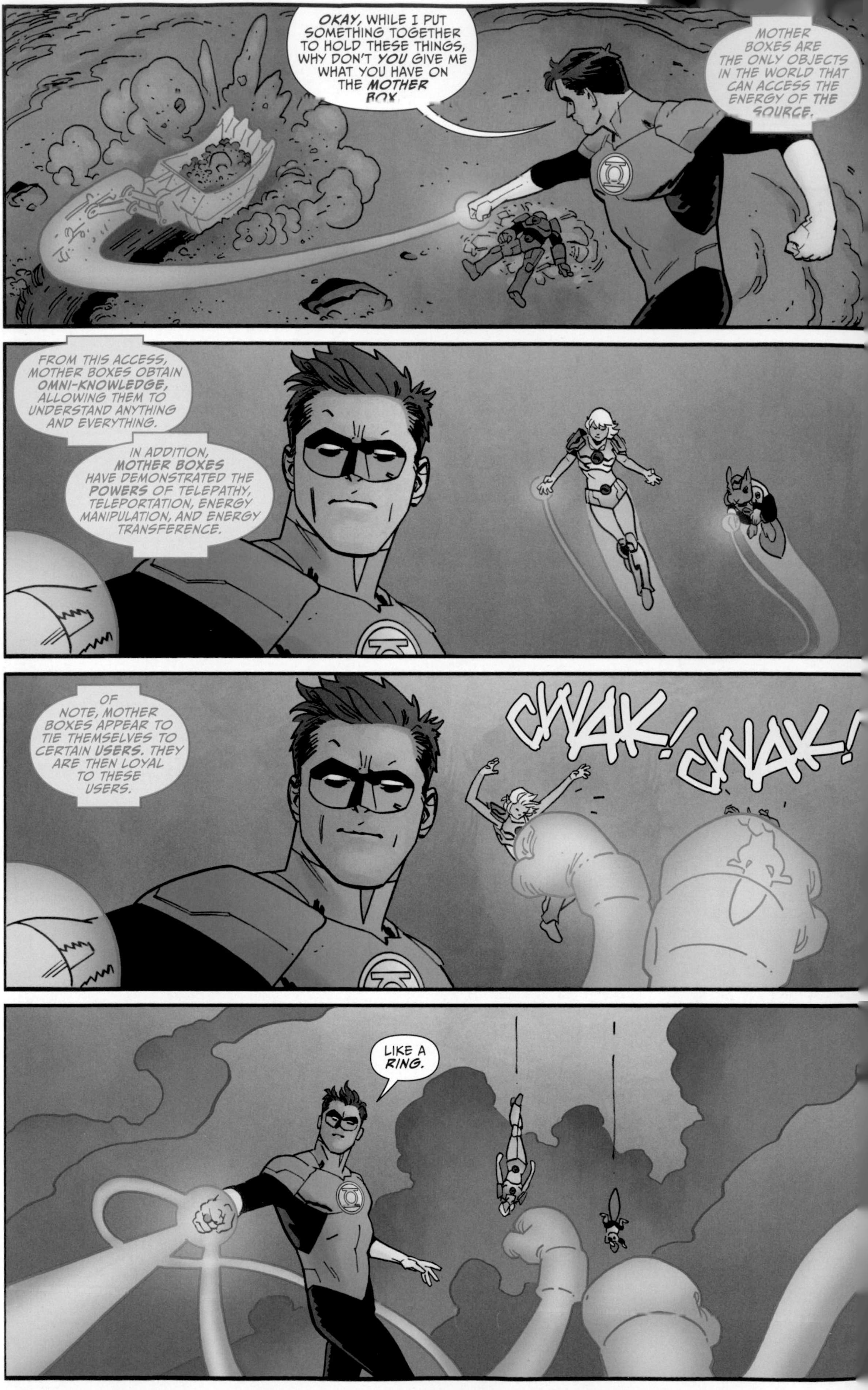

OKAY, WHILE I PUT SOMETHING TOGETHER TO HOLD THESE THINGS, WHY DON'T YOU GIVE ME WHAT YOU HAVE ON THE MOTHER BOX.
MOTHER BOXES ARE THE ONLY OBJECTS IN THE WORLD THAT CAN ACCESS THE ENERGY OF THE SOURCE.
FROM THIS ACCESS, MOTHER BOXES OBTAIN OMNI-KNOWLEDGE, ALLOWING THEM TO UNDERSTAND ANYTHING AND EVERYTHING.
IN ADDITION, MOTHER BOXES HAVE DEMONSTRATED THE POWERS OF TELEPATHY, TELEPORTATION, ENERGY MANIPULATION, AND ENERGY TRANSFERENCE.
OF NOTE, MOTHER BOXES APPEAR TO TIE THEMSELVES TO CERTAIN USERS. THEY ARE THEN LOYAL TO THESE USERS.
CWAK! CWAK!
LIKE A RING.

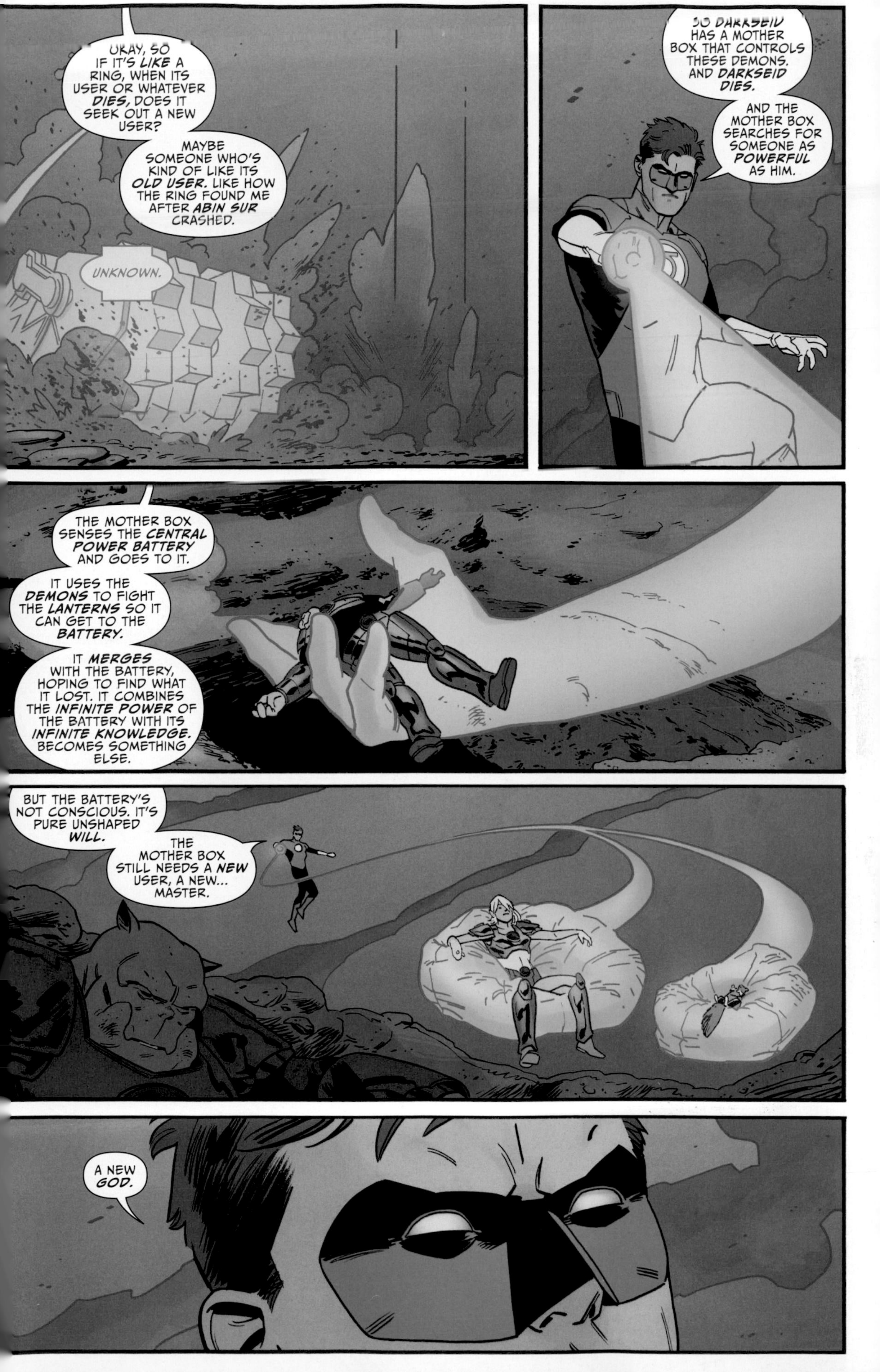
OKAY, SO IF IT'S LIKE A RING, WHEN ITS USER OR WHATEVER DIES, DOES IT SEEK OUT A NEW USER?
MAYBE SOMEONE WHO'S KIND OF LIKE ITS OLD USER. LIKE HOW THE RING FOUND ME AFTER ABIN SUR CRASHED.
UNKNOWN.
SO DARKSEID HAS A MOTHER BOX THAT CONTROLS THESE DEMONS. AND DARKSEID DIES.
AND THE MOTHER BOX SEARCHES FOR SOMEONE AS POWERFUL AS HIM.
THE MOTHER BOX SENSES THE CENTRAL POWER BATTERY AND GOES TO IT.
IT USES THE DEMONS TO FIGHT THE LANTERNS SO IT CAN GET TO THE BATTERY.
IT MERGES WITH THE BATTERY, HOPING TO FIND WHAT IT LOST. IT COMBINES THE INFINITE POWER OF THE BATTERY WITH ITS INFINITE KNOWLEDGE. BECOMES SOMETHING ELSE.
BUT THE BATTERY'S NOT CONSCIOUS. IT'S PURE UNSHAPED WILL.
THE MOTHER BOX STILL NEEDS A NEW USER, A NEW... MASTER.
A NEW GOD.

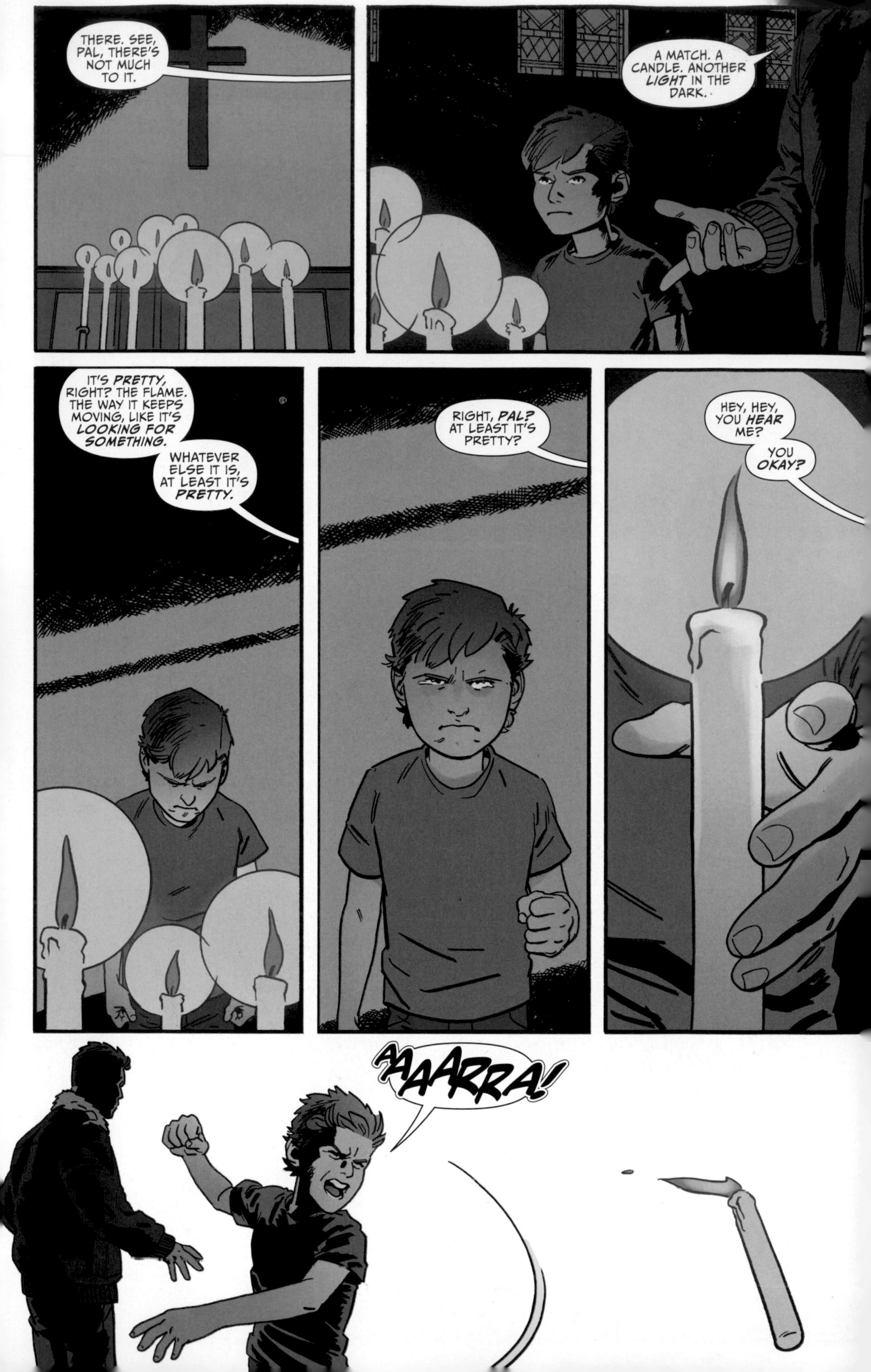
THERE. SEE, PAL, THERE'S NOT MUCH TO IT.
A MATCH. A CANDLE. ANOTHER LIGHT IN THE DARK.
IT'S PRETTY, RIGHT? THE FLAME. THE WAY IT KEEPS MOVING, LIKE IT'S LOOKING FOR SOMETHING.
WHATEVER ELSE IT IS, AT LEAST IT'S PRETTY.
RIGHT, PAL? AT LEAST IT'S PRETTY?
HEY, HEY, YOU HEAR ME?
YOU OKAY?
AAAARRA!

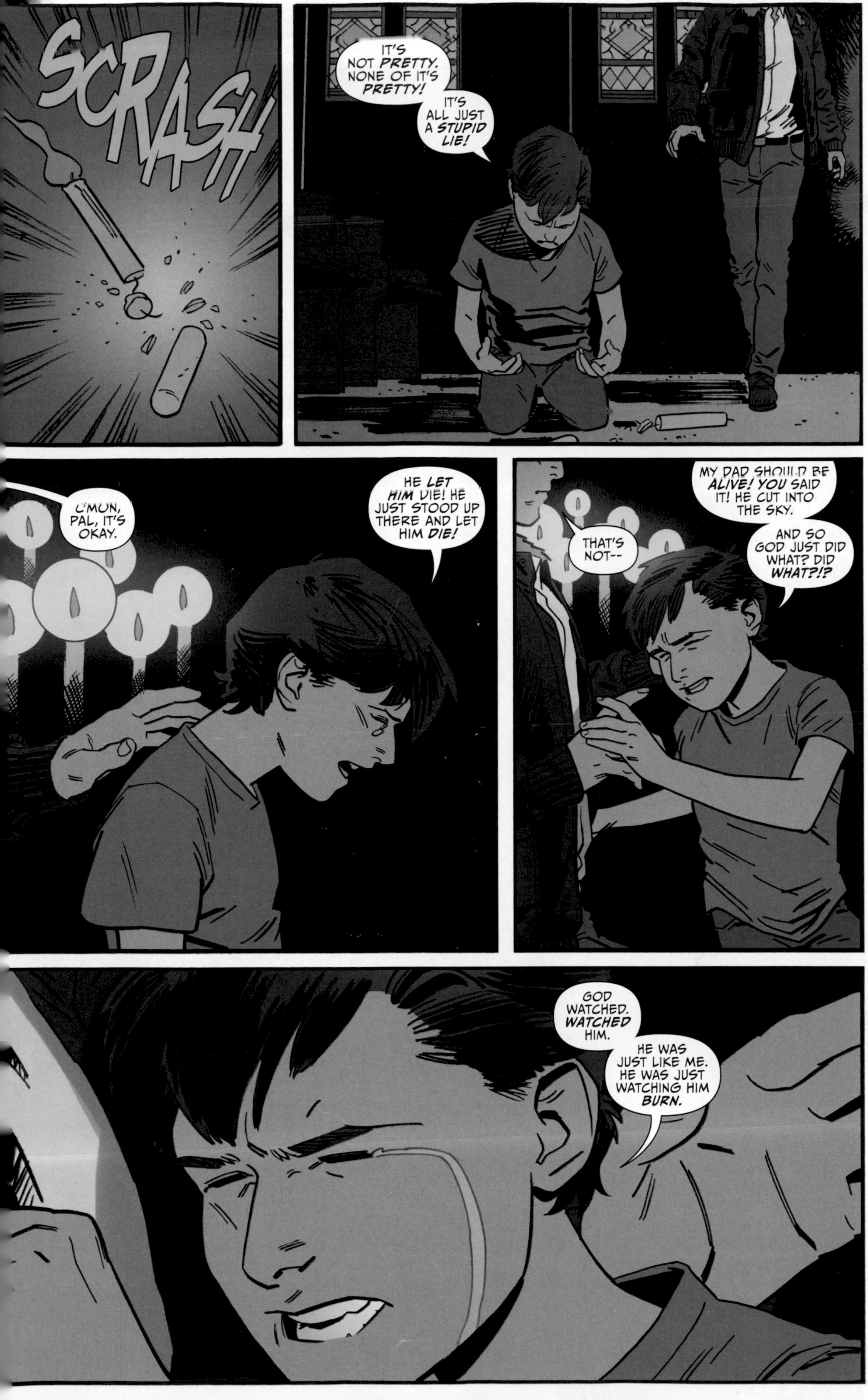
SCRASH
IT'S NOT PRETTY. NONE OF IT'S PRETTY!
IT'S ALL JUST A STUPID LIE!
C'MON, PAL, IT'S OKAY.
HE LET HIM DIE! HE JUST STOOD UP THERE AND LET HIM DIE!
MY DAD SHOULD BE ALIVE! YOU SAID IT! HE CUT INTO THE SKY.
THAT'S NOT--
AND SO GOD JUST DID WHAT? DID WHAT?!?
GOD WATCHED. WATCHED HIM.
HE WAS JUST LIKE ME. HE WAS JUST WATCHING HIM BURN.

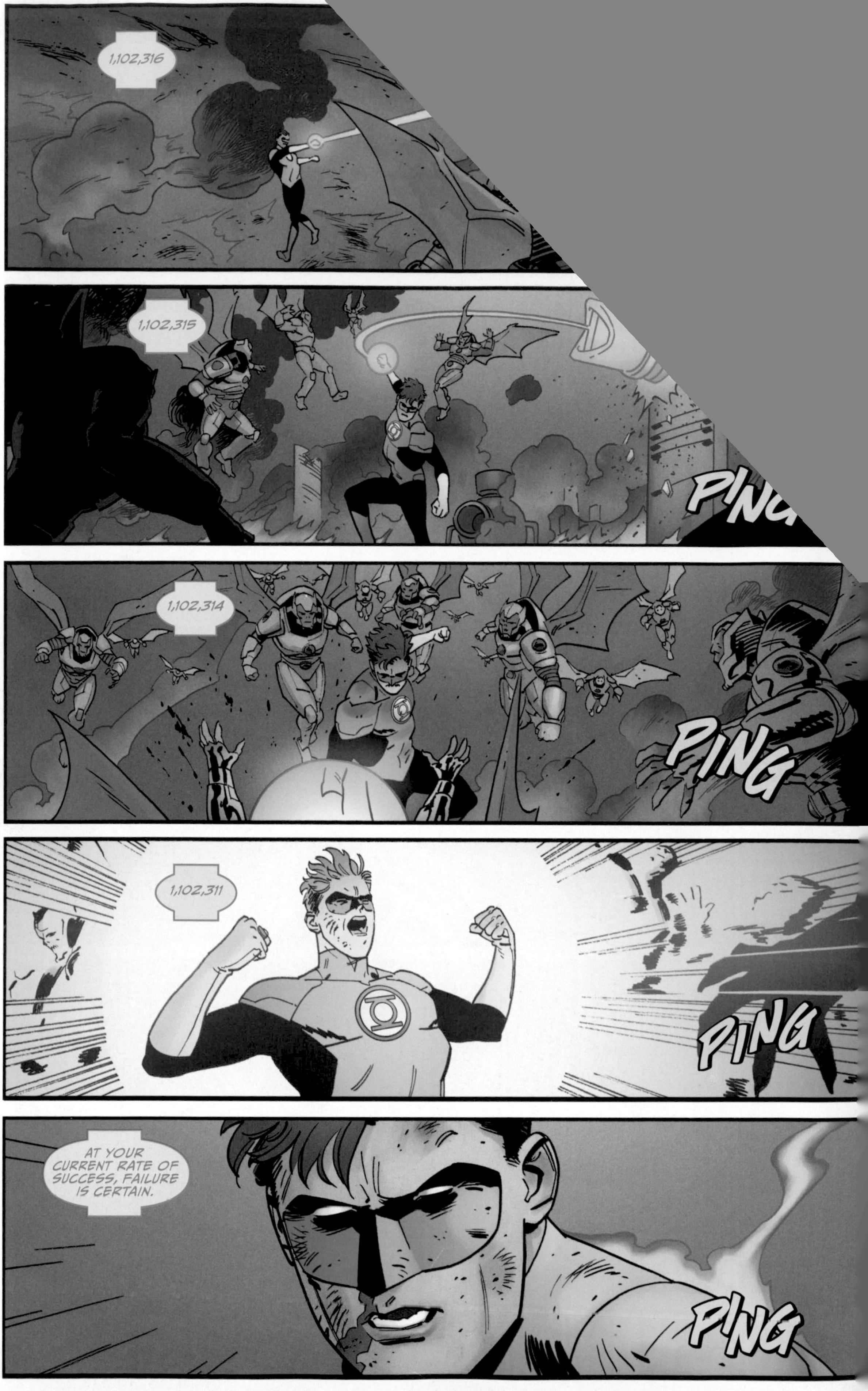
1,102,316
1,102,315
PING
1,102,314
PING
1,102,311
PING
AT YOUR CURRENT RATE OF SUCCESS, FAILURE IS CERTAIN.
PING

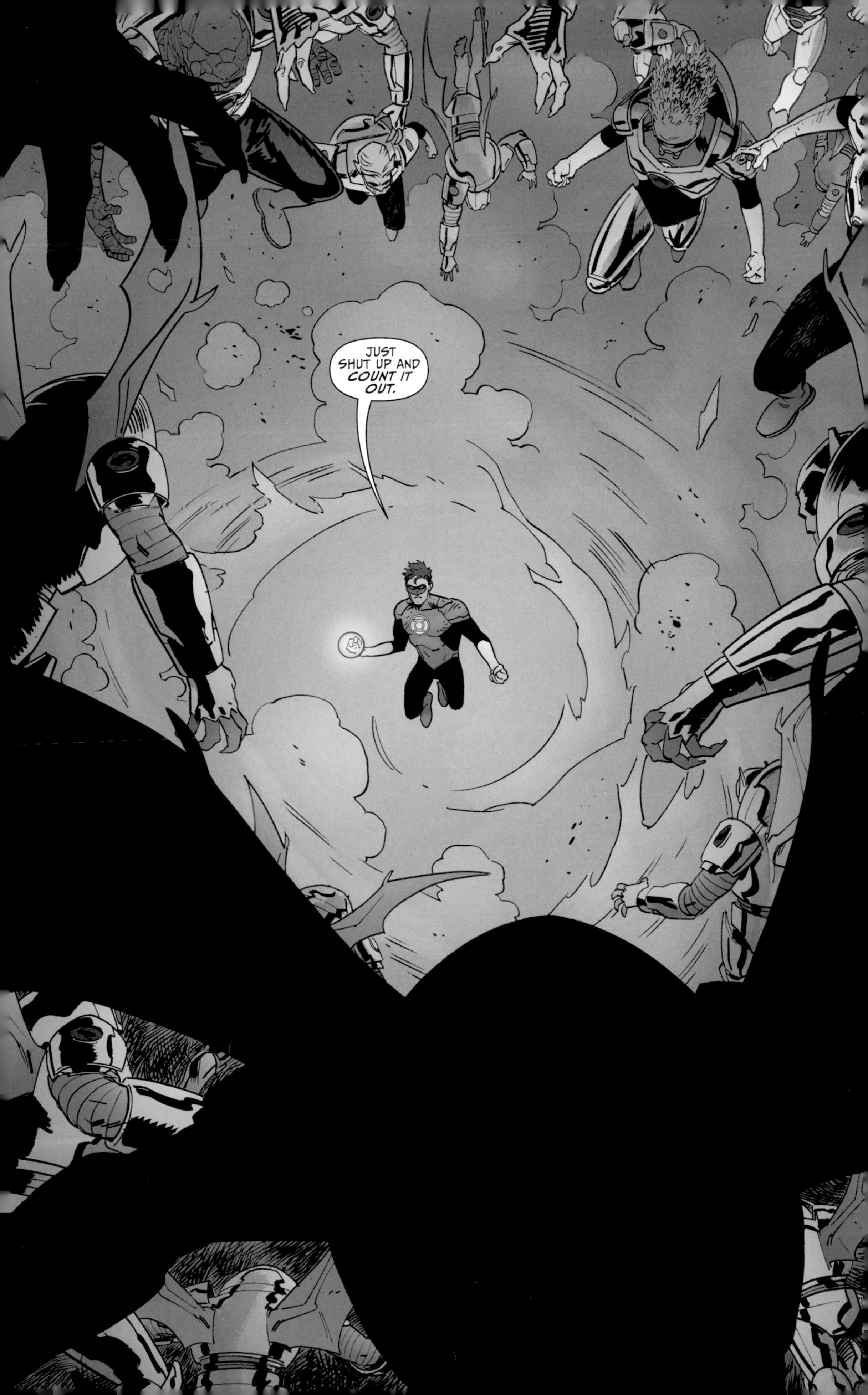
JUST SHUT UP AND COUNT IT OUT.

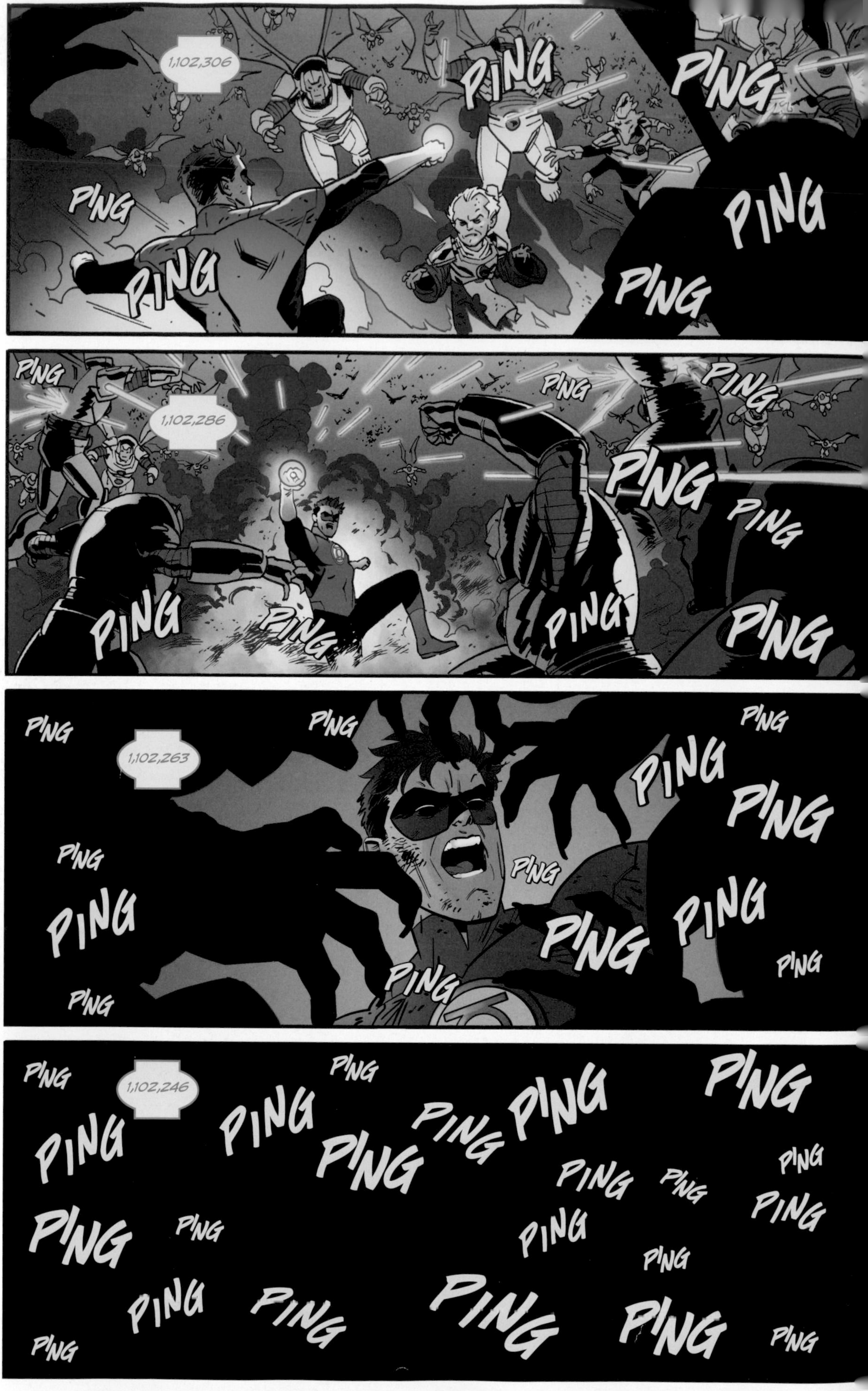
1,102,306
PING
PING
PING
PING
PING
PING
1,102,286
PING
PING
PING
PING
PING
PING
PING
PING
PING
1,102,263
PING
PING
PING
PING
PING
PING
PING
PING
PING
PING
PING
PING
PING
1,102,246
PING
PING
PING
PING
PING
PING
PING
PING
PING
PING
PING
PING
PING
PING
PING
PING
PING
PING
PING
PING
PING
PING

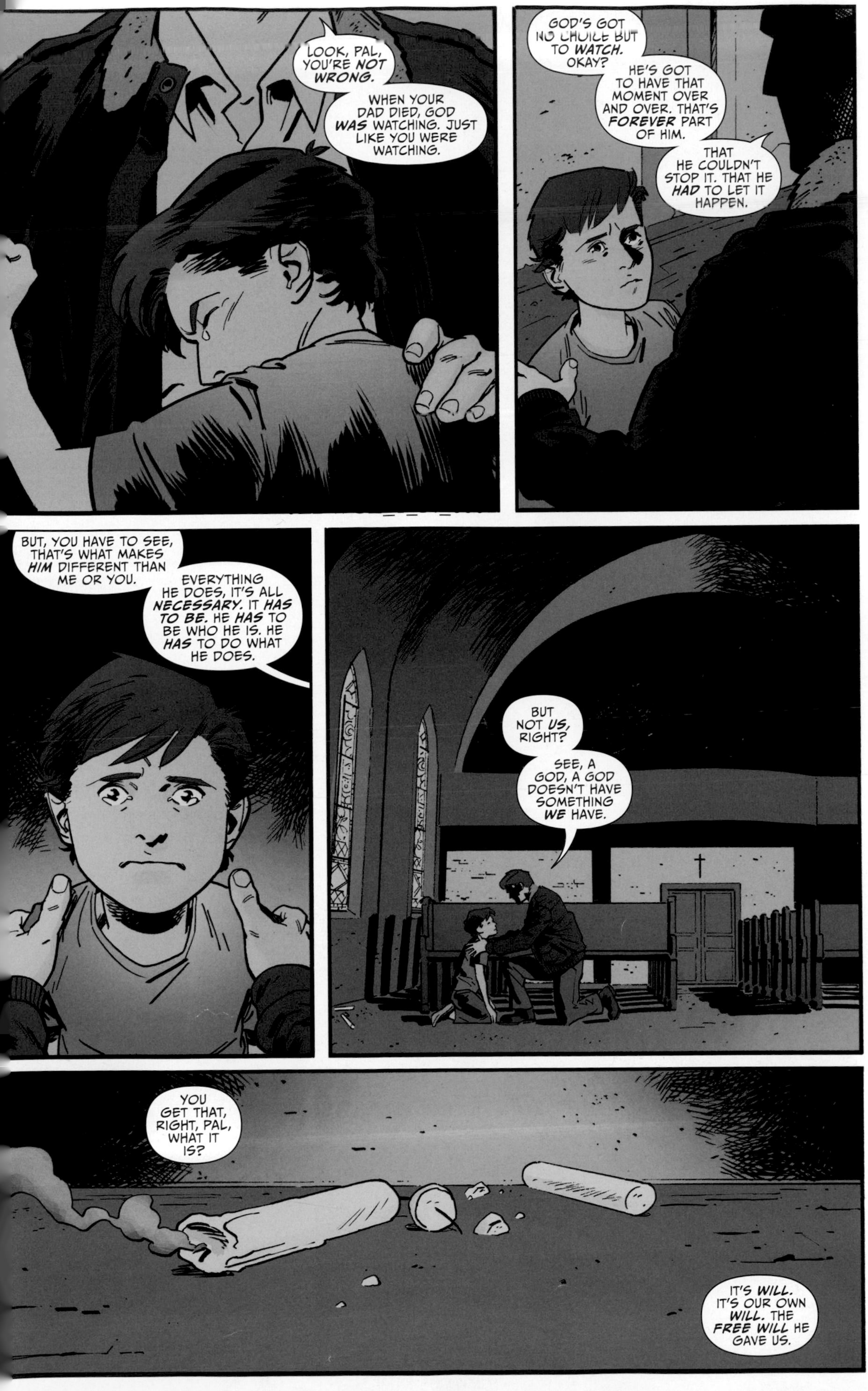
LOOK, PAL, YOU'RE NOT WRONG.
WHEN YOUR DAD DIED, GOD WAS WATCHING. JUST LIKE YOU WERE WATCHING.
GOD'S GOT NO CHOICE BUT TO WATCH. OKAY?
HE'S GOT TO HAVE THAT MOMENT OVER AND OVER. THAT'S FOREVER PART OF HIM.
THAT HE COULDN'T STOP IT. THAT HE HAD TO LET IT HAPPEN.
BUT, YOU HAVE TO SEE, THAT'S WHAT MAKES HIM DIFFERENT THAN ME OR YOU.
EVERYTHING HE DOES, IT'S ALL NECESSARY. IT HAS TO BE. HE HAS TO BE WHO HE IS. HE HAS TO DO WHAT HE DOES.
BUT NOT US, RIGHT?
SEE, A GOD, A GOD DOESN'T HAVE SOMETHING WE HAVE.
YOU GET THAT, RIGHT, PAL, WHAT IT IS?
IT'S WILL. IT'S OUR OWN WILL. THE FREE WILL HE GAVE US.

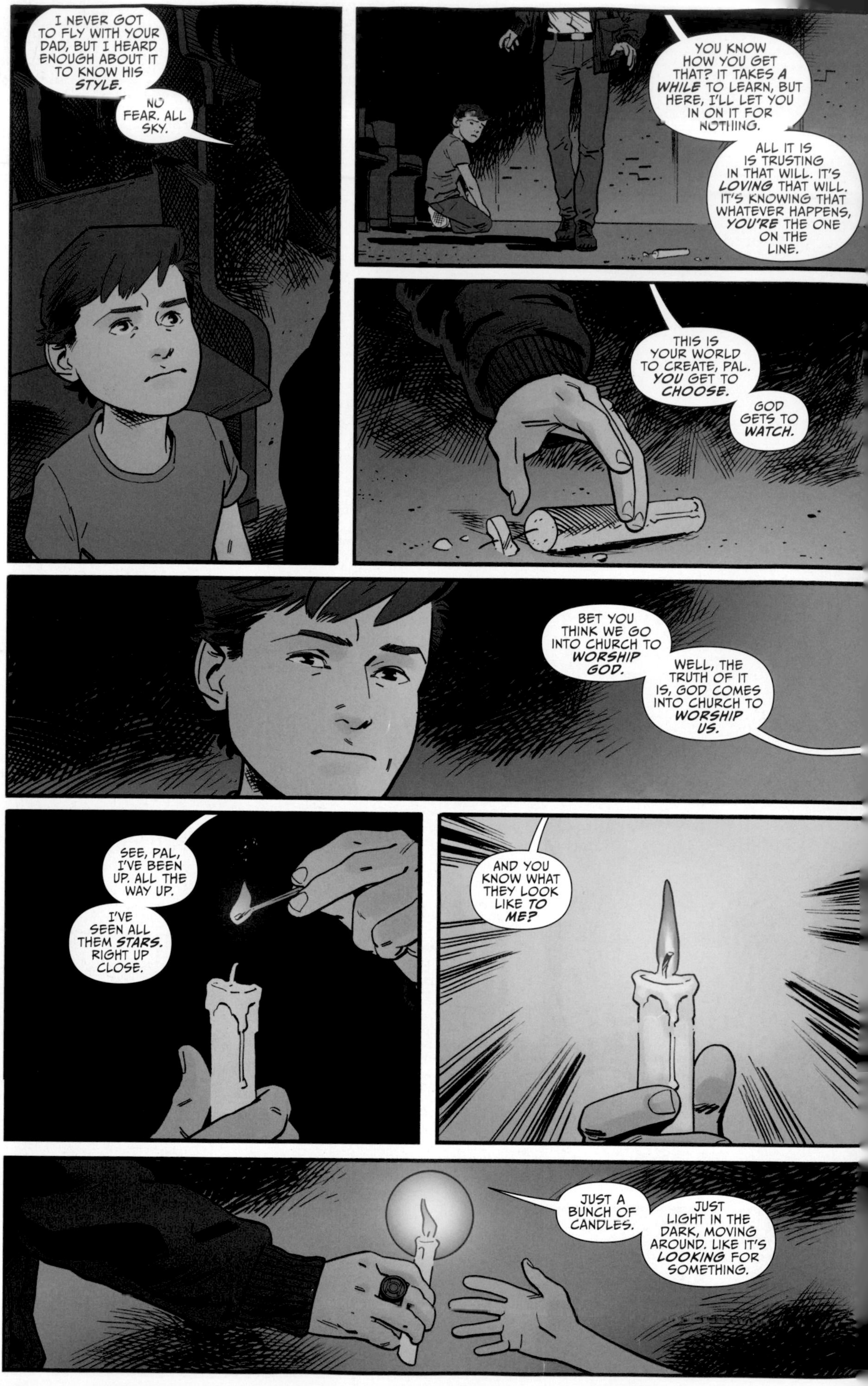
I NEVER GOT TO FLY WITH YOUR DAD, BUT I HEARD ENOUGH ABOUT IT TO KNOW HIS STYLE.
NO FEAR. ALL SKY.
YOU KNOW HOW YOU GET THAT? IT TAKES A WHILE TO LEARN, BUT HERE, I'LL LET YOU IN ON IT FOR NOTHING.
ALL IT IS IS TRUSTING IN THAT WILL. IT'S LOVING THAT WILL. IT'S KNOWING THAT WHATEVER HAPPENS, YOU'RE THE ONE ON THE LINE.
THIS IS YOUR WORLD TO CREATE, PAL. YOU GET TO CHOOSE.
GOD GETS TO WATCH.
BET YOU THINK WE GO INTO CHURCH TO WORSHIP GOD.
WELL, THE TRUTH OF IT IS, GOD COMES INTO CHURCH TO WORSHIP US.
SEE, PAL, I'VE BEEN UP. ALL THE WAY UP.
I'VE SEEN ALL THEM STARS. RIGHT UP CLOSE.
AND YOU KNOW WHAT THEY LOOK LIKE TO ME?
JUST A BUNCH OF CANDLES.
JUST LIGHT IN THE DARK, MOVING AROUND. LIKE IT'S LOOKING FOR SOMETHING.

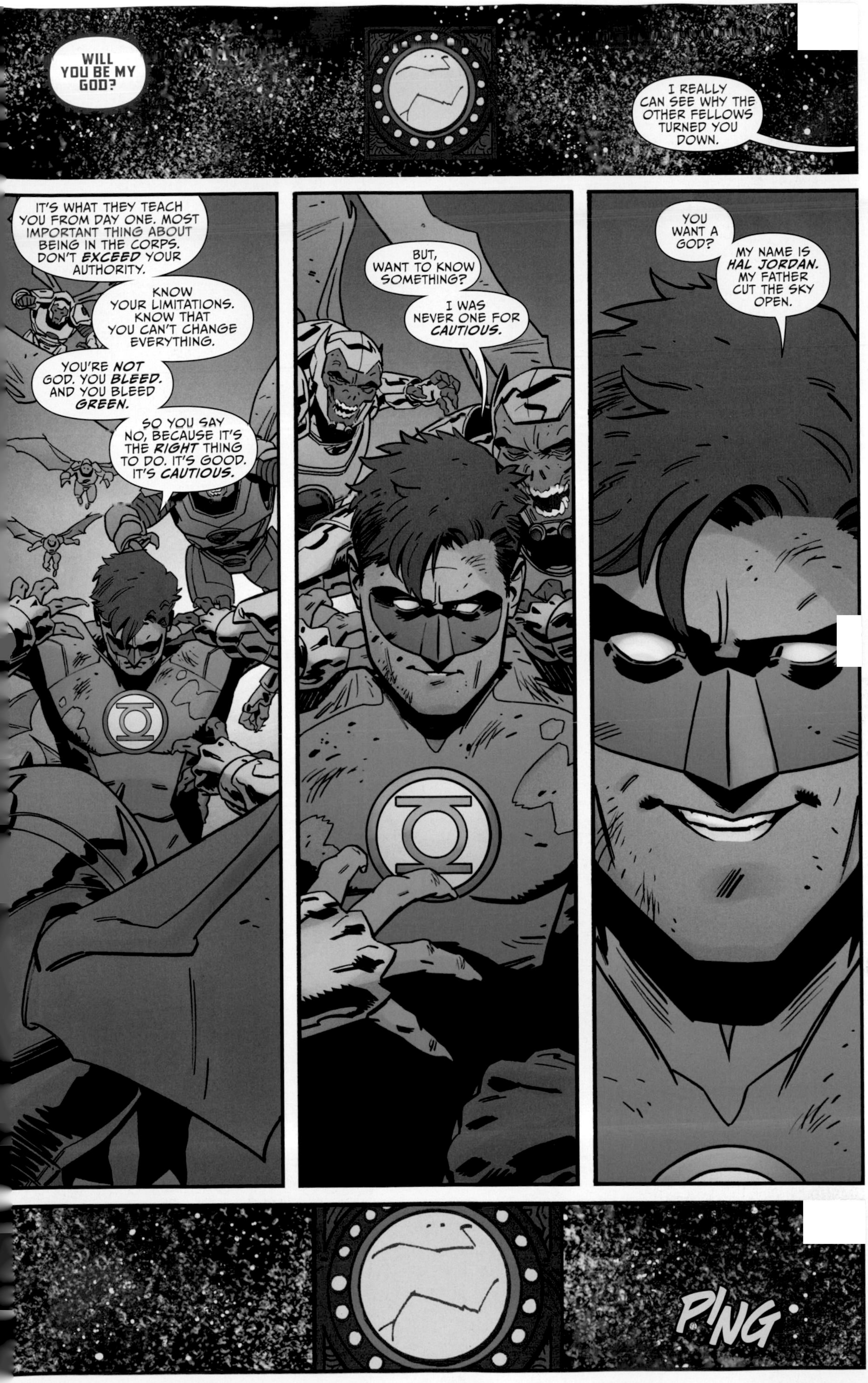
WILL YOU BE MY GOD?
I REALLY CAN SEE WHY THE OTHER FELLOWS TURNED YOU DOWN.
IT'S WHAT THEY TEACH YOU FROM DAY ONE. MOST IMPORTANT THING ABOUT BEING IN THE CORPS. DON'T EXCEED YOUR AUTHORITY.
KNOW YOUR LIMITATIONS. KNOW THAT YOU CAN'T CHANGE EVERYTHING.
YOU'RE NOT GOD. YOU BLEED. AND YOU BLEED GREEN.
SO YOU SAY NO, BECAUSE IT'S THE RIGHT THING TO DO. IT'S GOOD. IT'S CAUTIOUS.
BUT, WANT TO KNOW SOMETHING?
I WAS NEVER ONE FOR CAUTIOUS.
YOU WANT A GOD?
MY NAME IS HAL JORDAN. MY FATHER CUT THE SKY OPEN.
PING

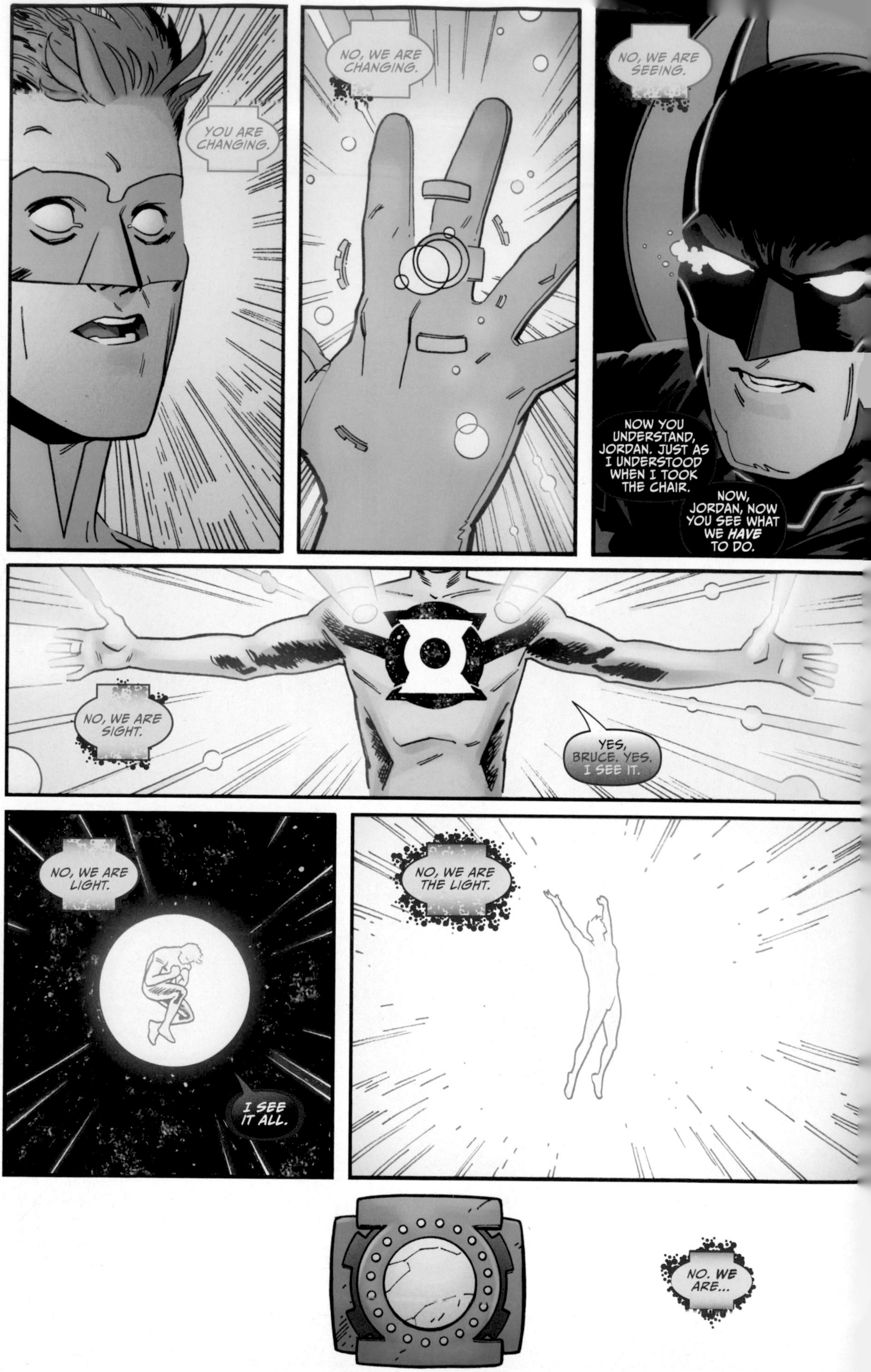
YOU ARE CHANGING.
NO, WE ARE CHANGING.
NO, WE ARE SEEING.
NOW YOU UNDERSTAND, JORDAN. JUST AS I UNDERSTOOD WHEN I TOOK THE CHAIR.
NOW, JORDAN, NOW YOU SEE WHAT WE HAVE TO DO.
NO, WE ARE SIGHT.
YES, BRUCE. YES. I SEE IT.
NO, WE ARE LIGHT.
I SEE IT ALL.
NO, WE ARE THE LIGHT.
NO. WE ARE...

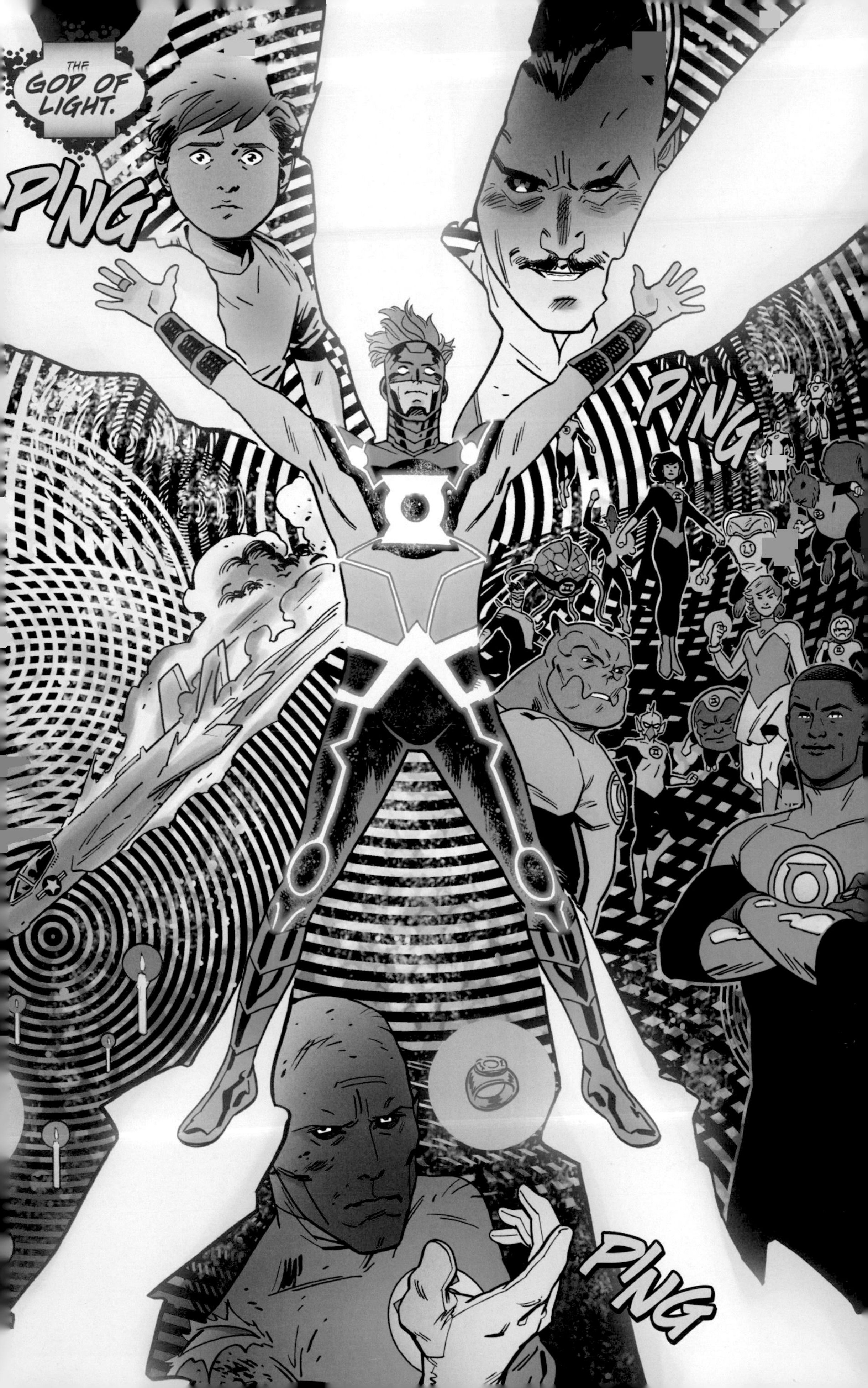
THE GOD OF LIGHT.
PING
PING
PING

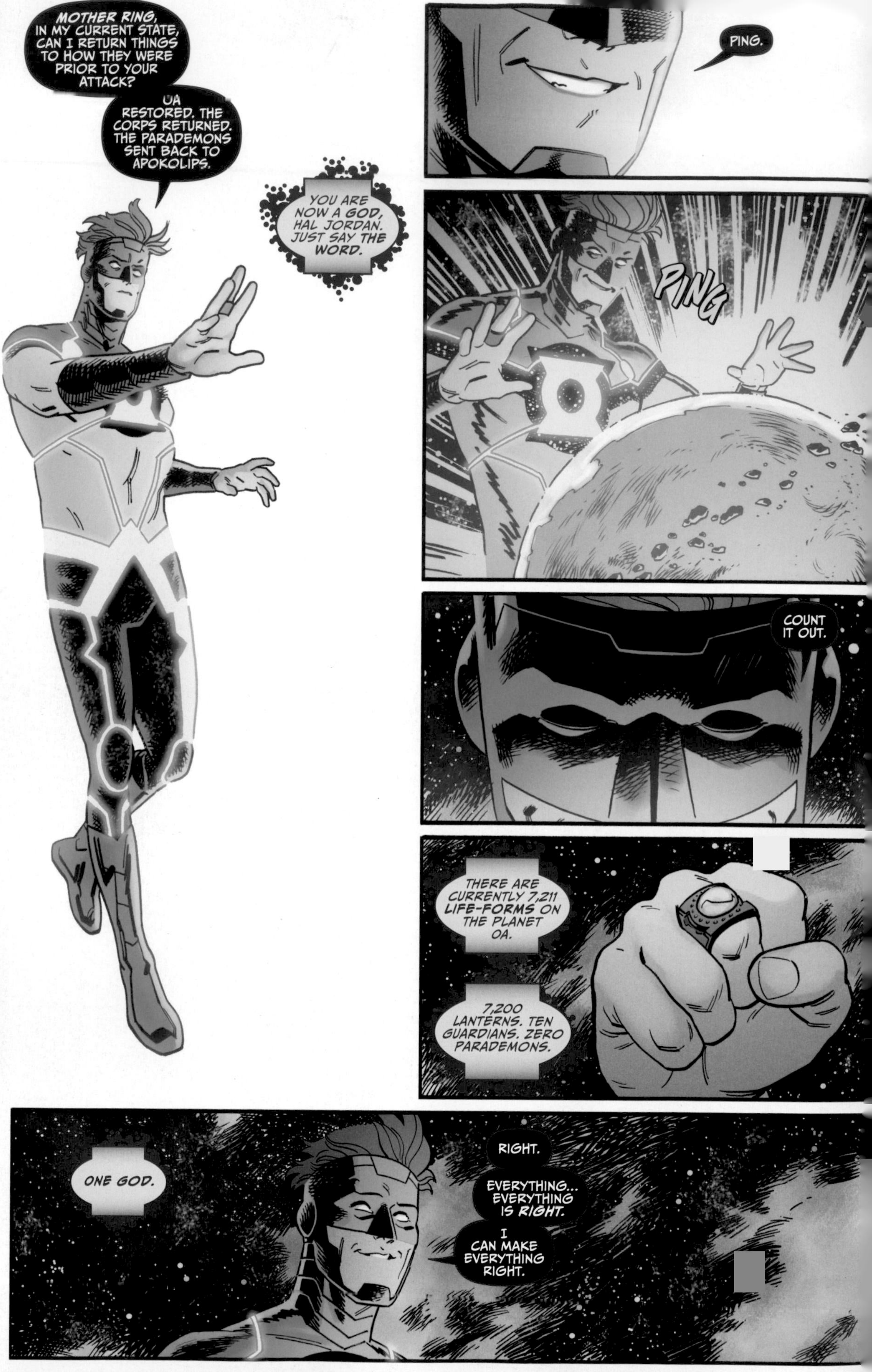

MOTHER RING, IN MY CURRENT STATE, CAN I RETURN THINGS TO HOW THEY WERE PRIOR TO YOUR ATTACK?
OA RESTORED. THE CORPS RETURNED. THE PARADEMONS SENT BACK TO APOKOLIPS.
YOU ARE NOW A GOD, HAL JORDAN. JUST SAY THE WORD.
PING.
PING
COUNT IT OUT.
THERE ARE CURRENTLY 7,211 LIFE-FORMS ON THE PLANET OA.
7,200 LANTERNS. TEN GUARDIANS. ZERO PARADEMONS.
ONE GOD.
RIGHT.
EVERYTHING... EVERYTHING IS RIGHT.
I CAN MAKE EVERYTHING RIGHT.

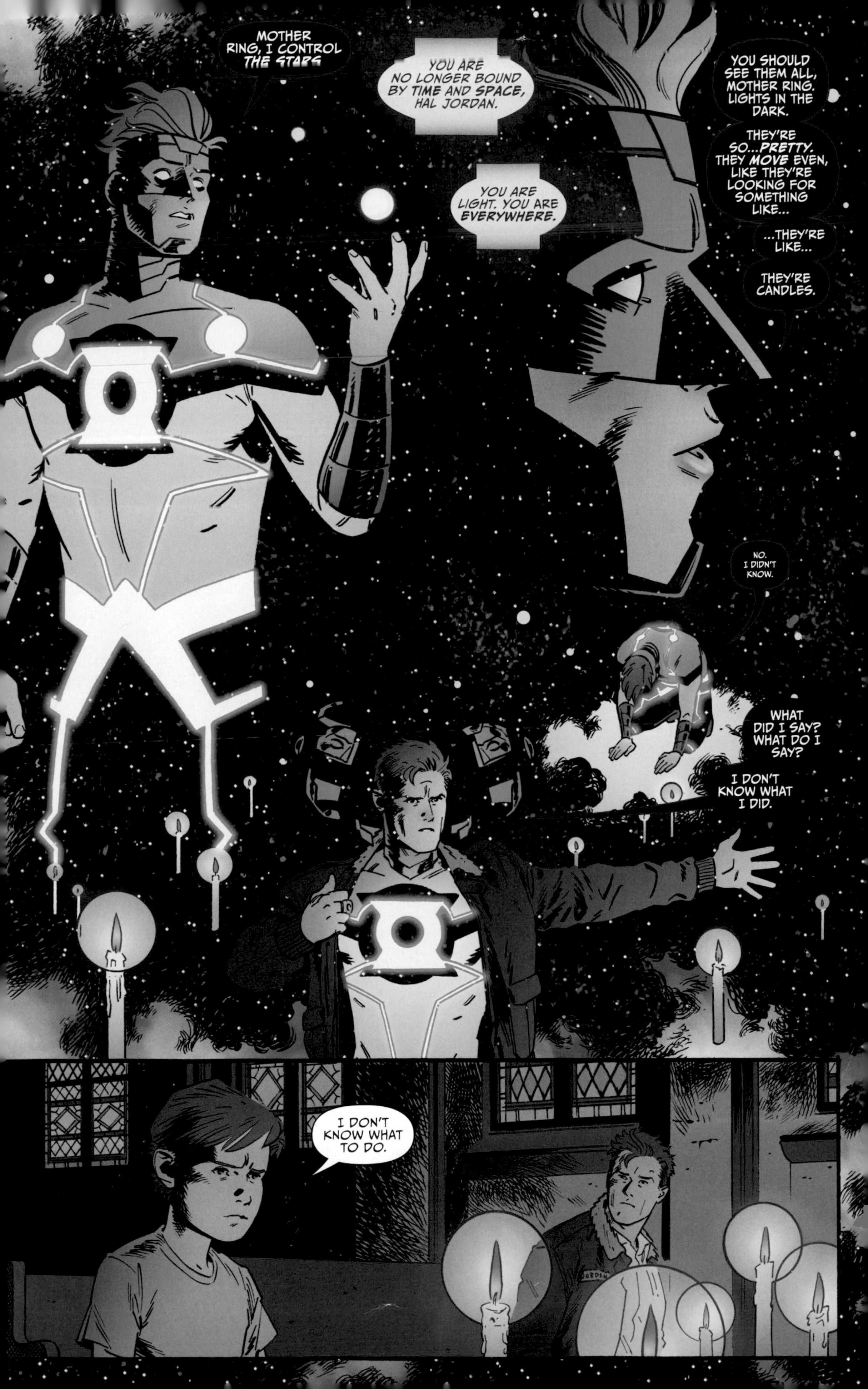
MOTHER RING, I CONTROL THE STARS
YOU ARE NO LONGER BOUND BY TIME AND SPACE, HAL JORDAN.
YOU ARE LIGHT. YOU ARE EVERYWHERE.
YOU SHOULD SEE THEM ALL, MOTHER RING. LIGHTS IN THE DARK.
THEY'RE SO...PRETTY. THEY MOVE EVEN, LIKE THEY'RE LOOKING FOR SOMETHING LIKE...
...THEY'RE LIKE...
THEY'RE CANDLES.
NO. I DIDN'T KNOW.
WHAT DID I SAY? WHAT DO I SAY?
I DON'T KNOW WHAT I DID.
I DON'T KNOW WHAT TO DO.
JORDAN

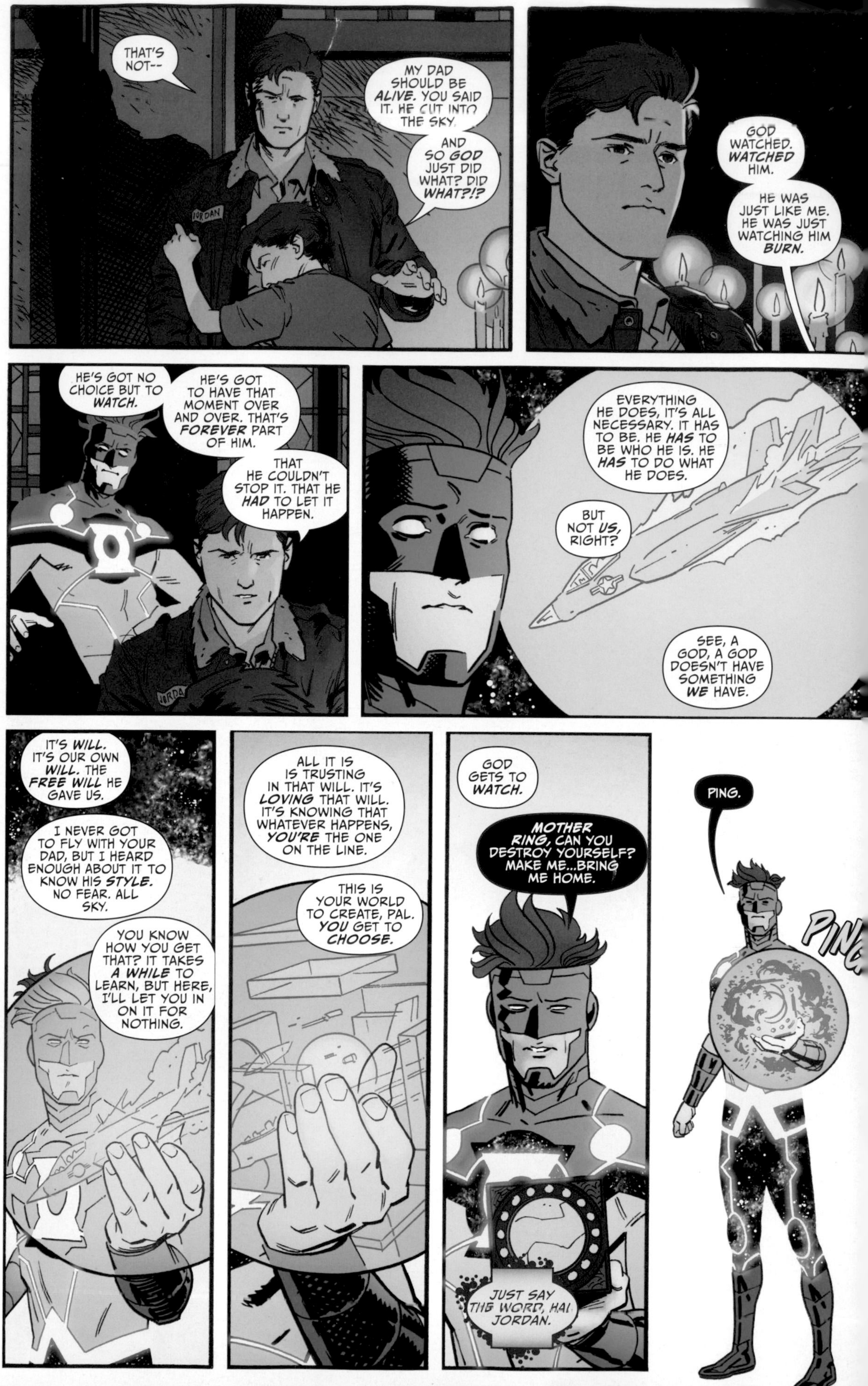
THAT'S NOT--
MY DAD SHOULD BE ALIVE. YOU SAID IT. HE CUT INTO THE SKY.
AND SO GOD JUST DID WHAT? DID WHAT?!?
JORDAN
GOD WATCHED. WATCHED HIM.
HE WAS JUST LIKE ME. HE WAS JUST WATCHING HIM BURN.
HE'S GOT NO CHOICE BUT TO WATCH.
HE'S GOT TO HAVE THAT MOMENT OVER AND OVER. THAT'S FOREVER PART OF HIM.
THAT HE COULDN'T STOP IT. THAT HE HAD TO LET IT HAPPEN.
EVERYTHING HE DOES, IT'S ALL NECESSARY. IT HAS TO BE. HE HAS TO BE WHO HE IS. HE HAS TO DO WHAT HE DOES.
BUT NOT US, RIGHT?
SEE, A GOD, A GOD DOESN'T HAVE SOMETHING WE HAVE.
IT'S WILL. IT'S OUR OWN WILL. THE FREE WILL HE GAVE US.
I NEVER GOT TO FLY WITH YOUR DAD, BUT I HEARD ENOUGH ABOUT IT TO KNOW HIS STYLE. NO FEAR. ALL SKY.
YOU KNOW HOW YOU GET THAT? IT TAKES A WHILE TO LEARN, BUT HERE, I'LL LET YOU IN ON IT FOR NOTHING.
ALL IT IS IS TRUSTING IN THAT WILL. IT'S LOVING THAT WILL. IT'S KNOWING THAT WHATEVER HAPPENS, YOU'RE THE ONE ON THE LINE.
THIS IS YOUR WORLD TO CREATE, PAL. YOU GET TO CHOOSE.
GOD GETS TO WATCH.
MOTHER RING, CAN YOU DESTROY YOURSELF? MAKE ME...BRING ME HOME.
JUST SAY THE WORD, HAL JORDAN.
PING.
PING

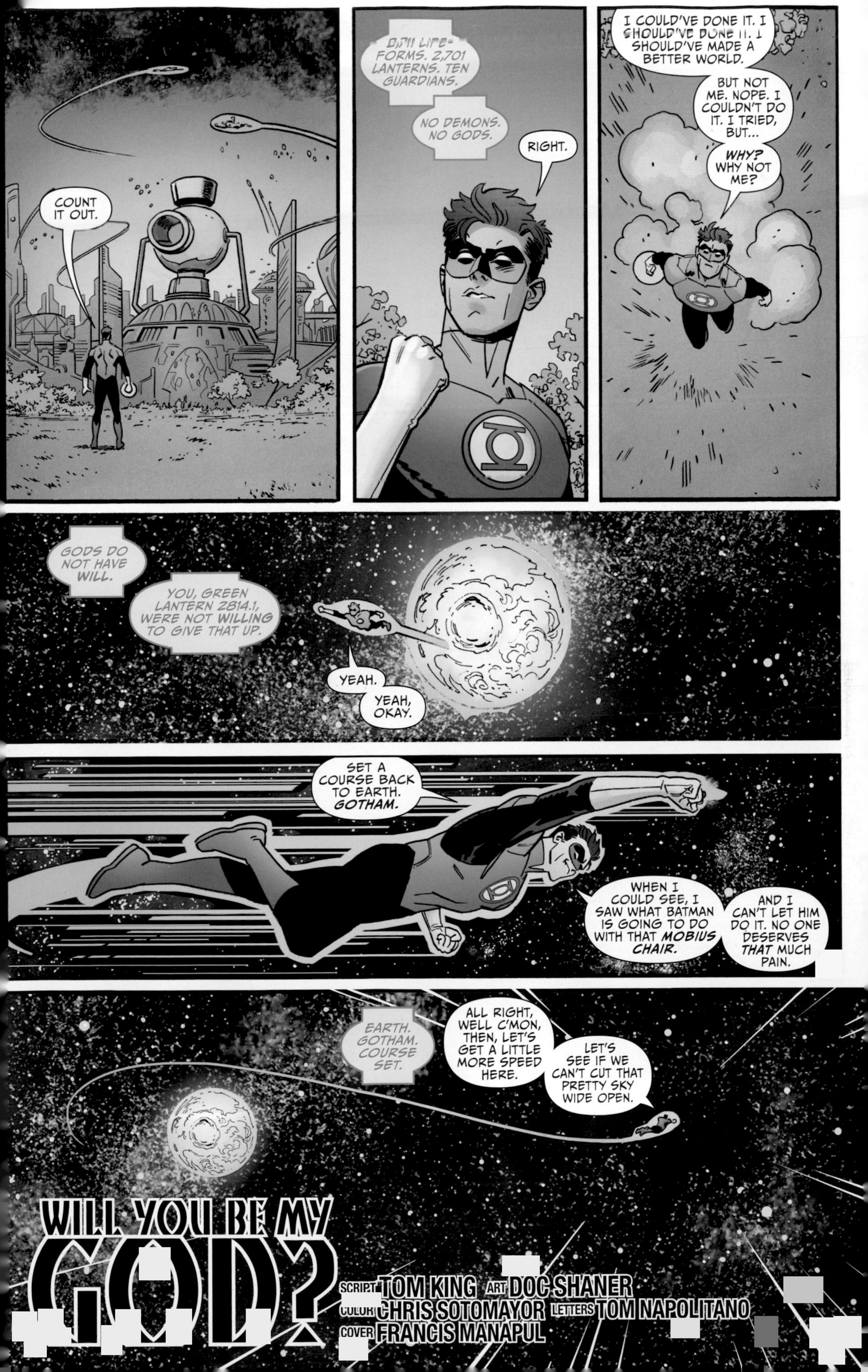
COUNT IT OUT.
FORMS. 2,701 LANTERNS. TEN GUARDIANS.
NO DEMONS. NO GODS.
RIGHT.
I COULD'VE DONE IT. I SHOULD'VE DONE IT. I SHOULD'VE MADE A BETTER WORLD.
BUT NOT ME. NOPE. I COULDN'T DO IT. I TRIED, BUT...
WHY? WHY NOT ME?
GODS DO NOT HAVE WILL.
YOU, GREEN LANTERN 2814.1, WERE NOT WILLING TO GIVE THAT UP.
YEAH.
YEAH, OKAY.
SET A COURSE BACK TO EARTH. GOTHAM.
WHEN I COULD SEE, I SAW WHAT BATMAN IS GOING TO DO WITH THAT MOBIUS CHAIR.
AND I CAN'T LET HIM DO IT. NO ONE DESERVES THAT MUCH PAIN.
EARTH. GOTHAM. COURSE SET.
ALL RIGHT, WELL C'MON, THEN, LET'S GET A LITTLE MORE SPEED HERE.
LET'S SEE IF WE CAN'T CUT THAT PRETTY SKY WIDE OPEN.
WILL YOU BE MY GOD?
SCRIPT TOM KING ART DOC SHANER
COLOR CHRIS SOTOMAYOR LETTERS TOM NAPOLITANO
COVER FRANCIS MANAPUL

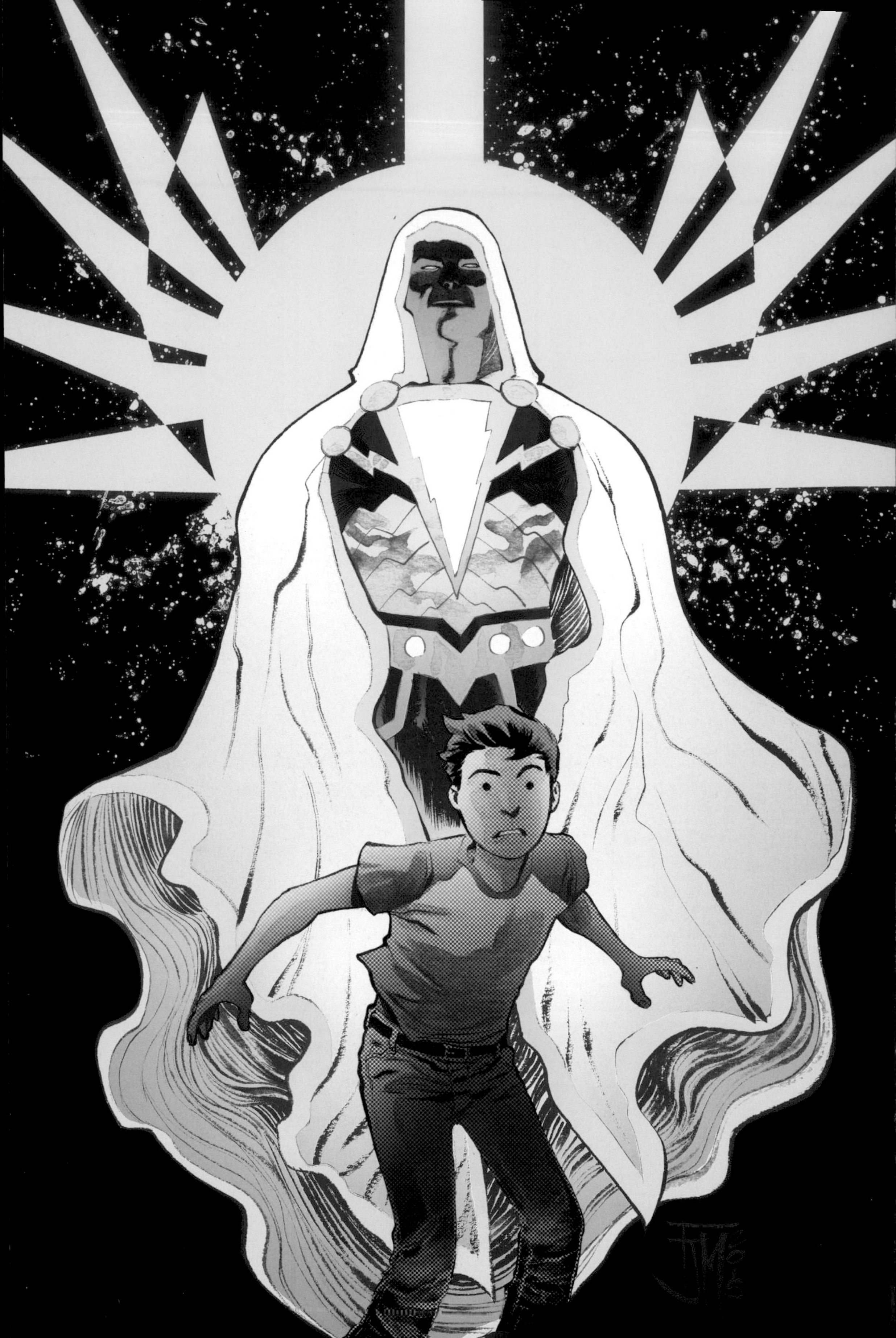

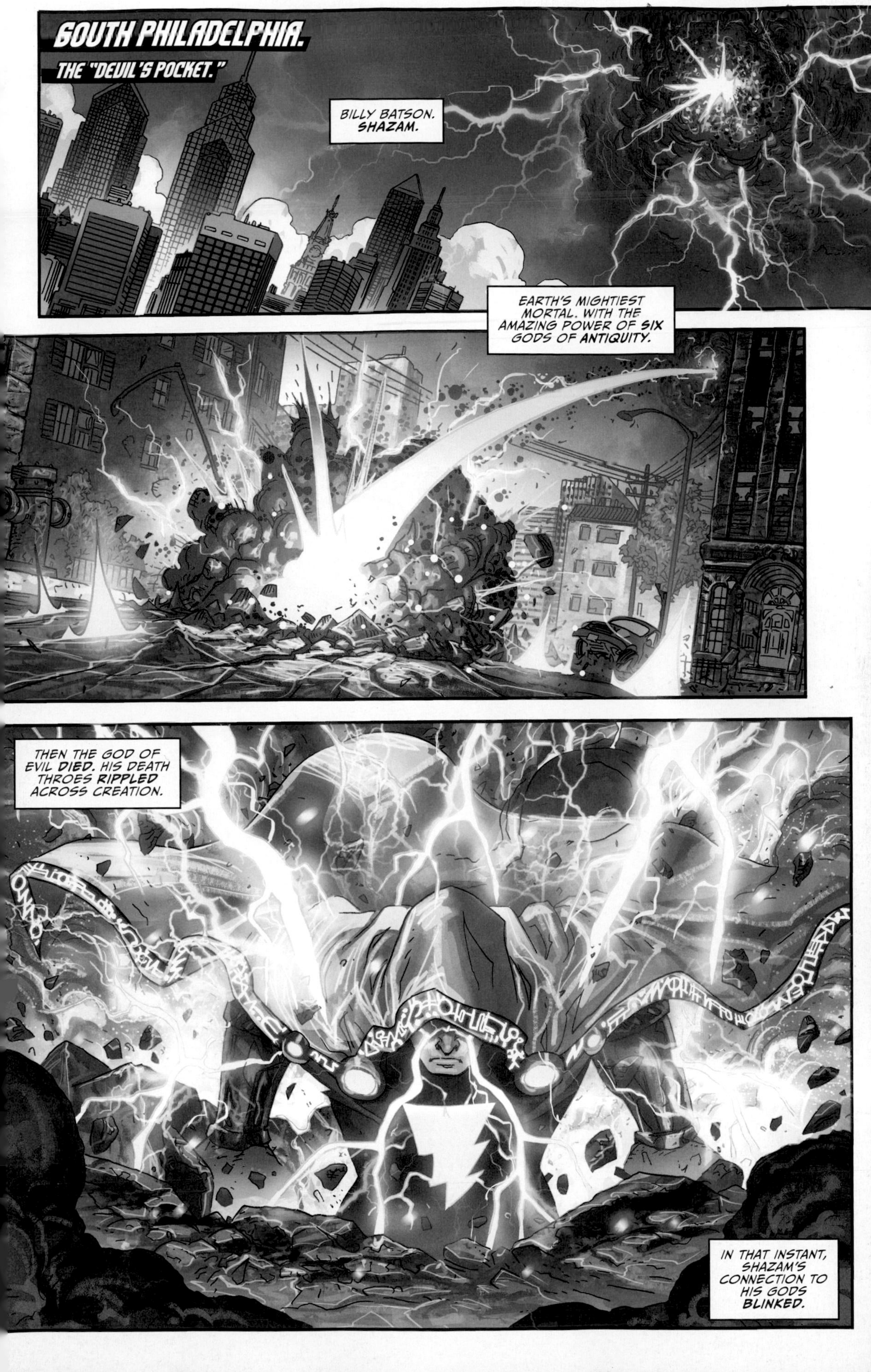
SOUTH PHILADELPHIA.
THE "DEVIL'S POCKET."
BILLY BATSON. SHAZAM.
EARTH'S MIGHTIEST MORTAL. WITH THE AMAZING POWER OF SIX GODS OF ANTIQUITY.
THEN THE GOD OF EVIL DIED. HIS DEATH THROES RIPPLED ACROSS CREATION.
IN THAT INSTANT, SHAZAM'S CONNECTION TO HIS GODS BLINKED.

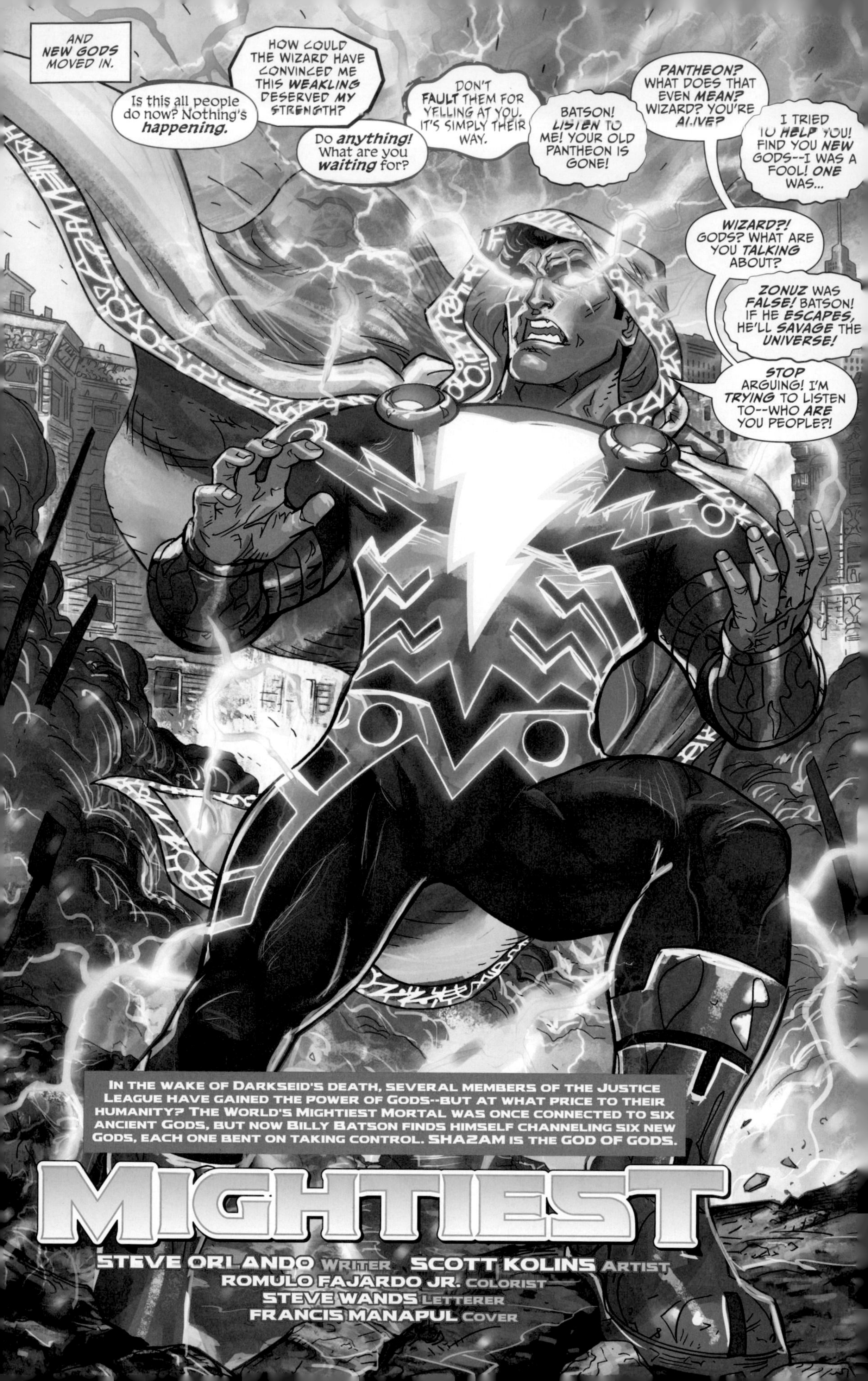
AND NEW GODS MOVED IN.
Is this all people do now? Nothing's happening.
HOW COULD THE WIZARD HAVE CONVINCED ME THIS WEAKLING DESERVED MY STRENGTH?
Do anything! What are you waiting for?
DON'T FAULT THEM FOR YELLING AT YOU. IT'S SIMPLY THEIR WAY.
BATSON! LISTEN TO ME! YOUR OLD PANTHEON IS GONE!
PANTHEON? WHAT DOES THAT EVEN MEAN? WIZARD? YOU'RE ALIVE?
I TRIED TO HELP YOU! FIND YOU NEW GODS--I WAS A FOOL! ONE WAS...
WIZARD?! GODS? WHAT ARE YOU TALKING ABOUT?
ZONUZ WAS FALSE! BATSON! IF HE ESCAPES, HE'LL SAVAGE THE UNIVERSE!
STOP ARGUING! I'M TRYING TO LISTEN TO--WHO ARE YOU PEOPLE?!
IN THE WAKE OF DARKSEID'S DEATH, SEVERAL MEMBERS OF THE JUSTICE LEAGUE HAVE GAINED THE POWER OF GODS--BUT AT WHAT PRICE TO THEIR HUMANITY? THE WORLD'S MIGHTIEST MORTAL WAS ONCE CONNECTED TO SIX ANCIENT GODS, BUT NOW BILLY BATSON FINDS HIMSELF CHANNELING SIX NEW GODS, EACH ONE BENT ON TAKING CONTROL. SHAZAM IS THE GOD OF GODS.
MIGHTIEST
STEVE ORLANDO WRITER SCOTT KOLINS ARTIST
ROMULO FAJARDO JR. COLORIST
STEVE WANDS LETTERER
FRANCIS MANAPUL COVER

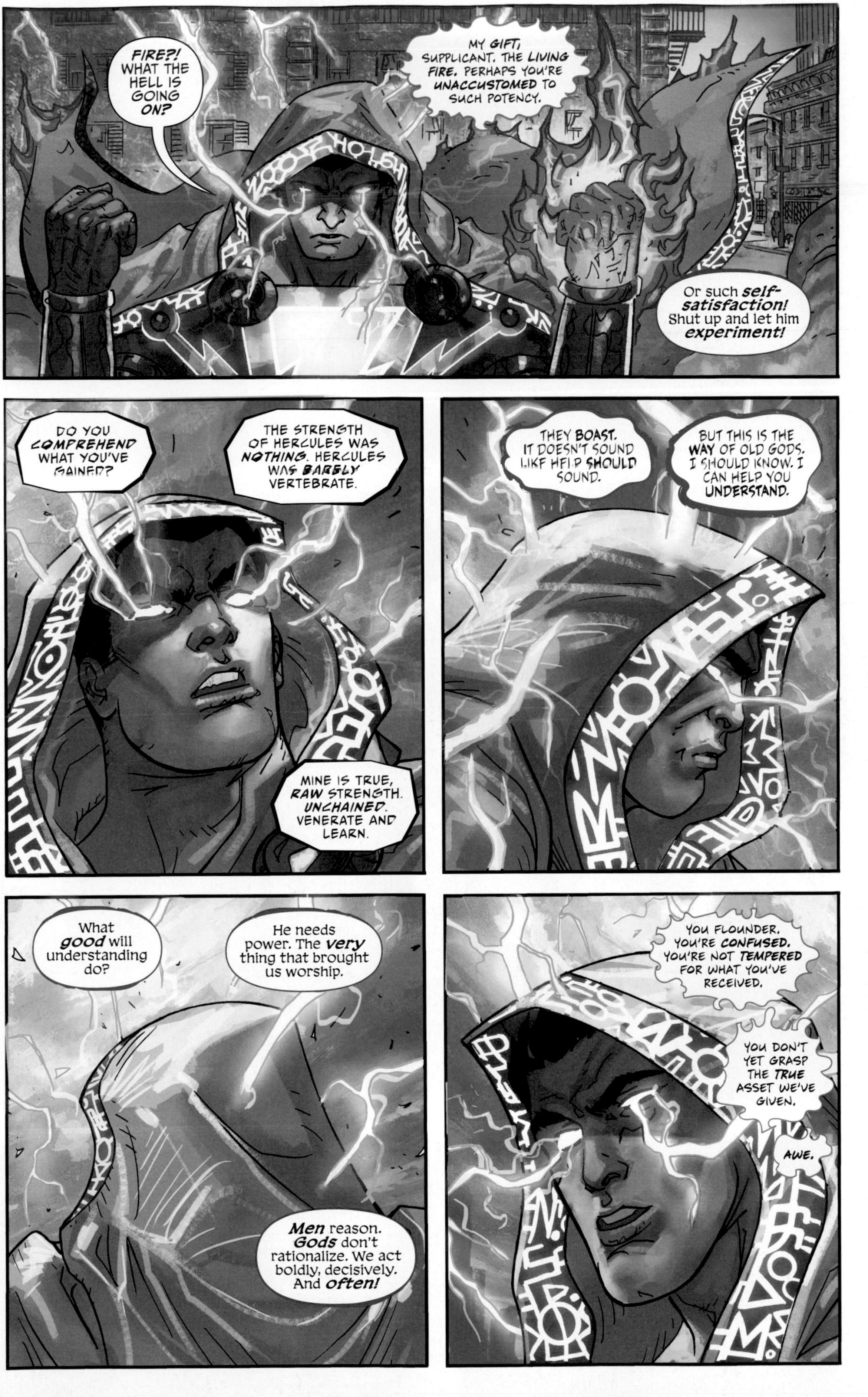
FIRE?! WHAT THE HELL IS GOING ON?
MY GIFT, SUPPLICANT. THE LIVING FIRE. PERHAPS YOU'RE UNACCUSTOMED TO SUCH POTENCY.
Or such self-satisfaction! Shut up and let him experiment!
DO YOU COMPREHEND WHAT YOU'VE GAINED?
THE STRENGTH OF HERCULES WAS NOTHING. HERCULES WAS BARELY VERTEBRATE.
MINE IS TRUE, RAW STRENGTH. UNCHAINED. VENERATE AND LEARN.
THEY BOAST. IT DOESN'T SOUND LIKE HELP SHOULD SOUND.
BUT THIS IS THE WAY OF OLD GODS. I SHOULD KNOW. I CAN HELP YOU UNDERSTAND.
What good will understanding do?
He needs power. The very thing that brought us worship.
Men reason. Gods don't rationalize. We act boldly, decisively. And often!
YOU FLOUNDER. YOU'RE CONFUSED. YOU'RE NOT TEMPERED FOR WHAT YOU'VE RECEIVED.
YOU DON'T YET GRASP THE TRUE ASSET WE'VE GIVEN.
AWE.

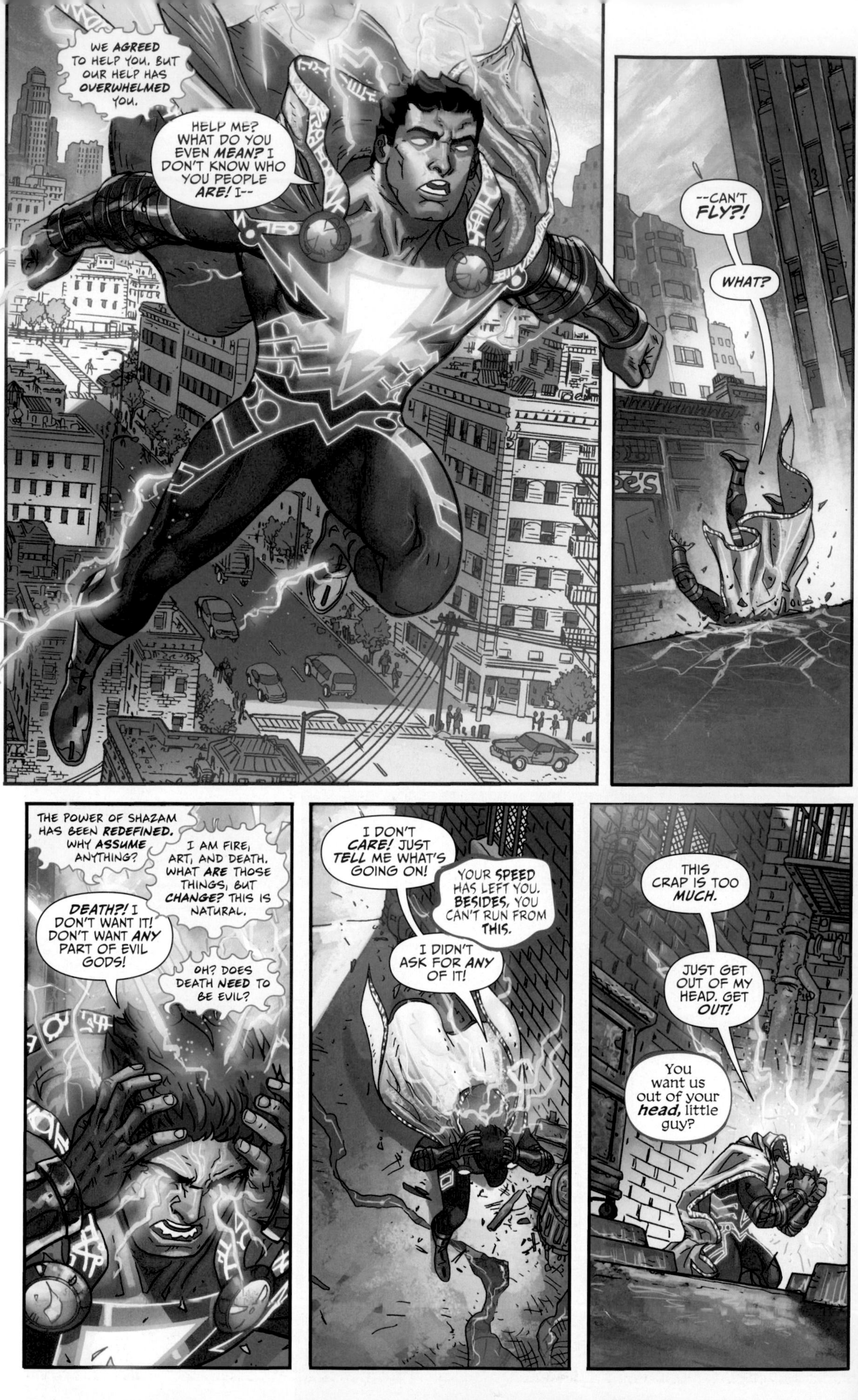
WE AGREED TO HELP YOU. BUT OUR HELP HAS OVERWHELMED YOU.
HELP ME? WHAT DO YOU EVEN MEAN? I DON'T KNOW WHO YOU PEOPLE ARE! I--
--CAN'T FLY?!
WHAT?
THE POWER OF SHAZAM HAS BEEN REDEFINED. WHY ASSUME ANYTHING?
I AM FIRE, ART, AND DEATH. WHAT ARE THOSE THINGS, BUT CHANGE? THIS IS NATURAL.
DEATH?! I DON'T WANT IT! DON'T WANT ANY PART OF EVIL GODS!
OH? DOES DEATH NEED TO BE EVIL?
I DON'T CARE! JUST TELL ME WHAT'S GOING ON!
YOUR SPEED HAS LEFT YOU. BESIDES, YOU CAN'T RUN FROM THIS.
I DIDN'T ASK FOR ANY OF IT!
THIS CRAP IS TOO MUCH.
JUST GET OUT OF MY HEAD. GET OUT!
You want us out of your head, little guy?

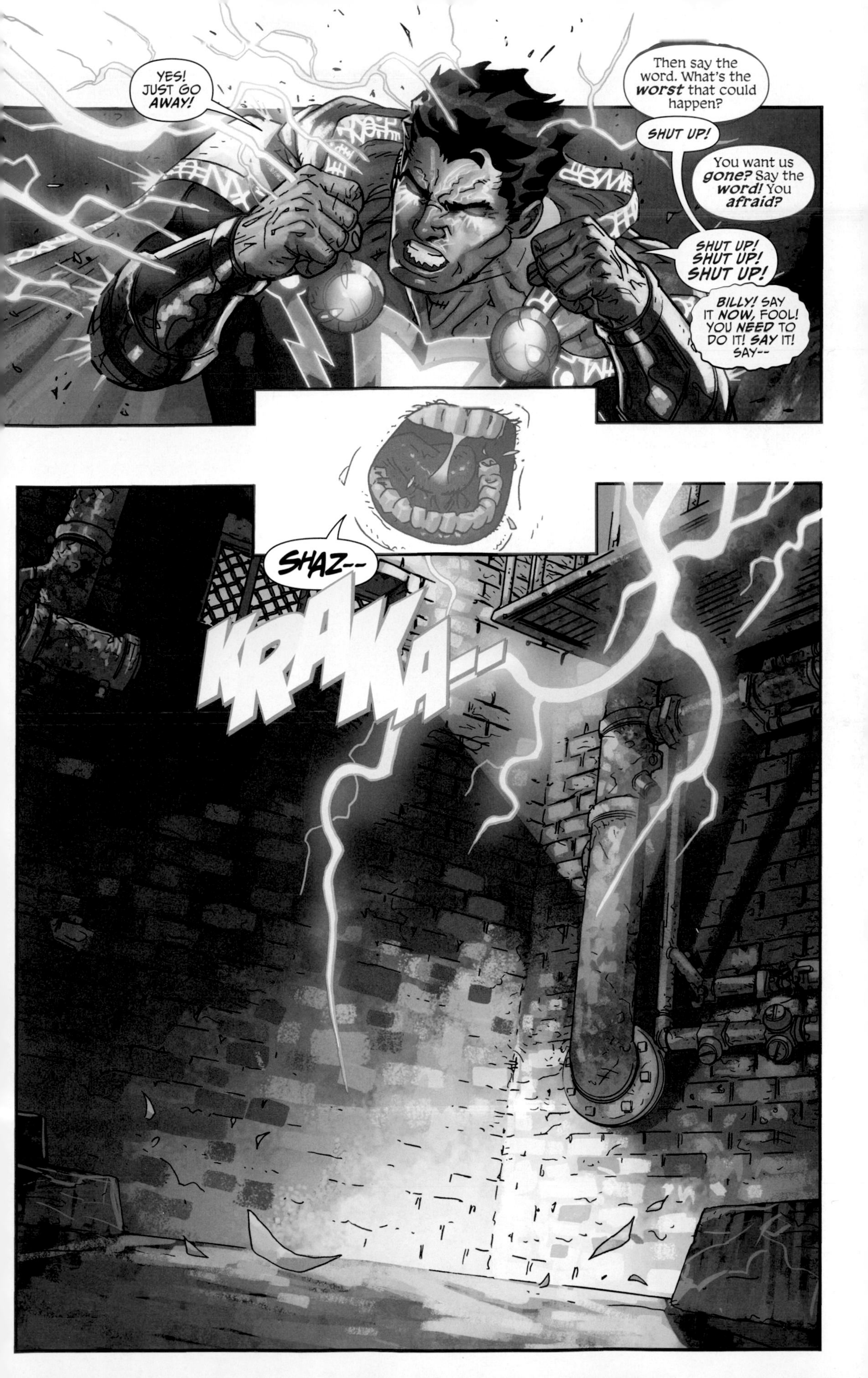
YES! JUST GO AWAY!
Then say the word. What's the worst that could happen?
SHUT UP!
You want us gone? Say the word! You afraid?
SHUT UP! SHUT UP! SHUT UP!
BILLY! SAY IT NOW, FOOL! YOU NEED TO DO IT! SAY IT! SAY--
SHAZ--
KRAKA--

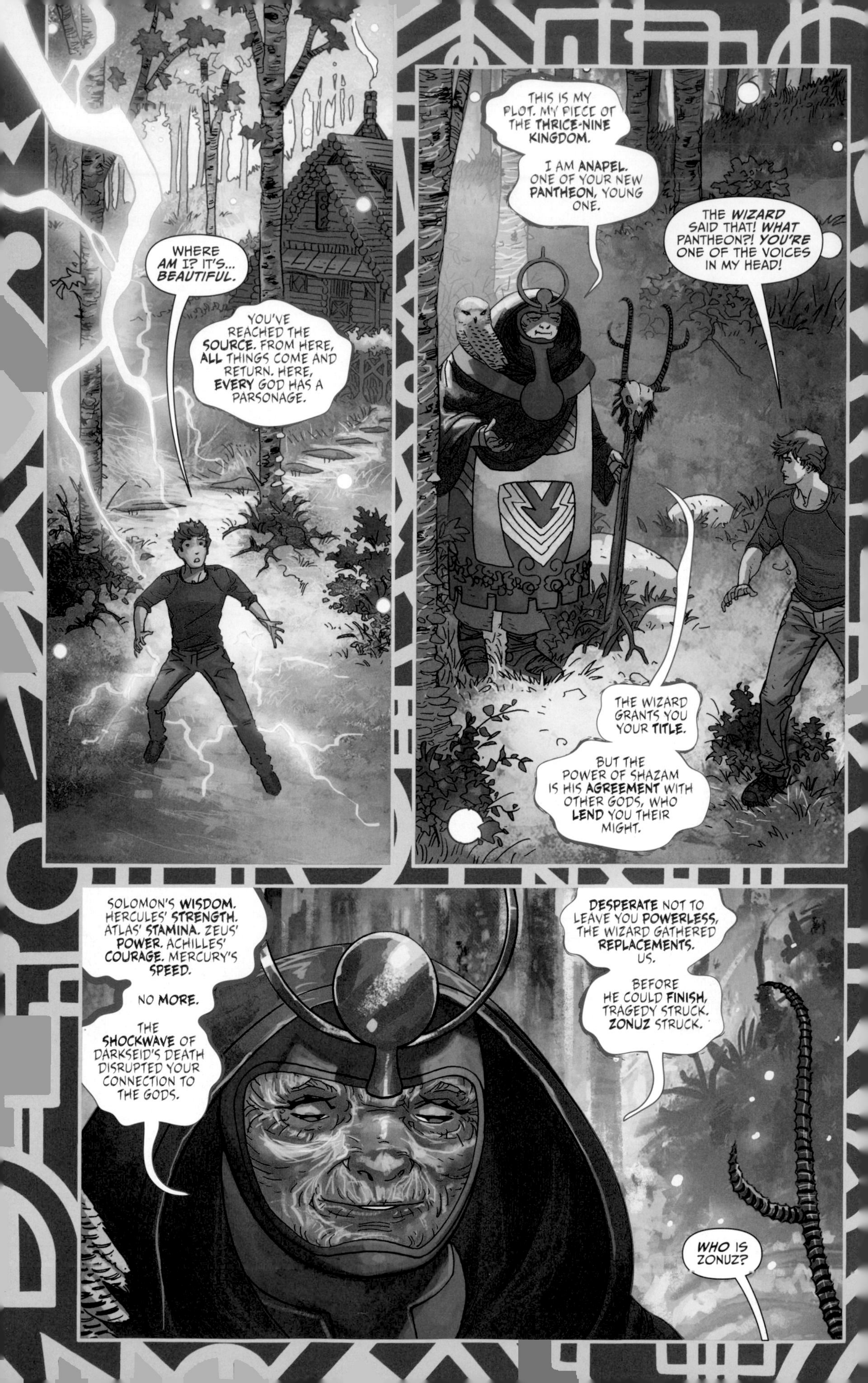

WHERE AM I? IT'S... BEAUTIFUL.
YOU'VE REACHED THE SOURCE. FROM HERE, ALL THINGS COME AND RETURN. HERE, EVERY GOD HAS A PARSONAGE.
THIS IS MY PLOT. MY PIECE OF THE THRICE-NINE KINGDOM.
I AM ANAPEL. ONE OF YOUR NEW PANTHEON, YOUNG ONE.
THE WIZARD SAID THAT! WHAT PANTHEON?! YOU'RE ONE OF THE VOICES IN MY HEAD!
THE WIZARD GRANTS YOU YOUR TITLE.
BUT THE POWER OF SHAZAM IS HIS AGREEMENT WITH OTHER GODS, WHO LEND YOU THEIR MIGHT.
SOLOMON'S WISDOM. HERCULES' STRENGTH. ATLAS' STAMINA. ZEUS' POWER. ACHILLES' COURAGE. MERCURY'S SPEED.
NO MORE.
THE SHOCKWAVE OF DARKSEID'S DEATH DISRUPTED YOUR CONNECTION TO THE GODS.
DESPERATE NOT TO LEAVE YOU POWERLESS, THE WIZARD GATHERED REPLACEMENTS. US.
BEFORE HE COULD FINISH, TRAGEDY STRUCK. ZONUZ STRUCK.
WHO IS ZONUZ?

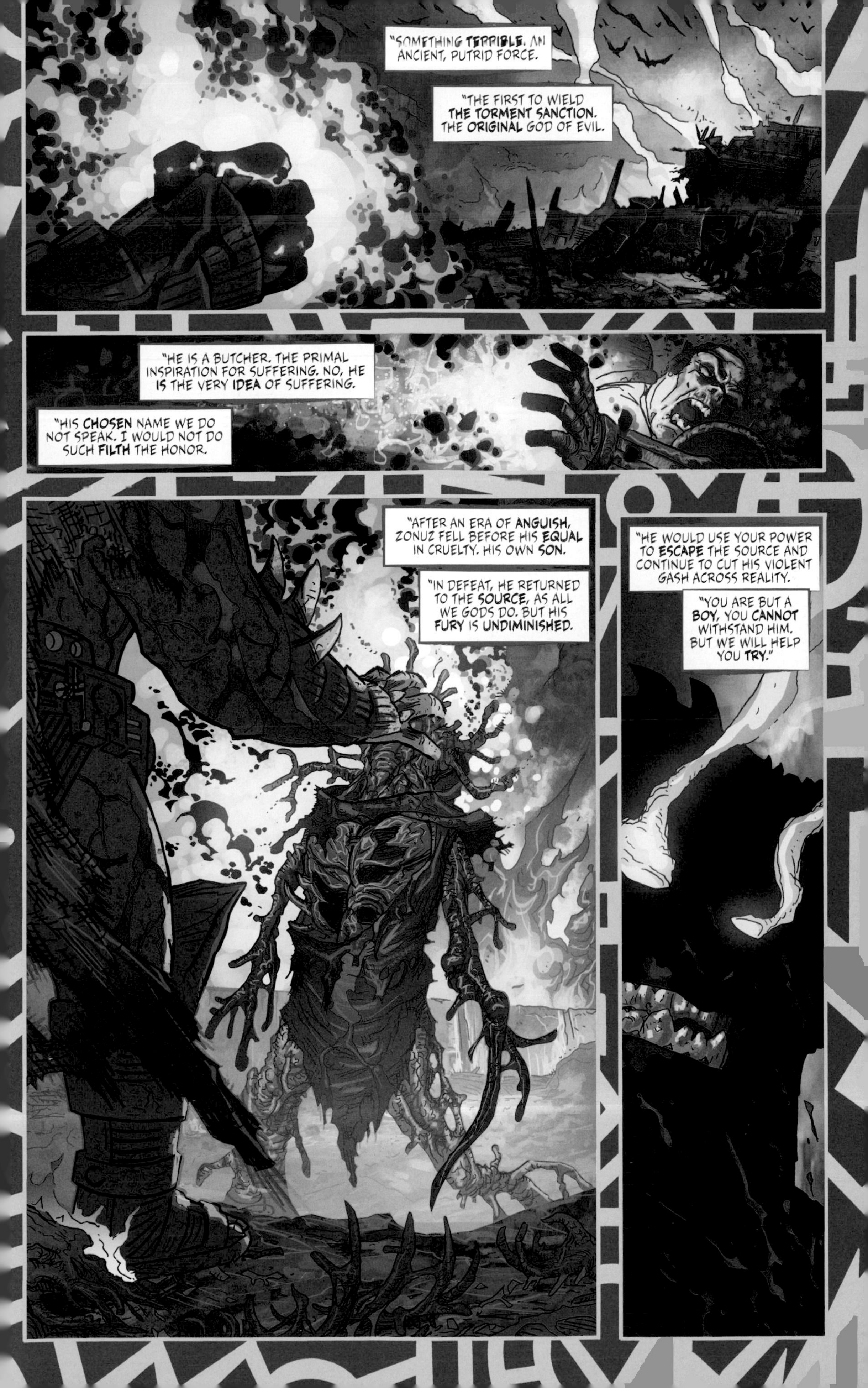
"SOMETHING TERRIBLE. AN ANCIENT, PUTRID FORCE.
"THE FIRST TO WIELD THE TORMENT SANCTION. THE ORIGINAL GOD OF EVIL.
"HE IS A BUTCHER. THE PRIMAL INSPIRATION FOR SUFFERING. NO, HE IS THE VERY IDEA OF SUFFERING.
"HIS CHOSEN NAME WE DO NOT SPEAK. I WOULD NOT DO SUCH FILTH THE HONOR.
"AFTER AN ERA OF ANGUISH, ZONUZ FELL BEFORE HIS EQUAL IN CRUELTY. HIS OWN SON.
"IN DEFEAT, HE RETURNED TO THE SOURCE, AS ALL WE GODS DO. BUT HIS FURY IS UNDIMINISHED.
"HE WOULD USE YOUR POWER TO ESCAPE THE SOURCE AND CONTINUE TO CUT HIS VIOLENT GASH ACROSS REALITY.
"YOU ARE BUT A BOY, YOU CANNOT WITHSTAND HIM. BUT WE WILL HELP YOU TRY."

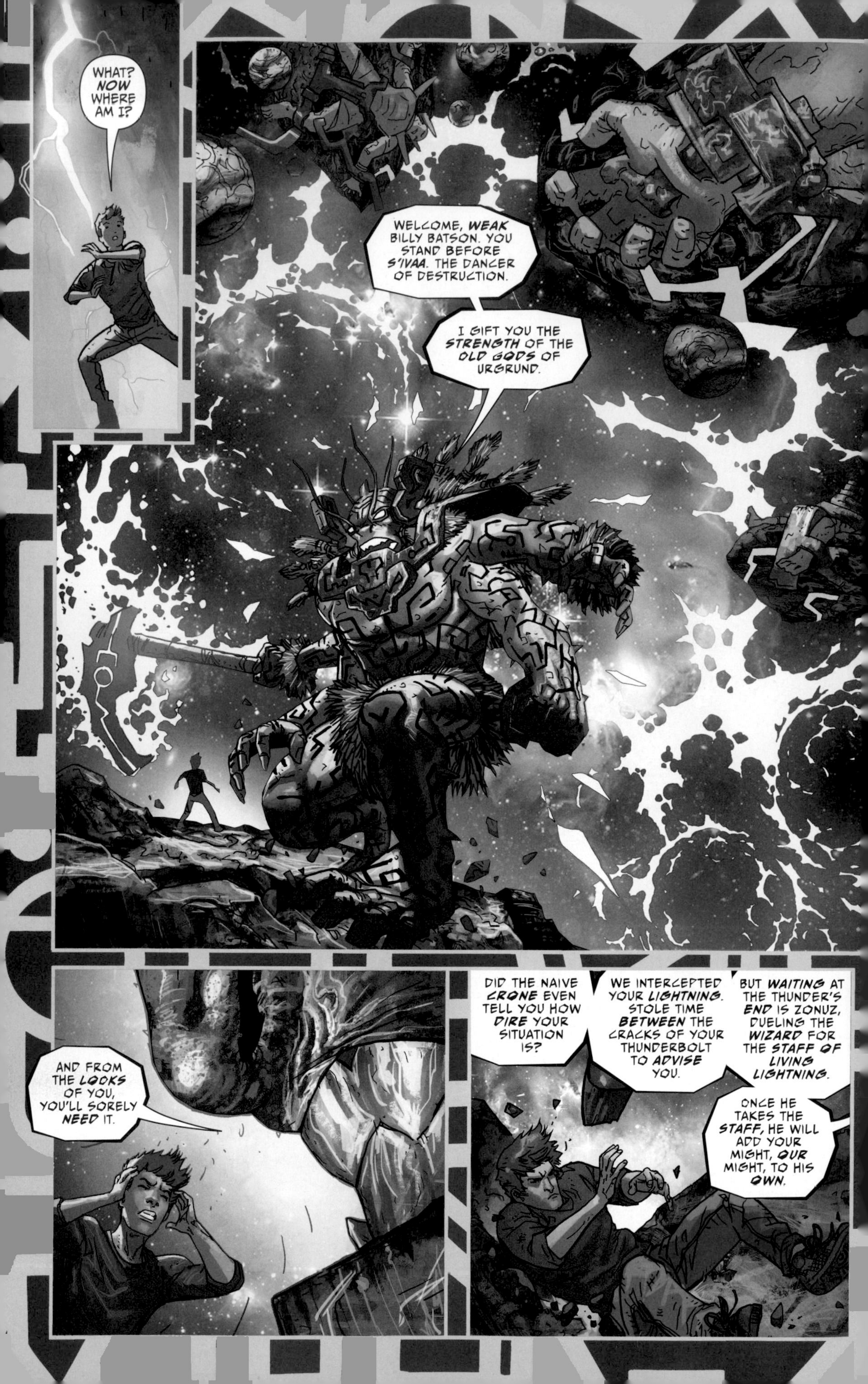
WHAT? NOW WHERE AM I?
WELCOME, WEAK BILLY BATSON. YOU STAND BEFORE S'IVAA. THE DANCER OF DESTRUCTION.
I GIFT YOU THE STRENGTH OF THE OLD GODS OF URGRUND.
AND FROM THE LOOKS OF YOU, YOU'LL SORELY NEED IT.
DID THE NAIVE CRONE EVEN TELL YOU HOW DIRE YOUR SITUATION IS?
WE INTERCEPTED YOUR LIGHTNING. STOLE TIME BETWEEN THE CRACKS OF YOUR THUNDERBOLT TO ADVISE YOU.
BUT WAITING AT THE THUNDER'S END IS ZONUZ, DUELING THE WIZARD FOR THE STAFF OF LIVING LIGHTNING.
ONCE HE TAKES THE STAFF, HE WILL ADD YOUR MIGHT, OUR MIGHT, TO HIS OWN.

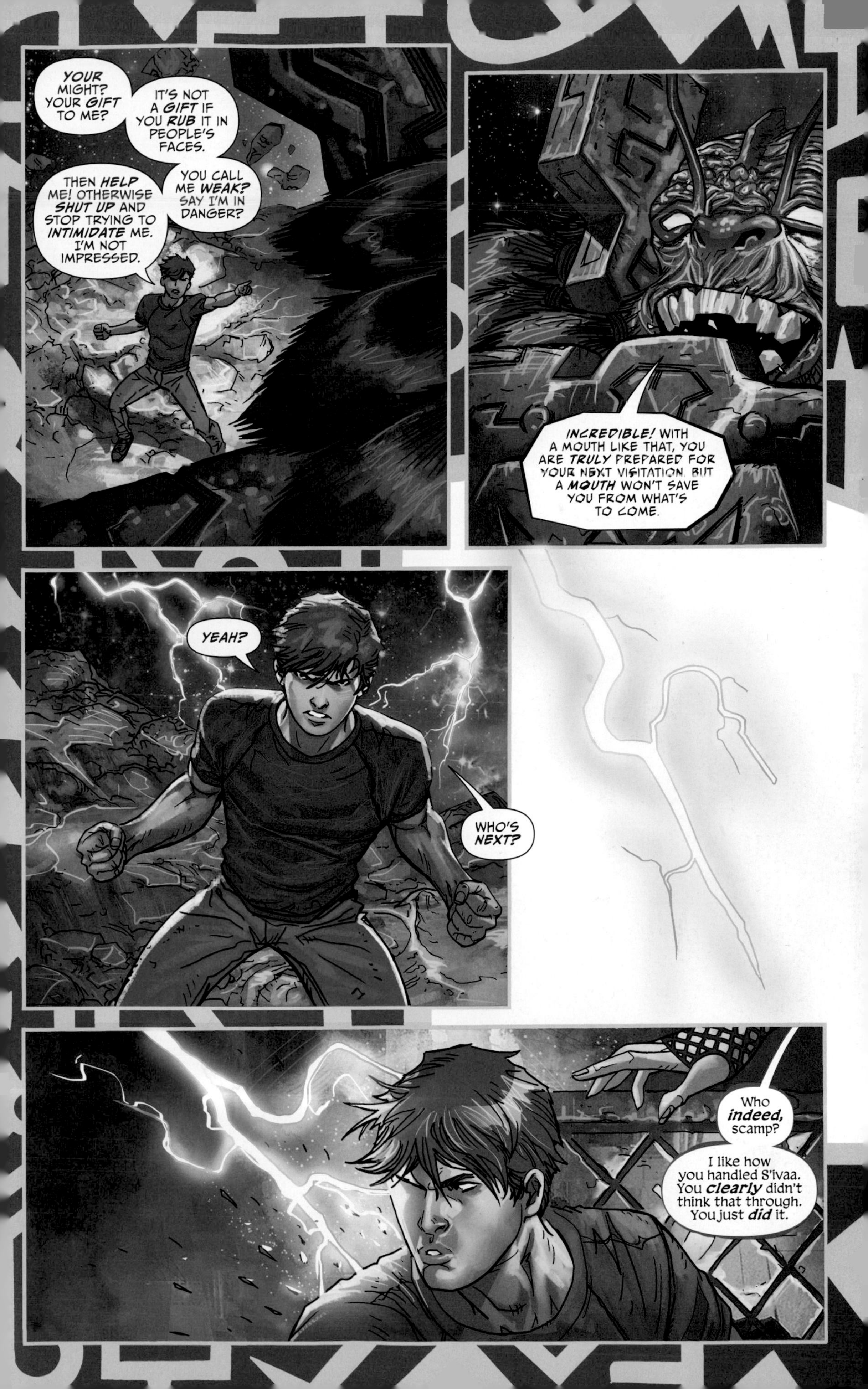
YOUR MIGHT? YOUR GIFT TO ME?
IT'S NOT A GIFT IF YOU RUB IT IN PEOPLE'S FACES.
YOU CALL ME WEAK? SAY I'M IN DANGER?
THEN HELP ME! OTHERWISE SHUT UP AND STOP TRYING TO INTIMIDATE ME. I'M NOT IMPRESSED.
INCREDIBLE! WITH A MOUTH LIKE THAT, YOU ARE TRULY PREPARED FOR YOUR NEXT VISITATION. BUT A MOUTH WON'T SAVE YOU FROM WHAT'S TO COME.
YEAH?
WHO'S NEXT?
Who indeed, scamp?
I like how you handled S'ivaa. You clearly didn't think that through. You just did it.

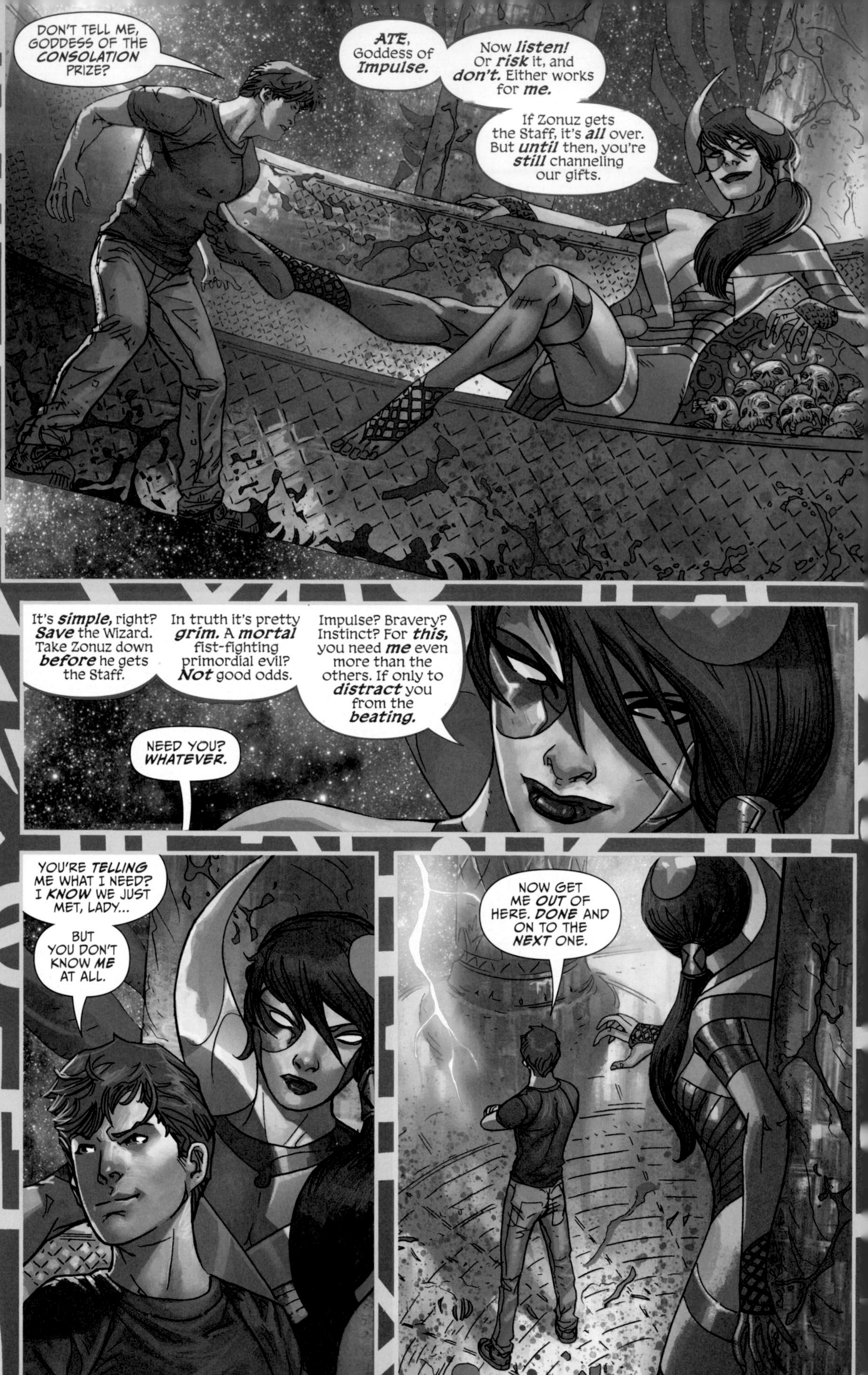

DON'T TELL ME, GODDESS OF THE CONSOLATION PRIZE?
ATE, Goddess of Impulse.
Now listen! Or risk it, and don't. Either works for me.
If Zonuz gets the Staff, it's all over. But until then, you're still channeling our gifts.
It's simple, right? Save the Wizard. Take Zonuz down before he gets the Staff.
In truth it's pretty grim. A mortal fist-fighting primordial evil? Not good odds.
Impulse? Bravery? Instinct? For this, you need me even more than the others. If only to distract you from the beating.
NEED YOU? WHATEVER.
YOU'RE TELLING ME WHAT I NEED? I KNOW WE JUST MET, LADY...
BUT YOU DON'T KNOW ME AT ALL.
NOW GET ME OUT OF HERE. DONE AND ON TO THE NEXT ONE.

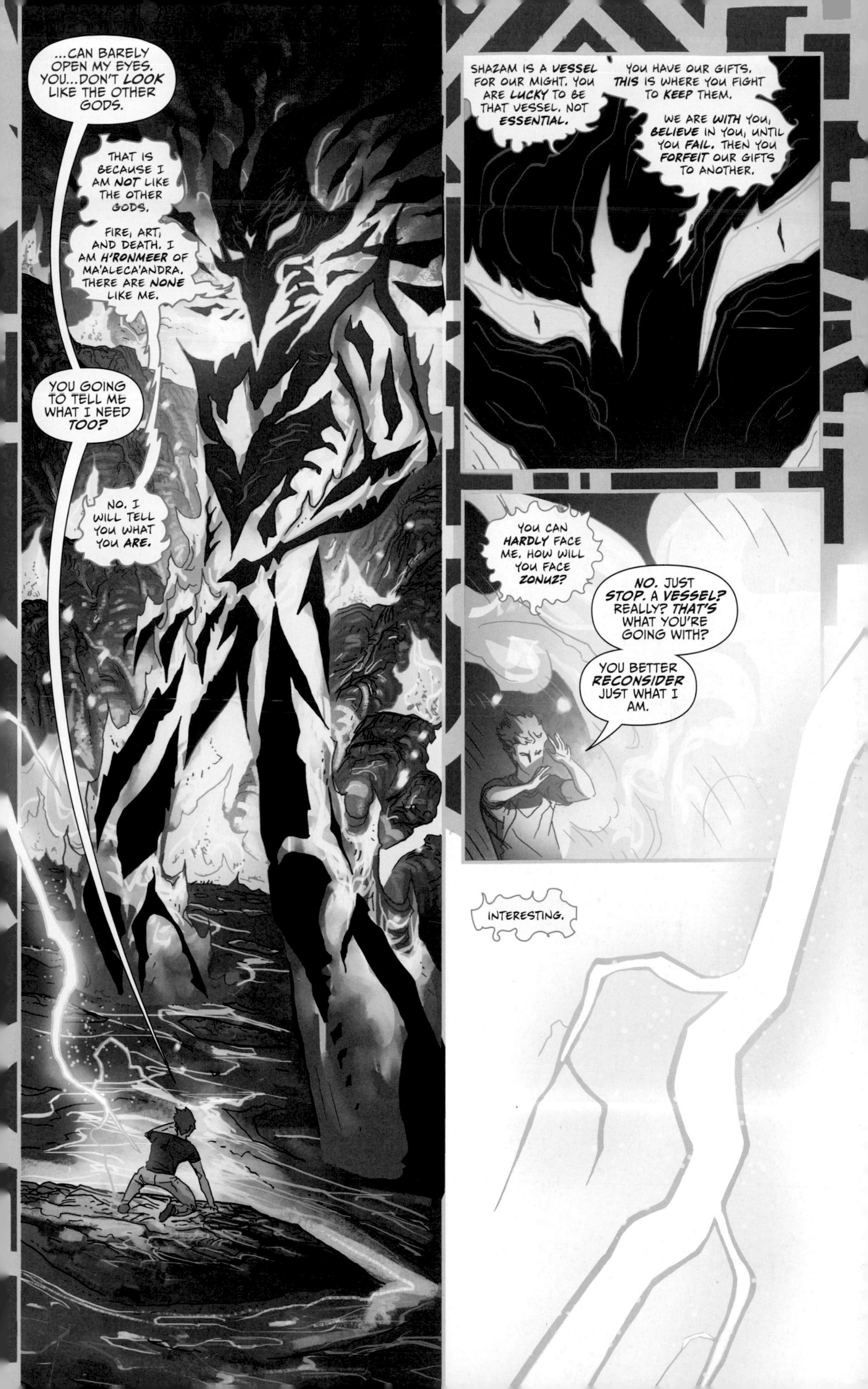
...CAN BARELY OPEN MY EYES. YOU...DON'T LOOK LIKE THE OTHER GODS.
THAT IS BECAUSE I AM NOT LIKE THE OTHER GODS.
FIRE, ART, AND DEATH. I AM H'RONMEER OF MA'ALECA'ANDRA. THERE ARE NONE LIKE ME.
YOU GOING TO TELL ME WHAT I NEED TOO?
NO. I WILL TELL YOU WHAT YOU ARE.
SHAZAM IS A VESSEL FOR OUR MIGHT. YOU ARE LUCKY TO BE THAT VESSEL. NOT ESSENTIAL.
YOU HAVE OUR GIFTS. THIS IS WHERE YOU FIGHT TO KEEP THEM.
WE ARE WITH YOU, BELIEVE IN YOU, UNTIL YOU FAIL. THEN YOU FORFEIT OUR GIFTS TO ANOTHER.
YOU CAN HARDLY FACE ME. HOW WILL YOU FACE ZONUZ?
NO. JUST STOP. A VESSEL? REALLY? THAT'S WHAT YOU'RE GOING WITH?
YOU BETTER RECONSIDER JUST WHAT I AM.
INTERESTING.

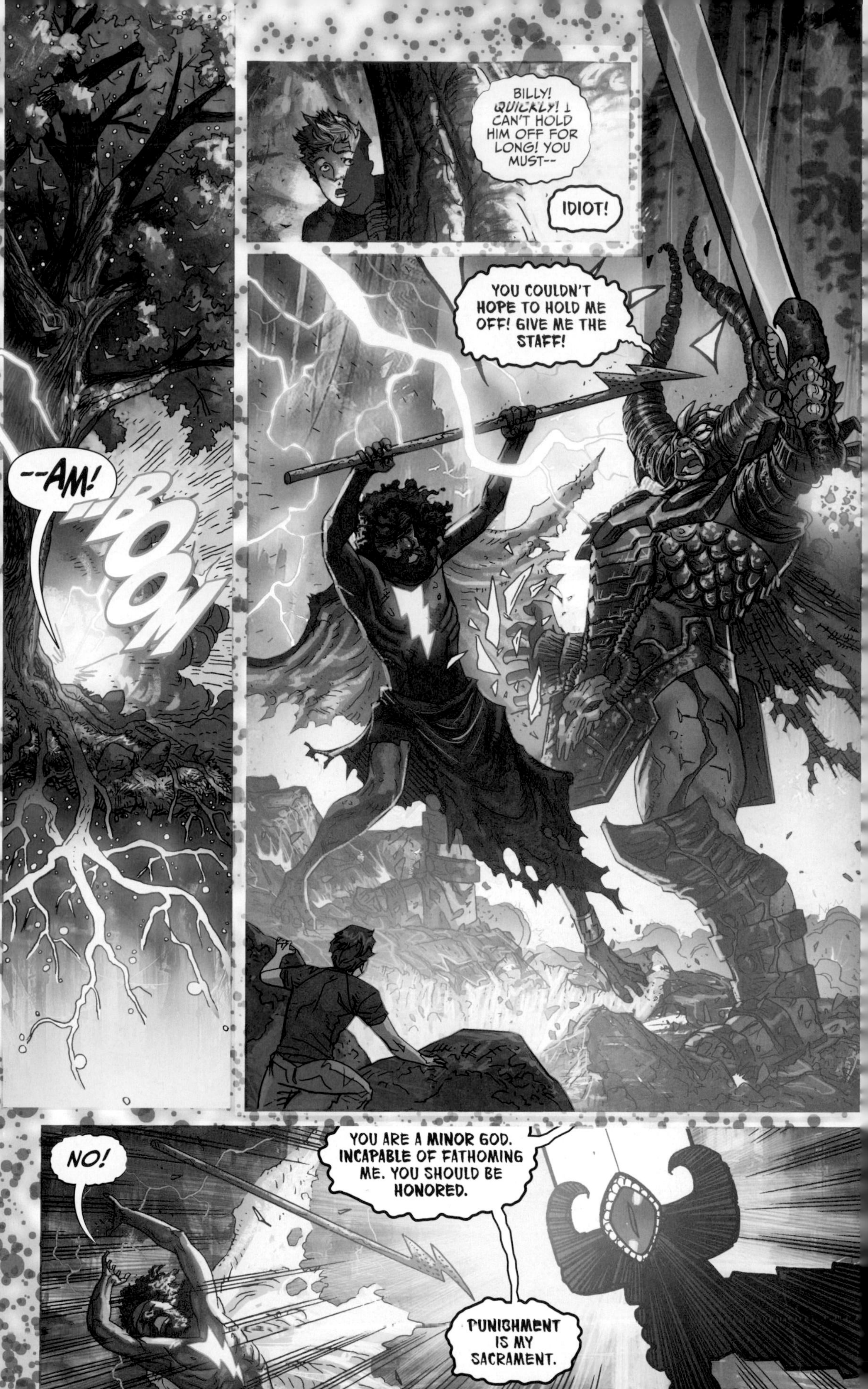
BILLY! QUICKLY! I CAN'T HOLD HIM OFF FOR LONG! YOU MUST--
IDIOT!
YOU COULDN'T HOPE TO HOLD ME OFF! GIVE ME THE STAFF!
--AM!
BOOM
NO!
YOU ARE A MINOR GOD. INCAPABLE OF FATHOMING ME. YOU SHOULD BE HONORED.
PUNISHMENT IS MY SACRAMENT.

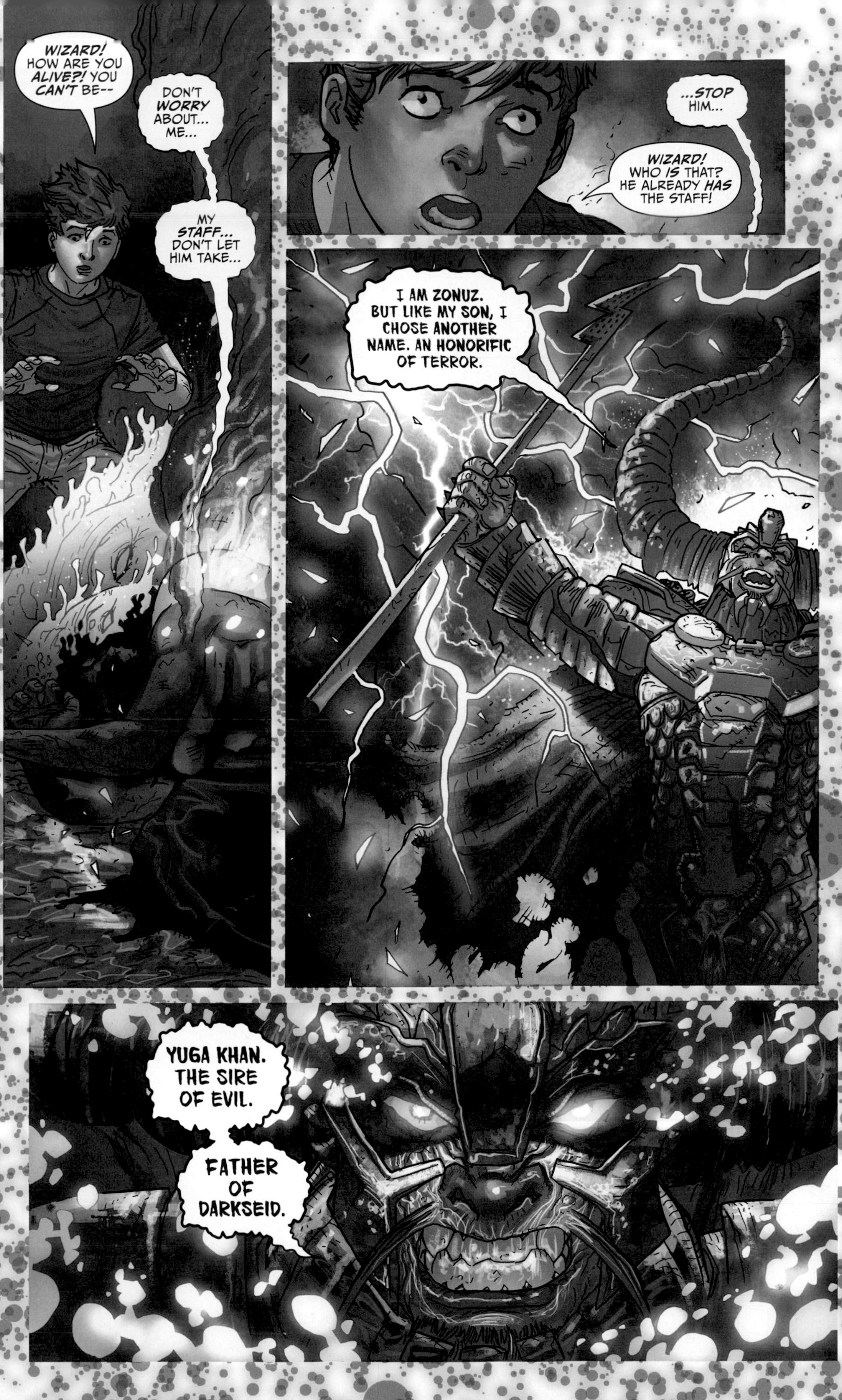
WIZARD! HOW ARE YOU ALIVE?! YOU CAN'T BE--
DON'T WORRY ABOUT... ME...
MY STAFF... DON'T LET HIM TAKE...
...STOP HIM...
WIZARD! WHO IS THAT? HE ALREADY HAS THE STAFF!
I AM ZONUZ. BUT LIKE MY SON, I CHOSE ANOTHER NAME. AN HONORIFIC OF TERROR.
YUGA KHAN. THE SIRE OF EVIL.
FATHER OF DARKSEID.

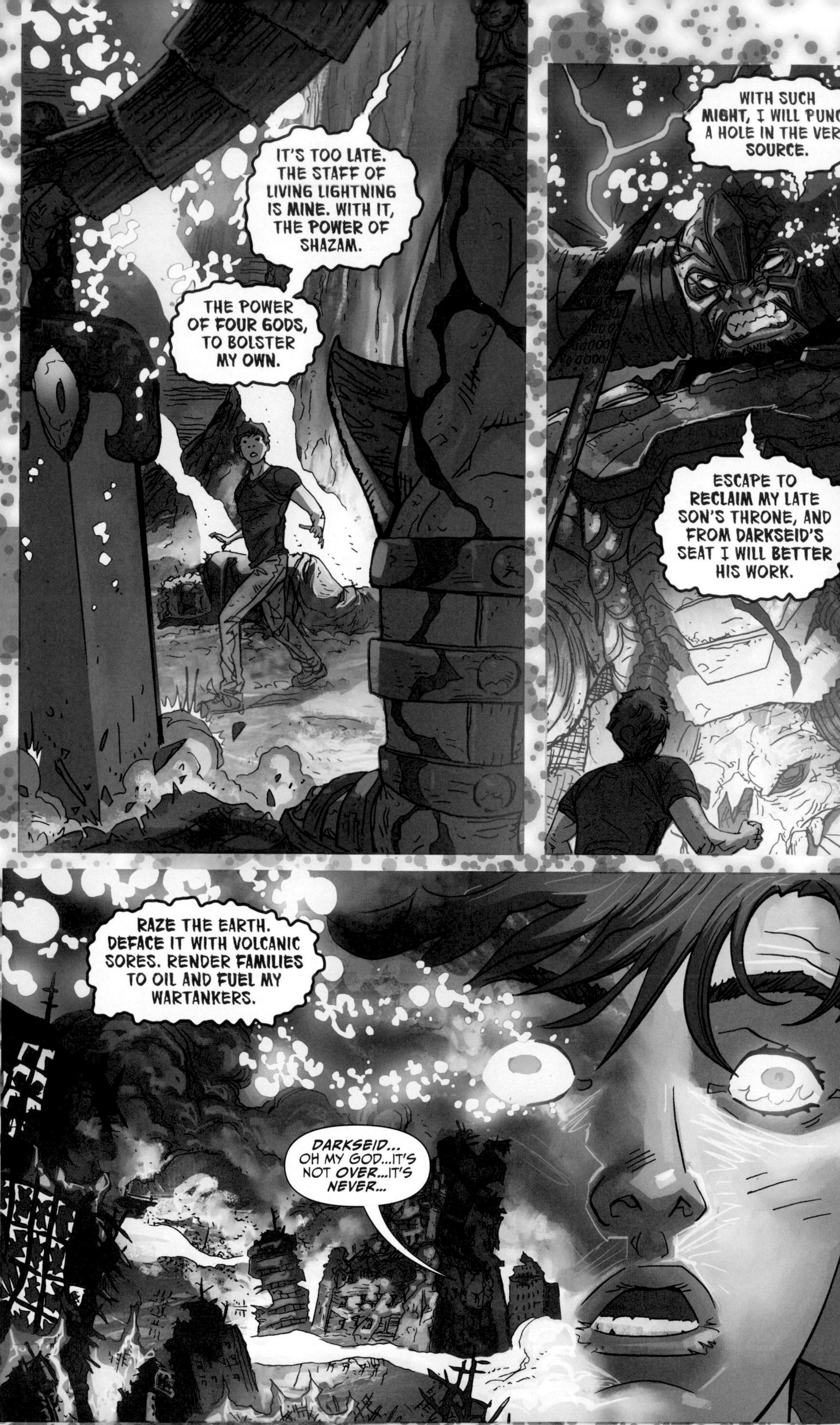
IT'S TOO LATE. THE STAFF OF LIVING LIGHTNING IS MINE. WITH IT, THE POWER OF SHAZAM.
THE POWER OF FOUR GODS, TO BOLSTER MY OWN.
WITH SUCH MIGHT, I WILL PUNCH A HOLE IN THE VERY SOURCE.
ESCAPE TO RECLAIM MY LATE SON'S THRONE, AND FROM DARKSEID'S SEAT I WILL BETTER HIS WORK.
RAZE THE EARTH. DEFACE IT WITH VOLCANIC SORES. RENDER FAMILIES TO OIL AND FUEL MY WARTANKERS.
DARKSEID... OH MY GOD...IT'S NOT OVER...IT'S NEVER...

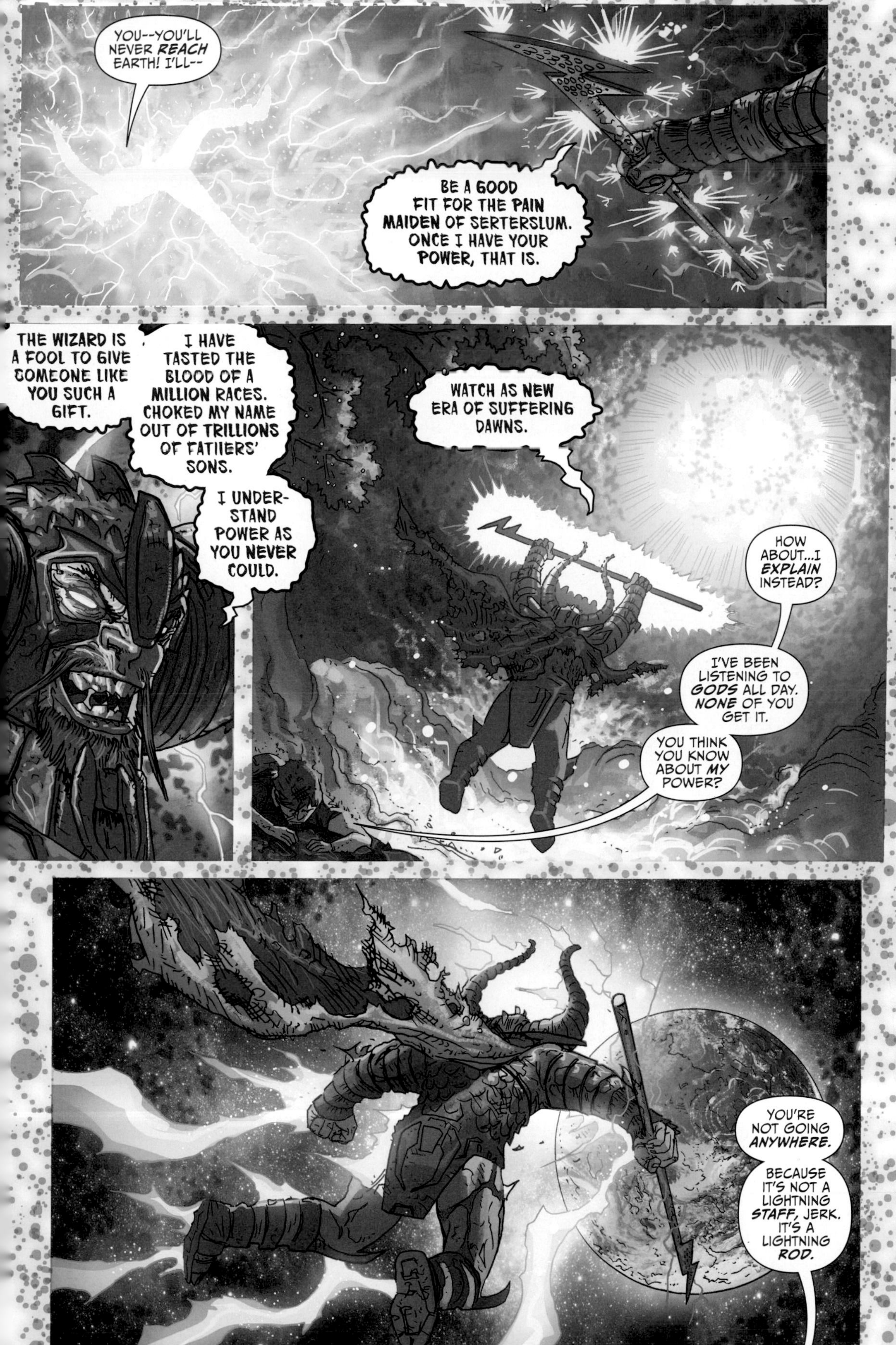
YOU--YOU'LL NEVER REACH EARTH! I'LL--
BE A GOOD FIT FOR THE PAIN MAIDEN OF SERTERSLUM. ONCE I HAVE YOUR POWER, THAT IS.
THE WIZARD IS A FOOL TO GIVE SOMEONE LIKE YOU SUCH A GIFT.
I HAVE TASTED THE BLOOD OF A MILLION RACES. CHOKED MY NAME OUT OF TRILLIONS OF FATHERS' SONS.
I UNDER-STAND POWER AS YOU NEVER COULD.
WATCH AS NEW ERA OF SUFFERING DAWNS.
HOW ABOUT...I EXPLAIN INSTEAD?
I'VE BEEN LISTENING TO GODS ALL DAY. NONE OF YOU GET IT.
YOU THINK YOU KNOW ABOUT MY POWER?
YOU'RE NOT GOING ANYWHERE.
BECAUSE IT'S NOT A LIGHTNING STAFF, JERK. IT'S A LIGHTNING ROD.

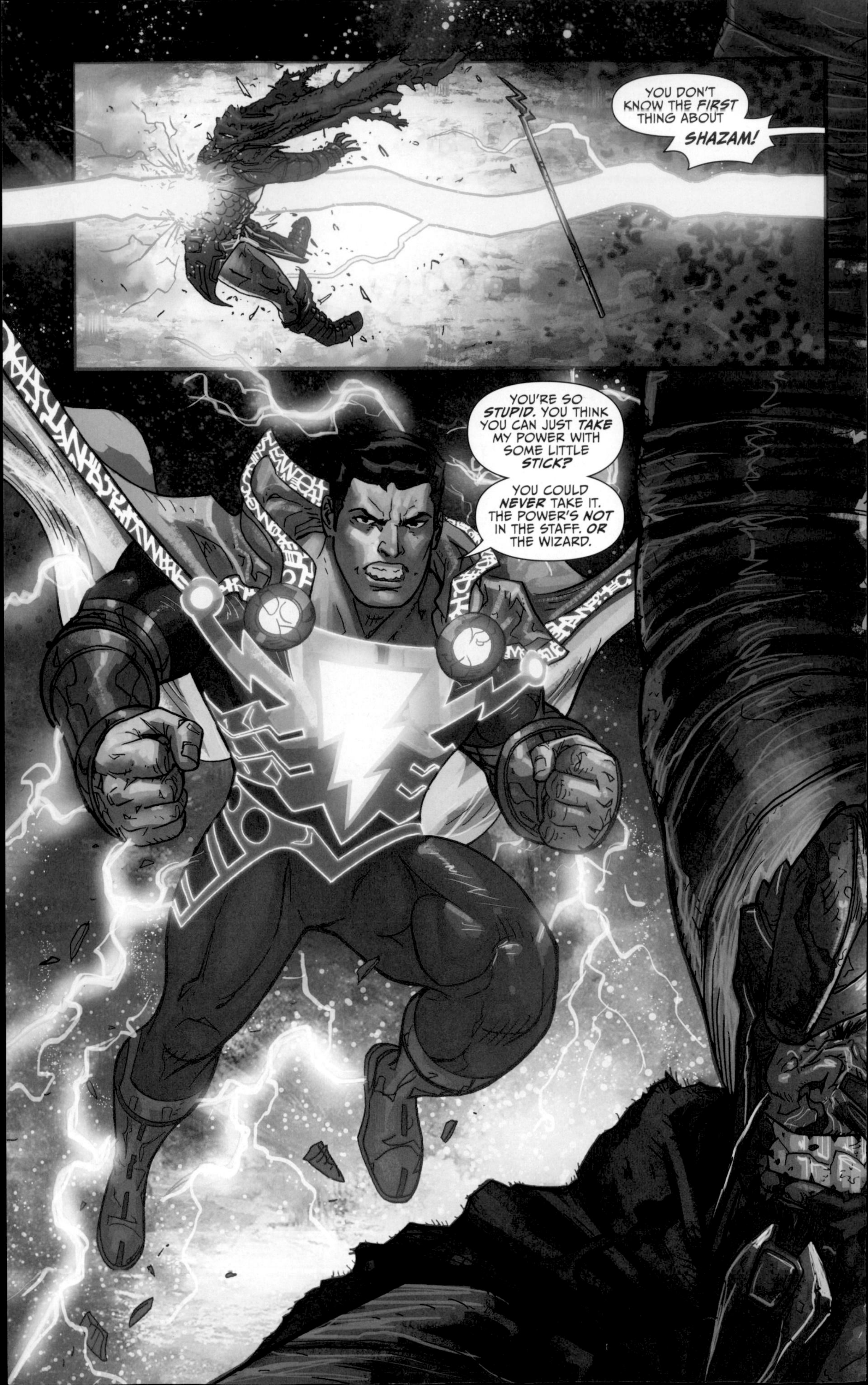
YOU DON'T KNOW THE FIRST THING ABOUT SHAZAM!
YOU'RE SO STUPID. YOU THINK YOU CAN JUST TAKE MY POWER WITH SOME LITTLE STICK?
YOU COULD NEVER TAKE IT. THE POWER'S NOT IN THE STAFF. OR THE WIZARD.

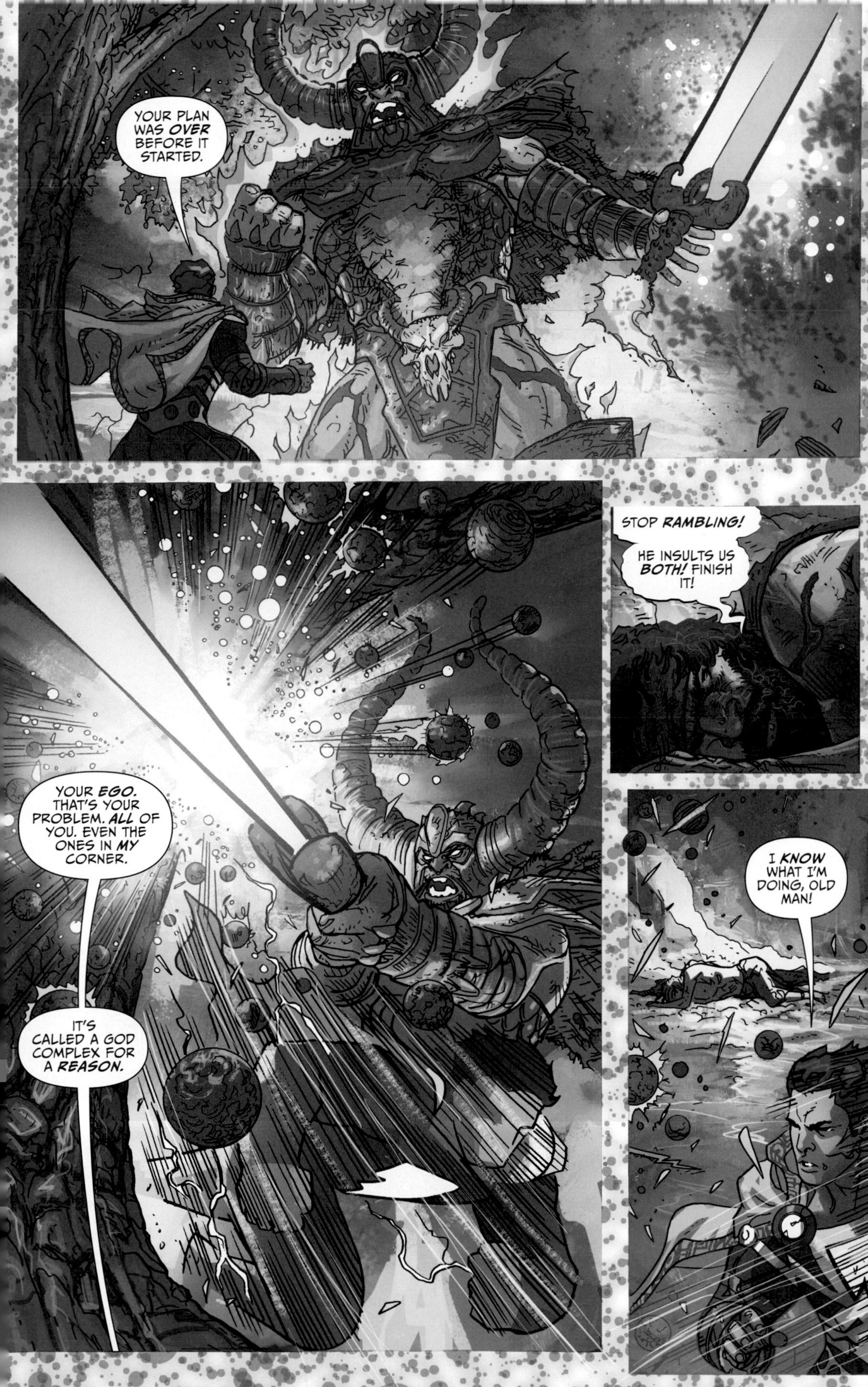
YOUR PLAN WAS OVER BEFORE IT STARTED.
YOUR EGO. THAT'S YOUR PROBLEM. ALL OF YOU. EVEN THE ONES IN MY CORNER.
IT'S CALLED A GOD COMPLEX FOR A REASON.
STOP RAMBLING!
HE INSULTS US BOTH! FINISH IT!
I KNOW WHAT I'M DOING, OLD MAN!

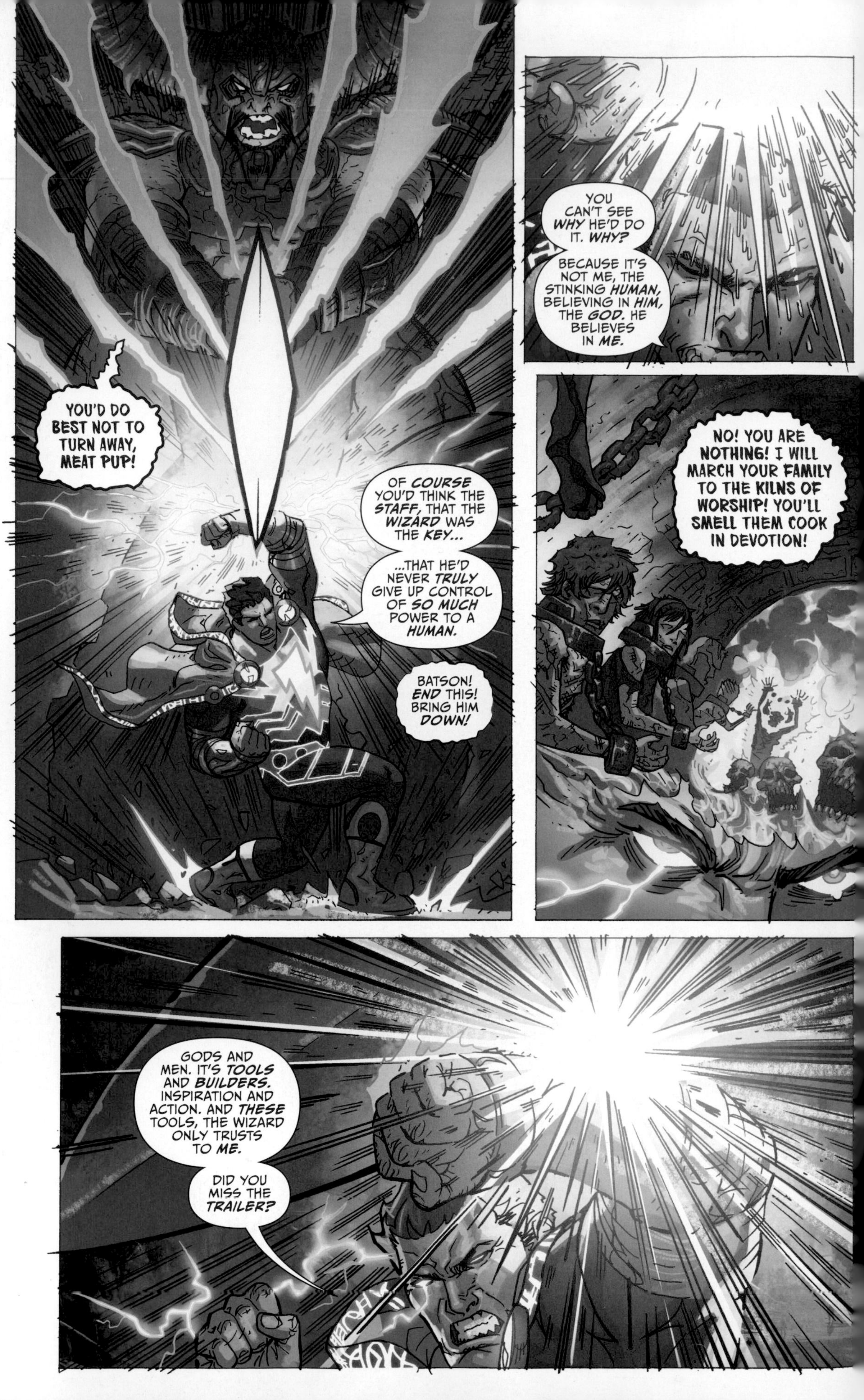
YOU'D DO BEST NOT TO TURN AWAY, MEAT PUP!
OF COURSE YOU'D THINK THE STAFF, THAT THE WIZARD WAS THE KEY...
...THAT HE'D NEVER TRULY GIVE UP CONTROL OF SO MUCH POWER TO A HUMAN.
BATSON! END THIS! BRING HIM DOWN!
YOU CAN'T SEE WHY HE'D DO IT. WHY?
BECAUSE IT'S NOT ME, THE STINKING HUMAN, BELIEVING IN HIM, THE GOD. HE BELIEVES IN ME.
NO! YOU ARE NOTHING! I WILL MARCH YOUR FAMILY TO THE KILNS OF WORSHIP! YOU'LL SMELL THEM COOK IN DEVOTION!
GODS AND MEN. IT'S TOOLS AND BUILDERS. INSPIRATION AND ACTION. AND THESE TOOLS, THE WIZARD ONLY TRUSTS TO ME.
DID YOU MISS THE TRAILER?

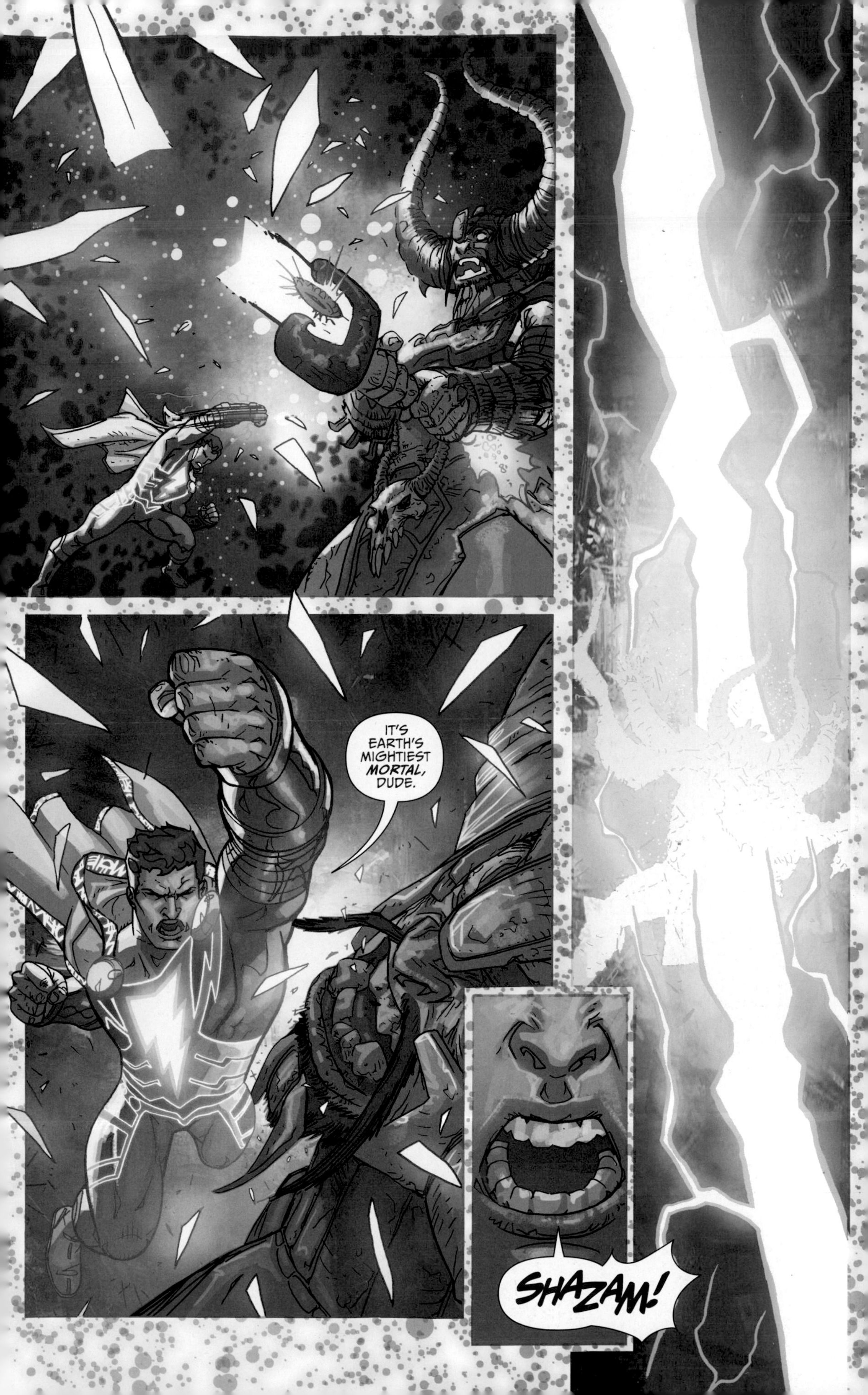
IT'S EARTH'S MIGHTIEST *MORTAL*, DUDE.
SHAZAM!

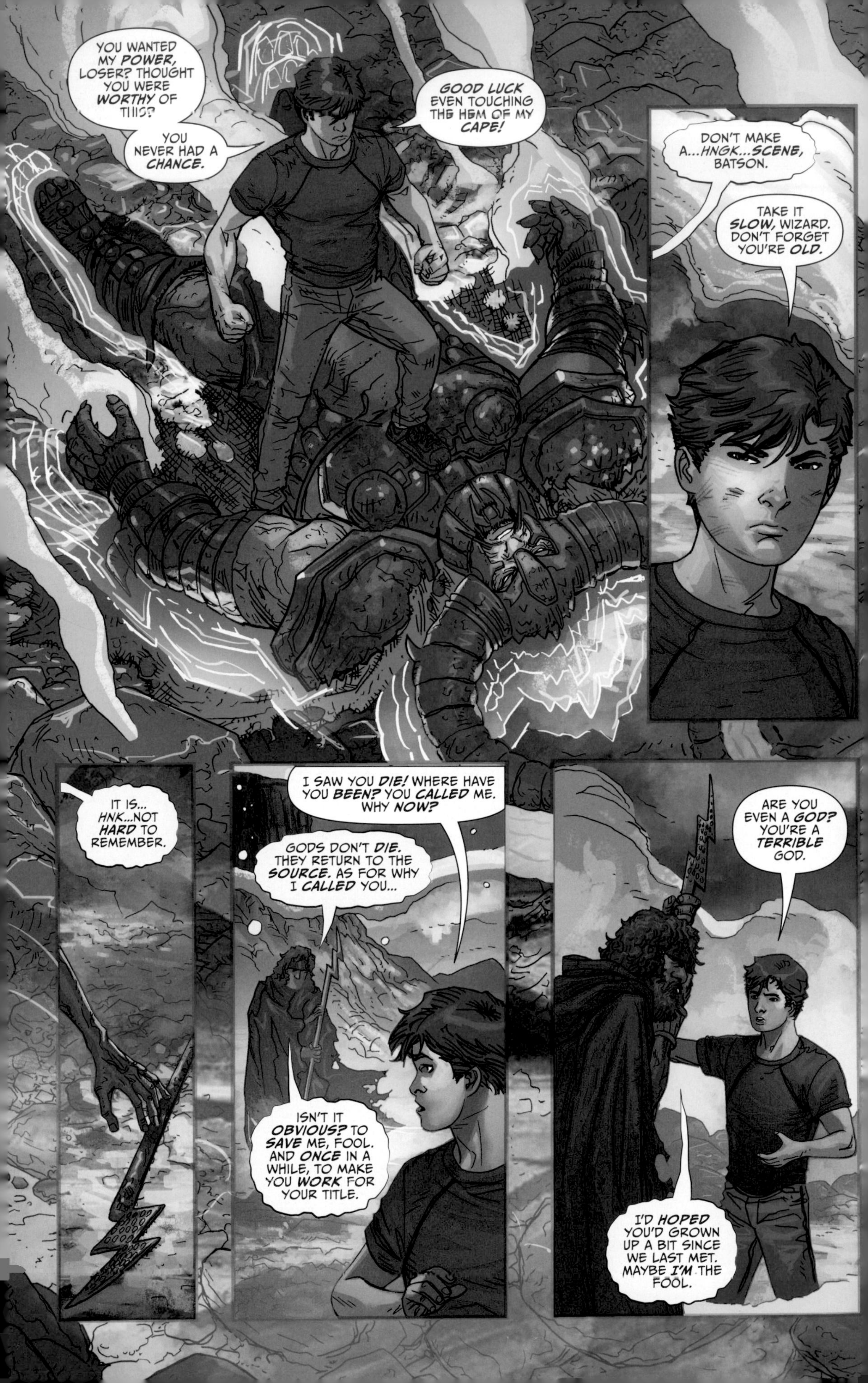
YOU WANTED MY POWER, LOSER? THOUGHT YOU WERE WORTHY OF THIS?
YOU NEVER HAD A CHANCE.
GOOD LUCK EVEN TOUCHING THE HEM OF MY CAPE!
DON'T MAKE A...HNGK...SCENE, BATSON.
TAKE IT SLOW, WIZARD. DON'T FORGET YOU'RE OLD.
IT IS... HNK...NOT HARD TO REMEMBER.
I SAW YOU DIE! WHERE HAVE YOU BEEN? YOU CALLED ME. WHY NOW?
GODS DON'T DIE. THEY RETURN TO THE SOURCE. AS FOR WHY I CALLED YOU...
ISN'T IT OBVIOUS? TO SAVE ME, FOOL. AND ONCE IN A WHILE, TO MAKE YOU WORK FOR YOUR TITLE.
ARE YOU EVEN A GOD? YOU'RE A TERRIBLE GOD.
I'D HOPED YOU'D GROWN UP A BIT SINCE WE LAST MET. MAYBE I'M THE FOOL.

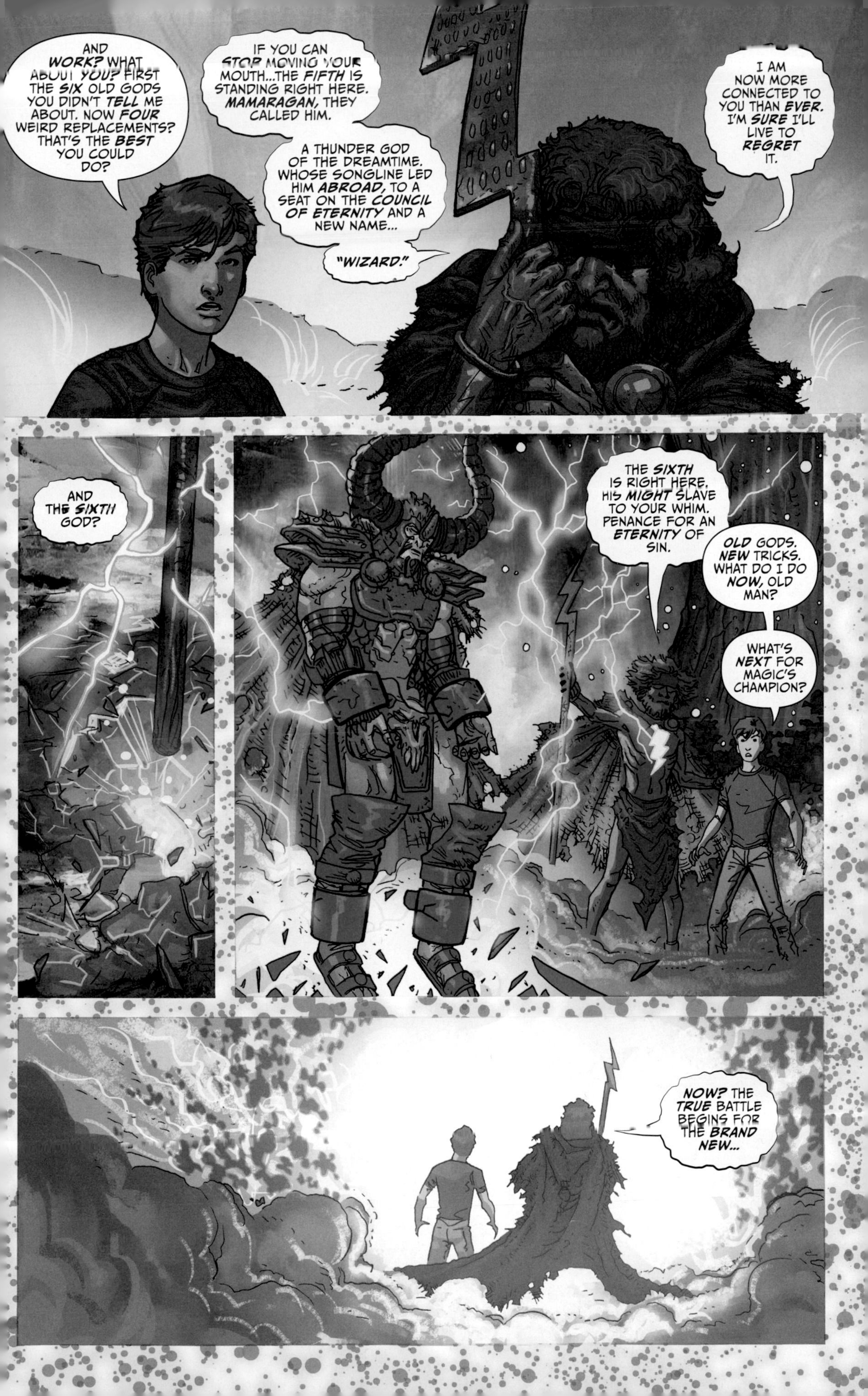

AND WORK? WHAT ABOUT YOU? FIRST THE SIX OLD GODS YOU DIDN'T TELL ME ABOUT. NOW FOUR WEIRD REPLACEMENTS? THAT'S THE BEST YOU COULD DO?
IF YOU CAN STOP MOVING YOUR MOUTH...THE FIFTH IS STANDING RIGHT HERE. MAMARAGAN, THEY CALLED HIM.
A THUNDER GOD OF THE DREAMTIME. WHOSE SONGLINE LED HIM ABROAD, TO A SEAT ON THE COUNCIL OF ETERNITY AND A NEW NAME...
"WIZARD."
I AM NOW MORE CONNECTED TO YOU THAN EVER. I'M SURE I'LL LIVE TO REGRET IT.
AND THE SIXTH GOD?
THE SIXTH IS RIGHT HERE. HIS MIGHT SLAVE TO YOUR WHIM. PENANCE FOR AN ETERNITY OF SIN.
OLD GODS. NEW TRICKS. WHAT DO I DO NOW, OLD MAN?
WHAT'S NEXT FOR MAGIC'S CHAMPION?
NOW? THE TRUE BATTLE BEGINS FOR THE BRAND NEW...

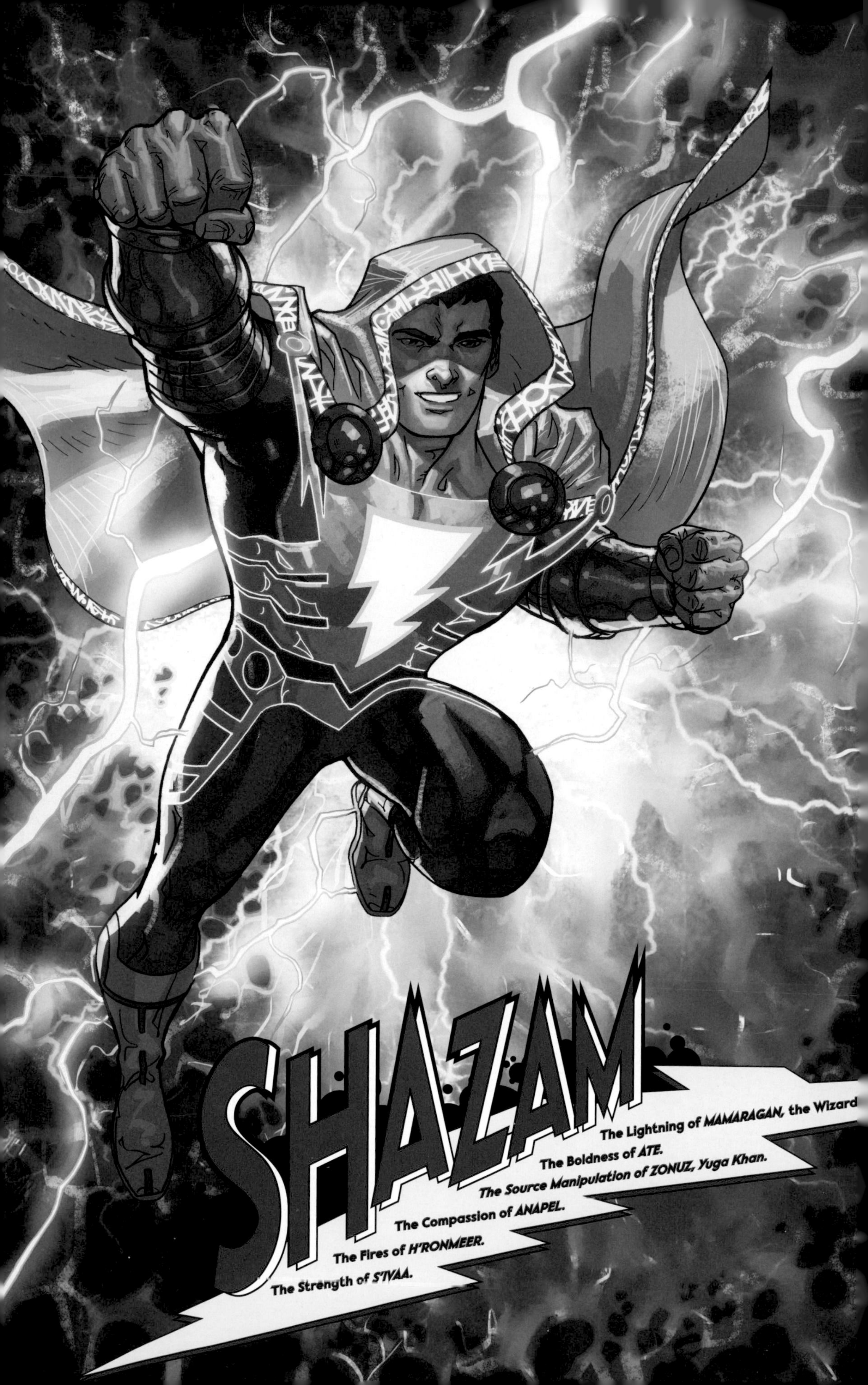
SHAZAM
The Lightning of MAMARAGAN, the Wizard
The Boldness of ATE.
The Source Manipulation of ZONUZ, Yuga Khan.
The Compassion of ANAPEL.
The Fires of H'RONMEER.
The Strength of S'IVAA.

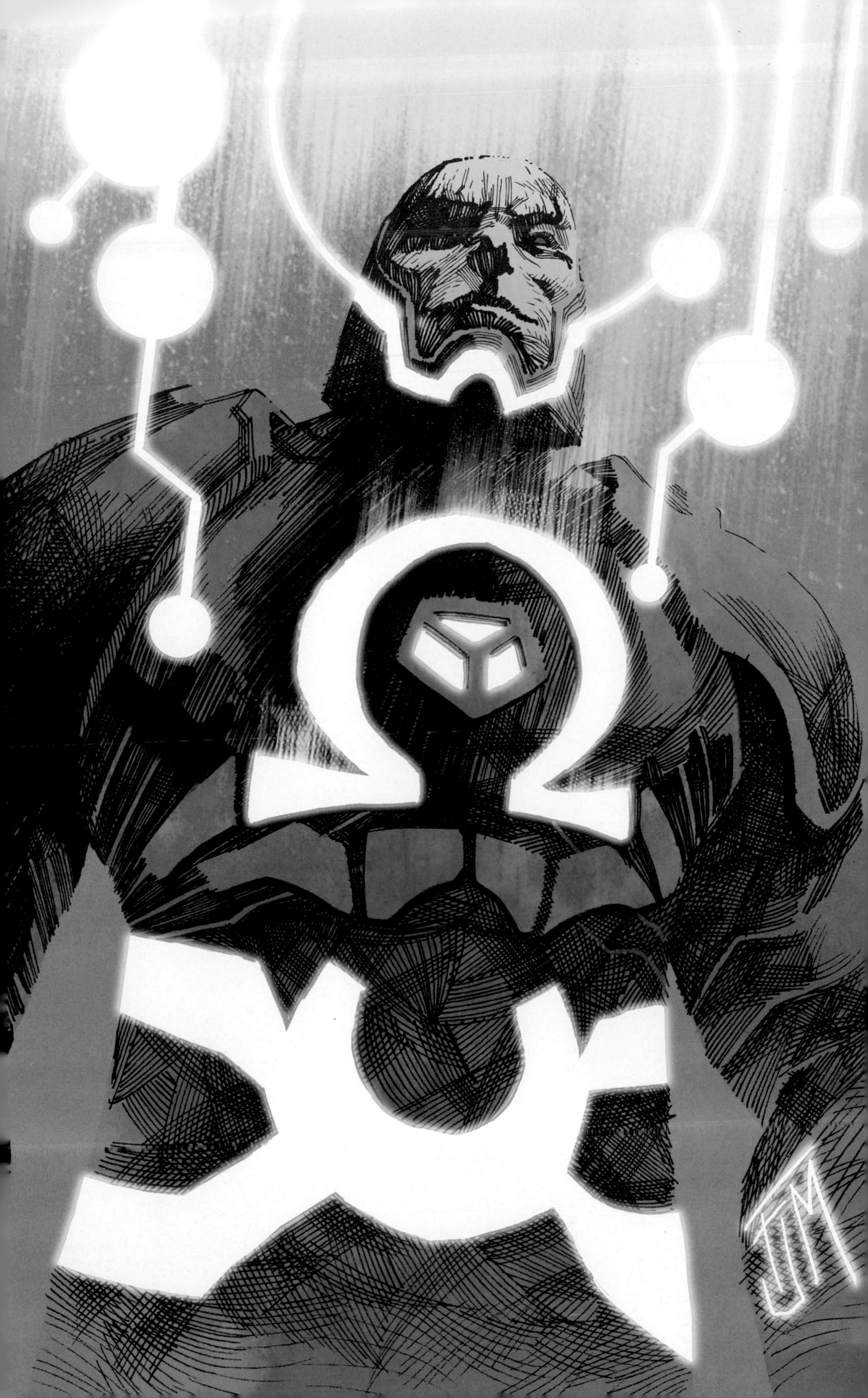

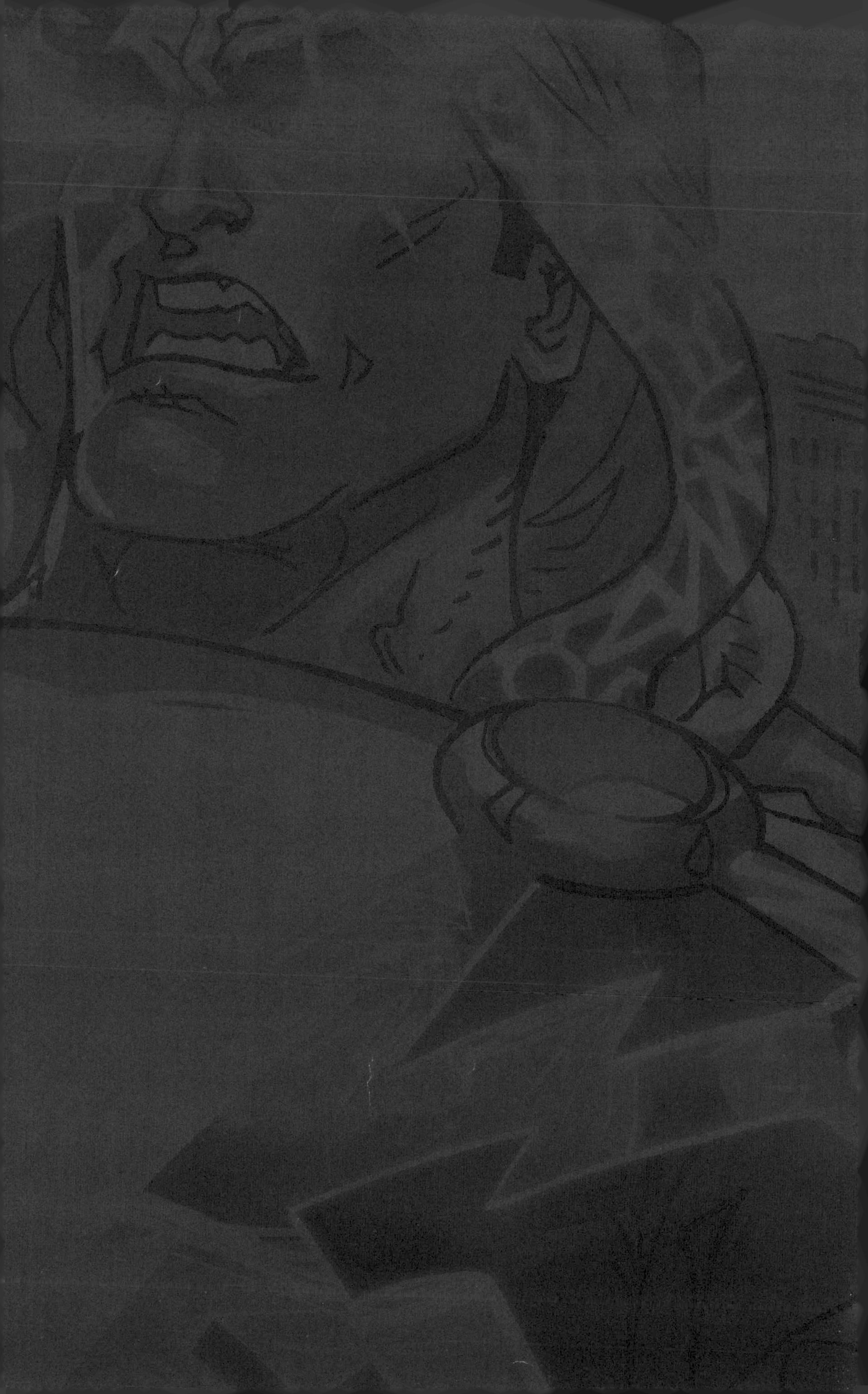

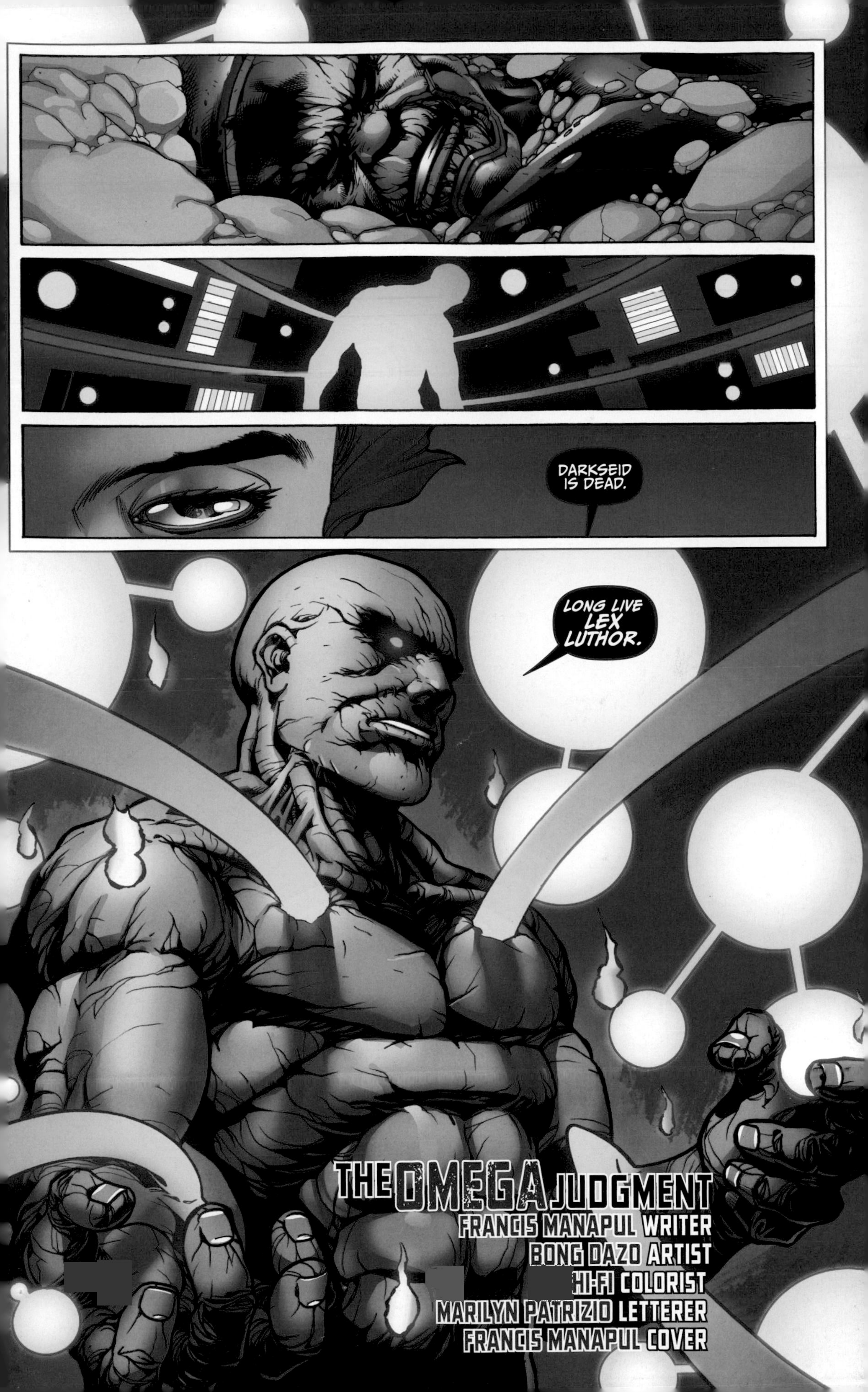
DARKSEID IS DEAD.
LONG LIVE LEX LUTHOR.
THE OMEGA JUDGMENT
FRANCIS MANAPUL WRITER
BONG DAZO ARTIST
[redacted] HI-FI COLORIST
MARILYN PATRIZIO LETTERER
FRANCIS MANAPUL COVER

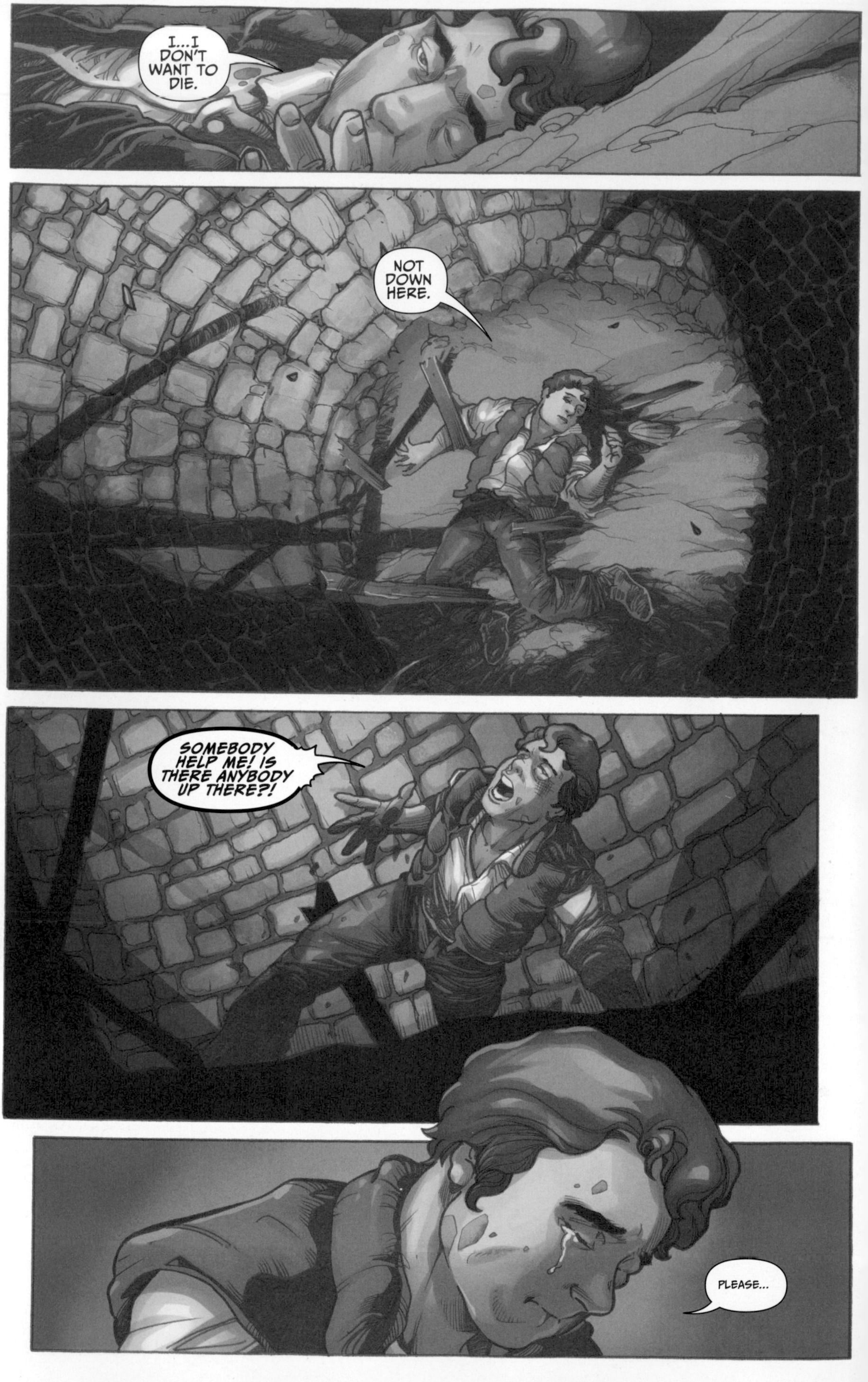
I...I DON'T WANT TO DIE.
NOT DOWN HERE.
SOMEBODY HELP ME! IS THERE ANYBODY UP THERE?!
PLEASE...

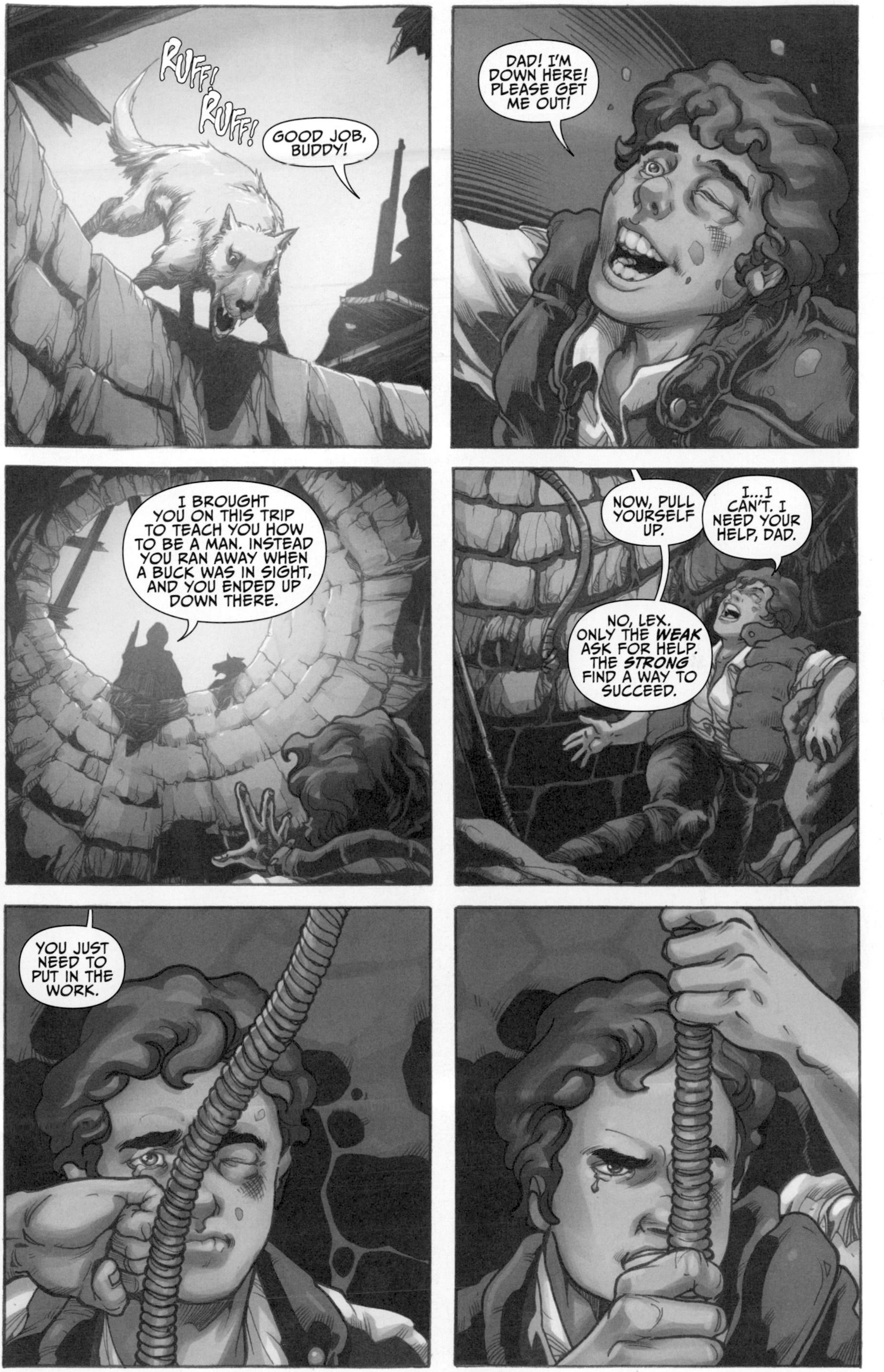
RUFF! RUFF!
GOOD JOB, BUDDY!
DAD! I'M DOWN HERE! PLEASE GET ME OUT!
I BROUGHT YOU ON THIS TRIP TO TEACH YOU HOW TO BE A MAN. INSTEAD YOU RAN AWAY WHEN A BUCK WAS IN SIGHT, AND YOU ENDED UP DOWN THERE.
NOW, PULL YOURSELF UP.
I...I CAN'T. I NEED YOUR HELP, DAD.
NO, LEX. ONLY THE WEAK ASK FOR HELP. THE STRONG FIND A WAY TO SUCCEED.
YOU JUST NEED TO PUT IN THE WORK.

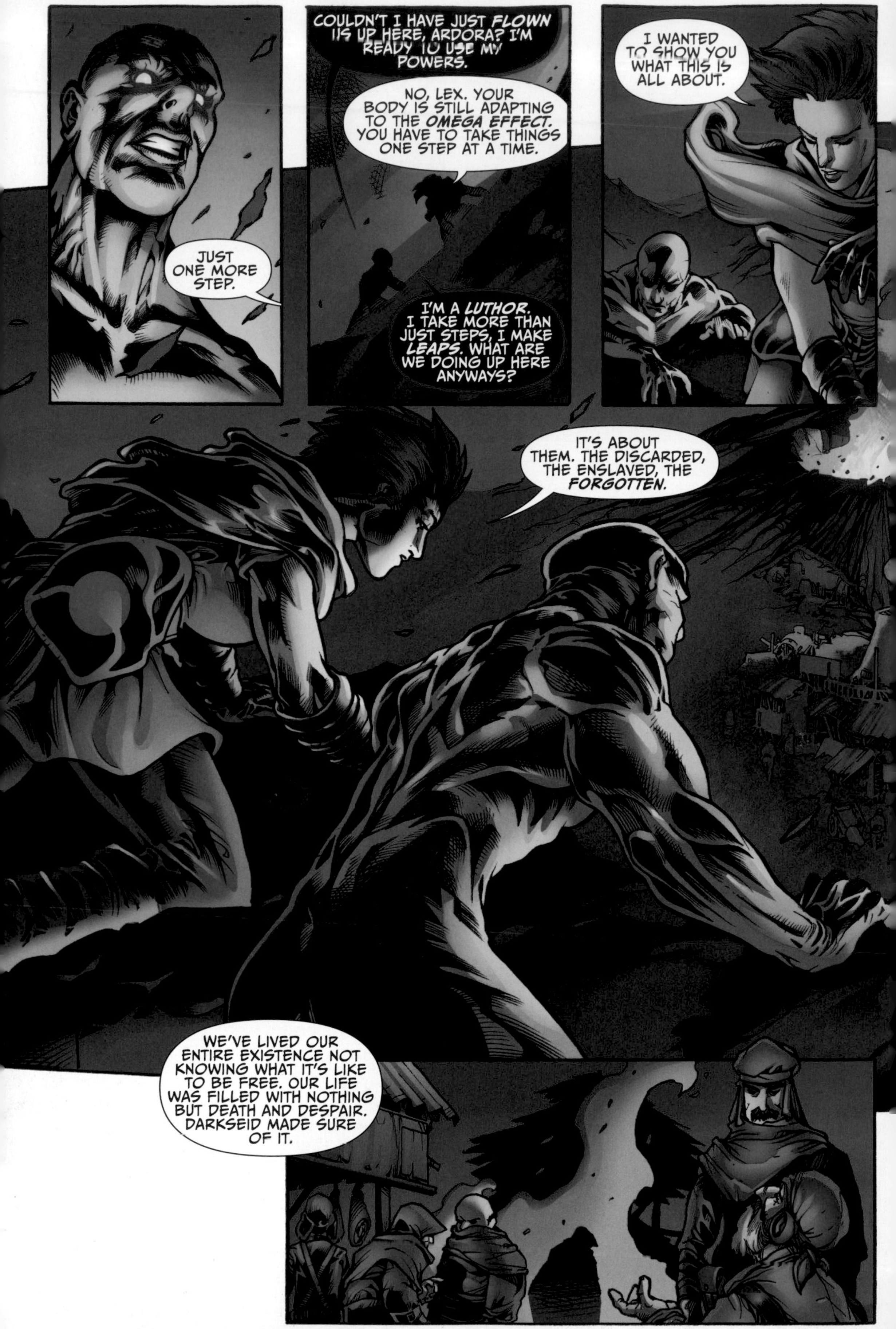

COULDN'T I HAVE JUST FLOWN US UP HERE, ARDORA? I'M READY TO USE MY POWERS.
NO, LEX. YOUR BODY IS STILL ADAPTING TO THE OMEGA EFFECT. YOU HAVE TO TAKE THINGS ONE STEP AT A TIME.
JUST ONE MORE STEP.
I'M A LUTHOR. I TAKE MORE THAN JUST STEPS, I MAKE LEAPS. WHAT ARE WE DOING UP HERE ANYWAYS?
I WANTED TO SHOW YOU WHAT THIS IS ALL ABOUT.
IT'S ABOUT THEM. THE DISCARDED, THE ENSLAVED, THE FORGOTTEN.
WE'VE LIVED OUR ENTIRE EXISTENCE NOT KNOWING WHAT IT'S LIKE TO BE FREE. OUR LIFE WAS FILLED WITH NOTHING BUT DEATH AND DESPAIR. DARKSEID MADE SURE OF IT.

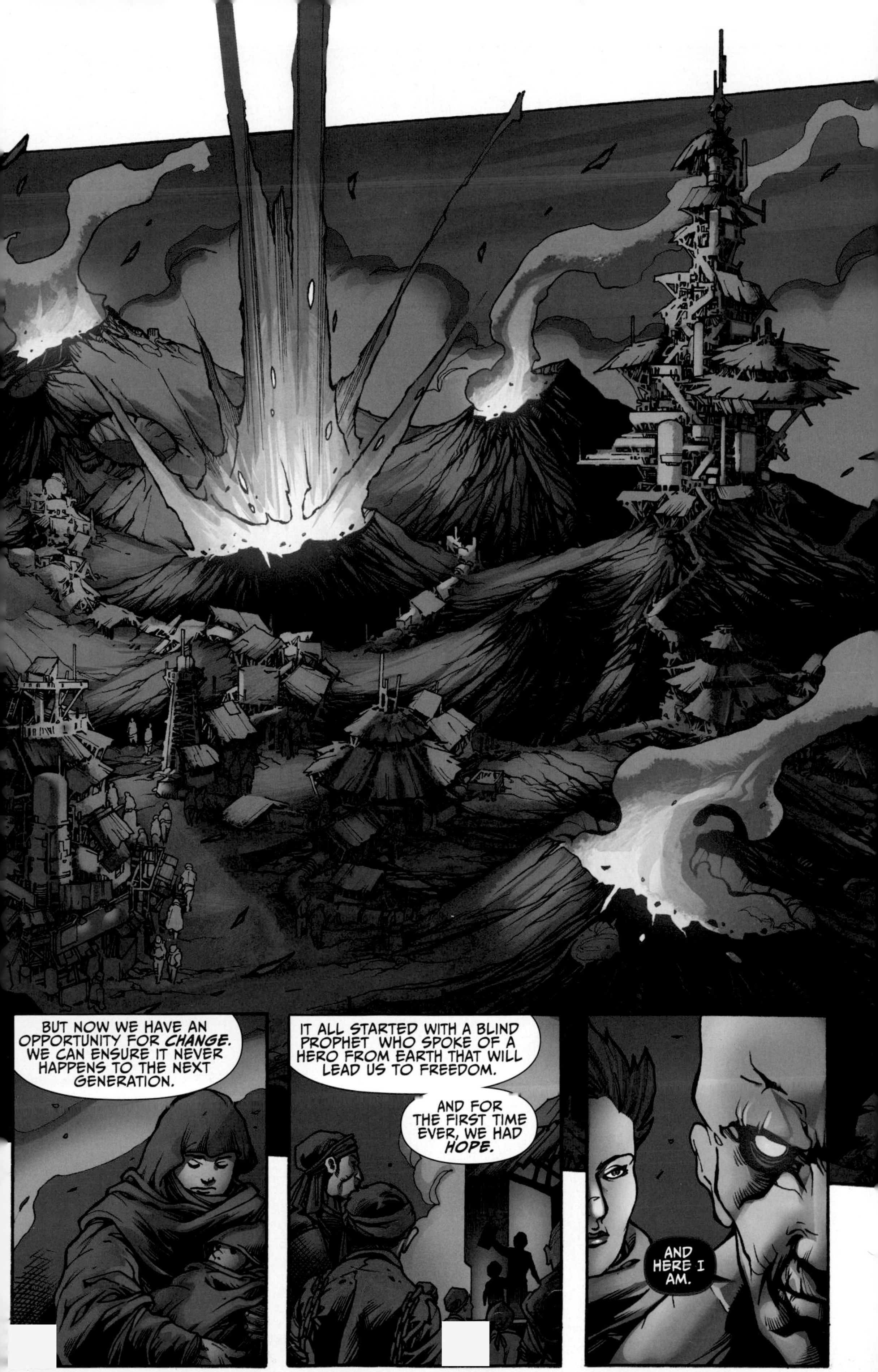
BUT NOW WE HAVE AN OPPORTUNITY FOR CHANGE. WE CAN ENSURE IT NEVER HAPPENS TO THE NEXT GENERATION.
IT ALL STARTED WITH A BLIND PROPHET WHO SPOKE OF A HERO FROM EARTH THAT WILL LEAD US TO FREEDOM.
AND FOR THE FIRST TIME EVER, WE HAD HOPE.
AND HERE I AM.

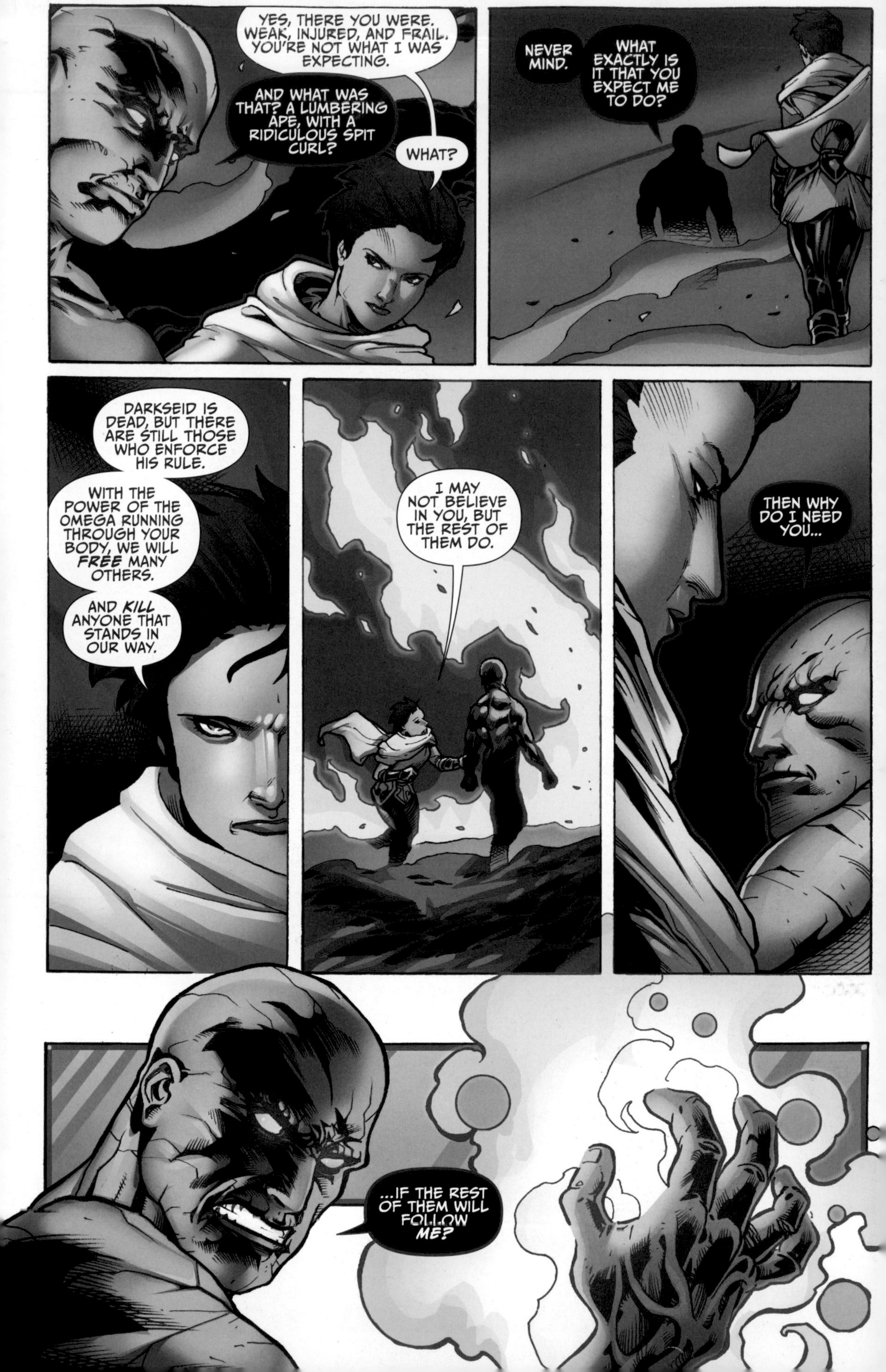
YES, THERE YOU WERE. WEAK, INJURED, AND FRAIL. YOU'RE NOT WHAT I WAS EXPECTING.
AND WHAT WAS THAT? A LUMBERING APE, WITH A RIDICULOUS SPIT CURL?
WHAT?
NEVER MIND.
WHAT EXACTLY IS IT THAT YOU EXPECT ME TO DO?
DARKSEID IS DEAD, BUT THERE ARE STILL THOSE WHO ENFORCE HIS RULE.
WITH THE POWER OF THE OMEGA RUNNING THROUGH YOUR BODY, WE WILL *FREE* MANY OTHERS.
AND *KILL* ANYONE THAT STANDS IN OUR WAY.
I MAY NOT BELIEVE IN YOU, BUT THE REST OF THEM DO.
THEN WHY DO I NEED YOU...
...IF THE REST OF THEM WILL FOLLOW *ME?*

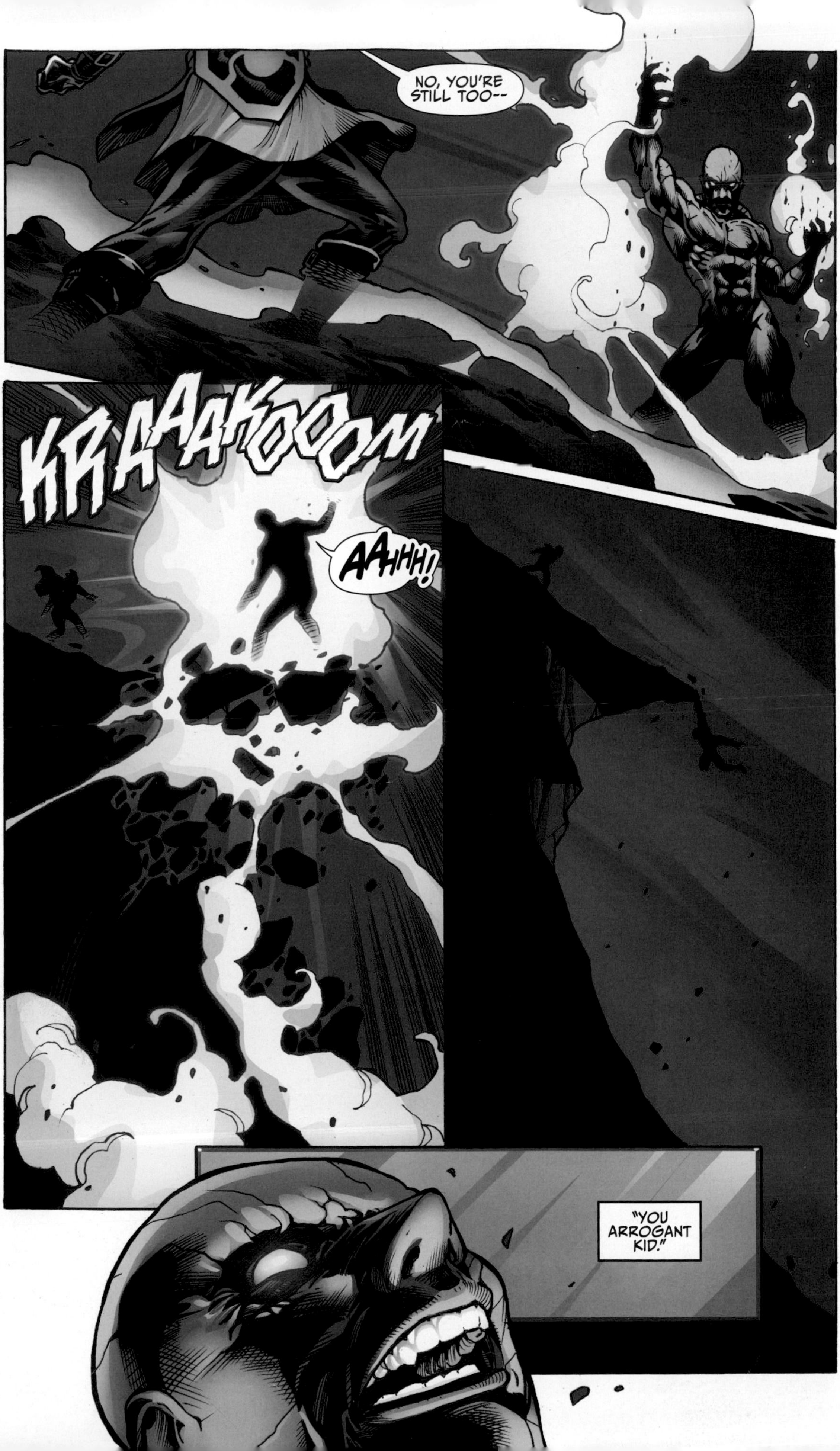
NO, YOU'RE STILL TOO--
KRAAAKOOOM
AAHHH!
"YOU ARROGANT KID."

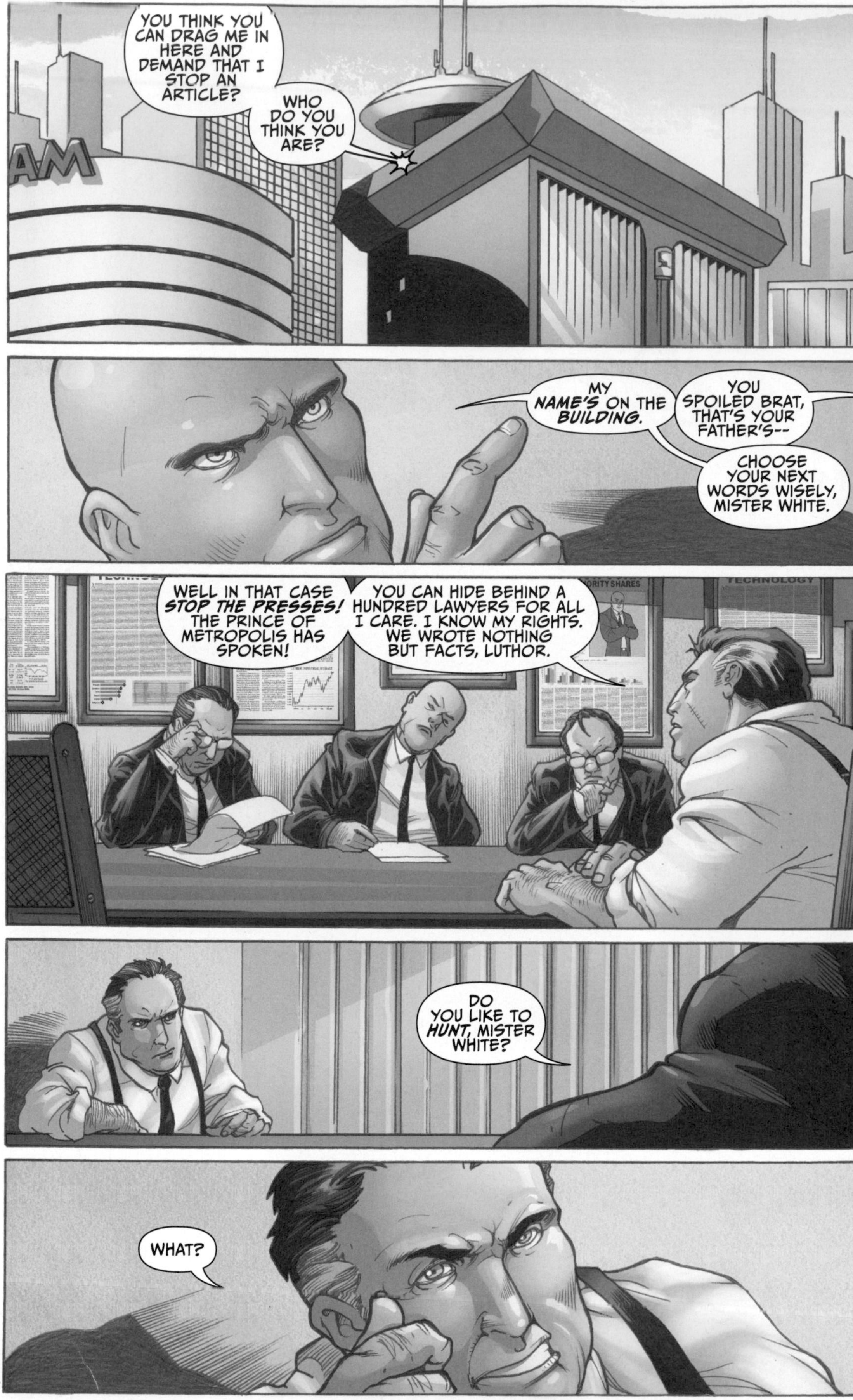
YOU THINK YOU CAN DRAG ME IN HERE AND DEMAND THAT I STOP AN ARTICLE?
WHO DO YOU THINK YOU ARE?
MY NAME'S ON THE BUILDING.
YOU SPOILED BRAT, THAT'S YOUR FATHER'S--
CHOOSE YOUR NEXT WORDS WISELY, MISTER WHITE.
WELL IN THAT CASE STOP THE PRESSES! THE PRINCE OF METROPOLIS HAS SPOKEN!
YOU CAN HIDE BEHIND A HUNDRED LAWYERS FOR ALL I CARE. I KNOW MY RIGHTS. WE WROTE NOTHING BUT FACTS, LUTHOR.
DO YOU LIKE TO HUNT, MISTER WHITE?
WHAT?

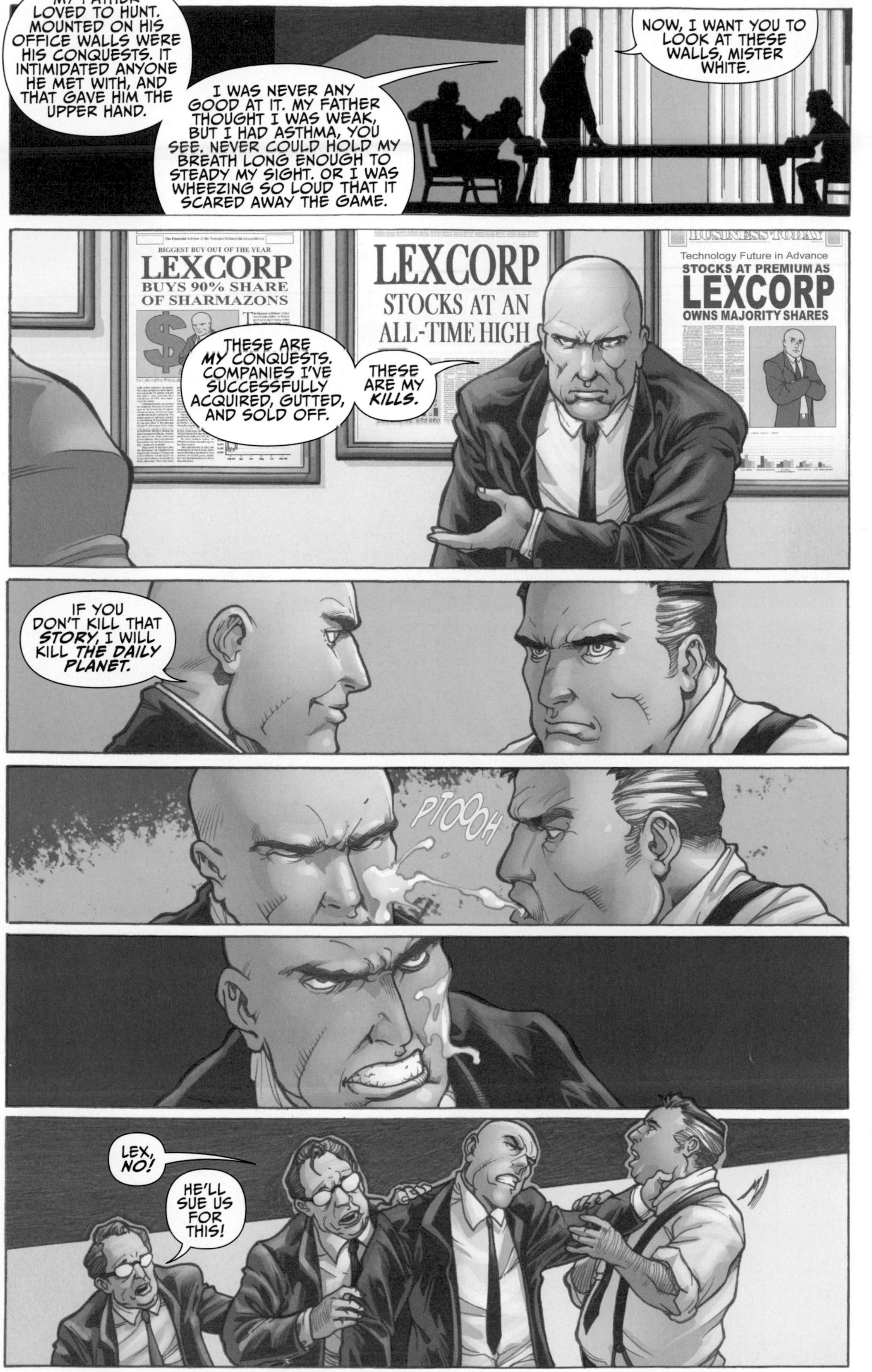
MY FATHER LOVED TO HUNT. MOUNTED ON HIS OFFICE WALLS WERE HIS CONQUESTS. IT INTIMIDATED ANYONE HE MET WITH, AND THAT GAVE HIM THE UPPER HAND.
I WAS NEVER ANY GOOD AT IT. MY FATHER THOUGHT I WAS WEAK, BUT I HAD ASTHMA, YOU SEE. NEVER COULD HOLD MY BREATH LONG ENOUGH TO STEADY MY SIGHT. OR I WAS WHEEZING SO LOUD THAT IT SCARED AWAY THE GAME.
NOW, I WANT YOU TO LOOK AT THESE WALLS, MISTER WHITE.
BIGGEST BUY OUT OF THE YEAR
LEXCORP
BUYS 90% SHARE OF SHARMAZONS
LEXCORP
STOCKS AT AN ALL-TIME HIGH
BUSINESS TODAY
Technology Future in Advance
STOCKS AT PREMIUM AS
LEXCORP
OWNS MAJORITY SHARES
THESE ARE MY CONQUESTS. COMPANIES I'VE SUCCESSFULLY ACQUIRED, GUTTED, AND SOLD OFF.
THESE ARE MY KILLS.
IF YOU DON'T KILL THAT STORY, I WILL KILL THE DAILY PLANET.
PTOOOH
LEX, NO!
HE'LL SUE US FOR THIS!

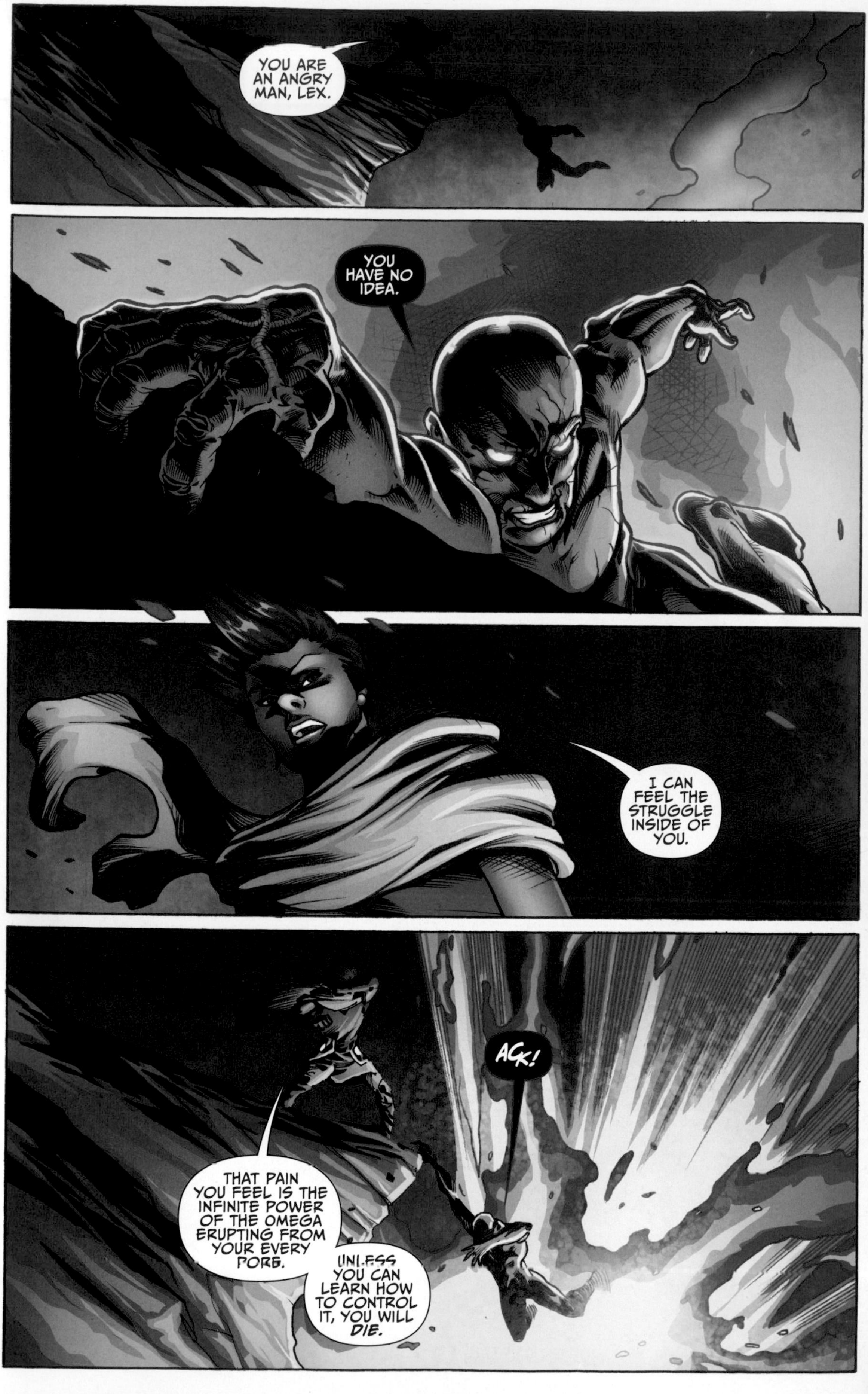
YOU ARE AN ANGRY MAN, LEX.
YOU HAVE NO IDEA.
I CAN FEEL THE STRUGGLE INSIDE OF YOU.
ACK!
THAT PAIN YOU FEEL IS THE INFINITE POWER OF THE OMEGA ERUPTING FROM YOUR EVERY PORE.
UNLESS YOU CAN LEARN HOW TO CONTROL IT, YOU WILL DIE.

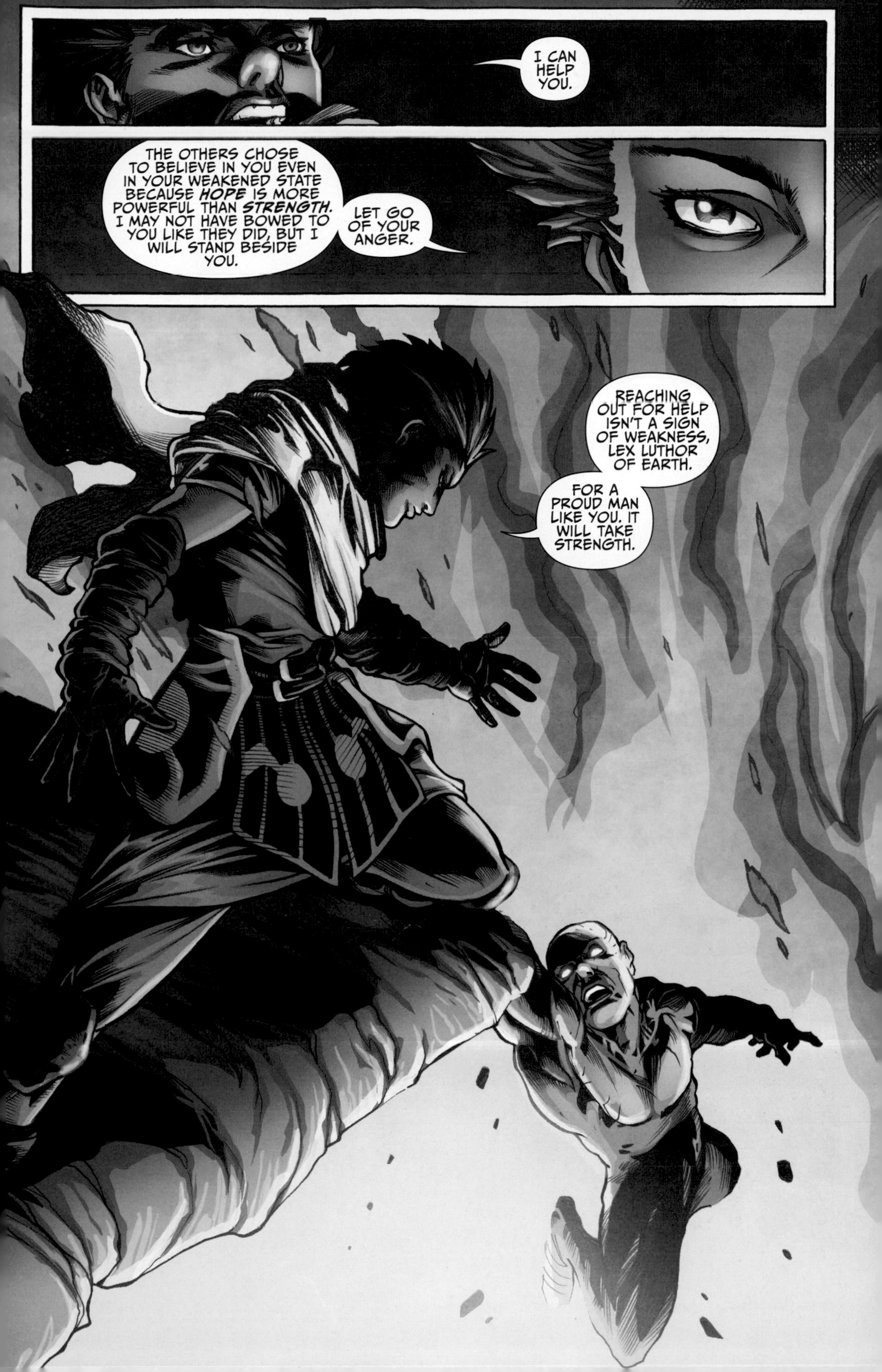
I CAN HELP YOU.
THE OTHERS CHOSE TO BELIEVE IN YOU EVEN IN YOUR WEAKENED STATE BECAUSE *HOPE* IS MORE POWERFUL THAN *STRENGTH*. I MAY NOT HAVE BOWED TO YOU LIKE THEY DID, BUT I WILL STAND BESIDE YOU.
LET GO OF YOUR ANGER.
REACHING OUT FOR HELP ISN'T A SIGN OF WEAKNESS, LEX LUTHOR OF EARTH.
FOR A PROUD MAN LIKE YOU. IT WILL TAKE STRENGTH.

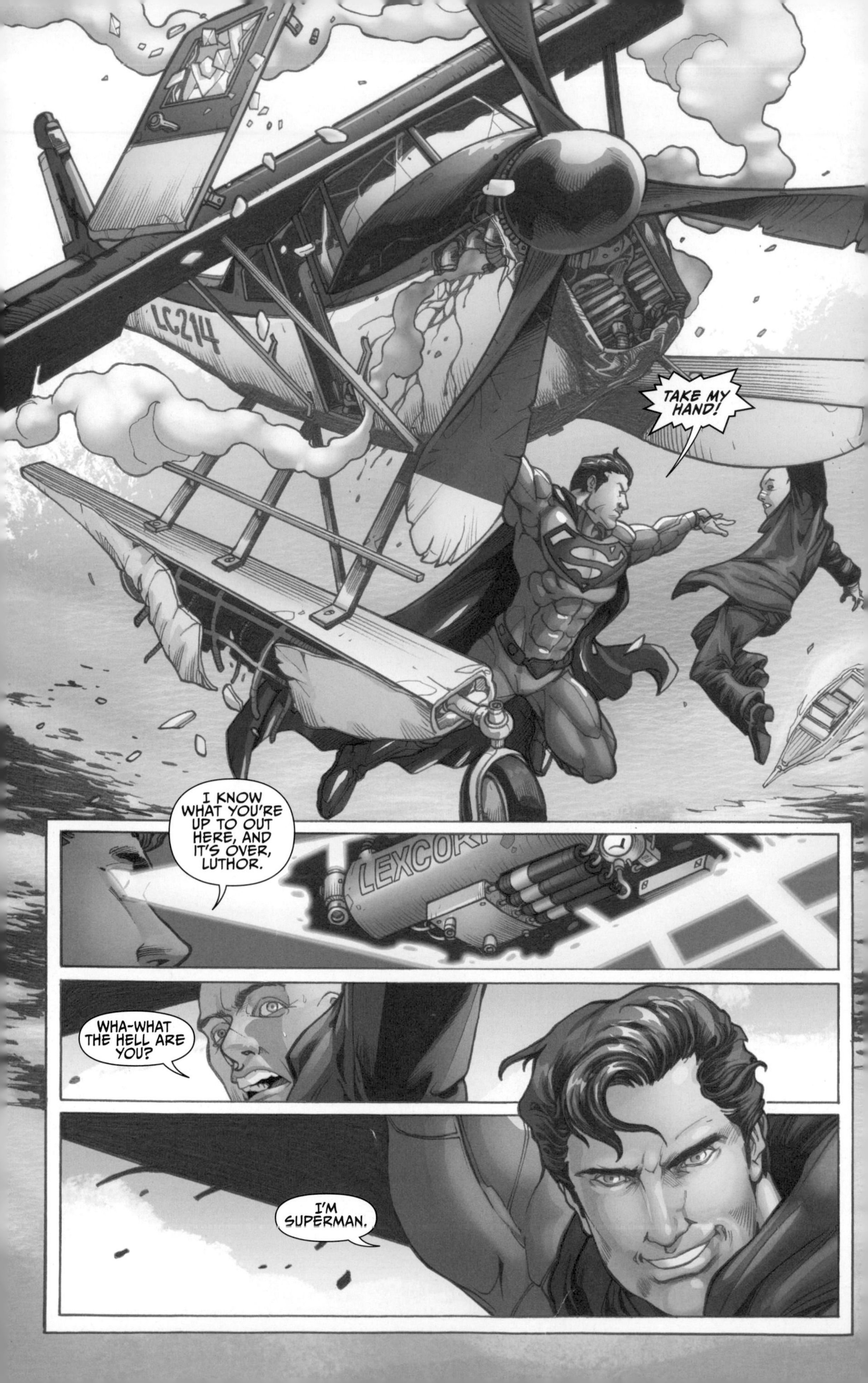
LC214
TAKE MY HAND!
I KNOW WHAT YOU'RE UP TO OUT HERE, AND IT'S OVER, LUTHOR.
LEXCORP
WHA-WHAT THE HELL ARE YOU?
I'M SUPERMAN.

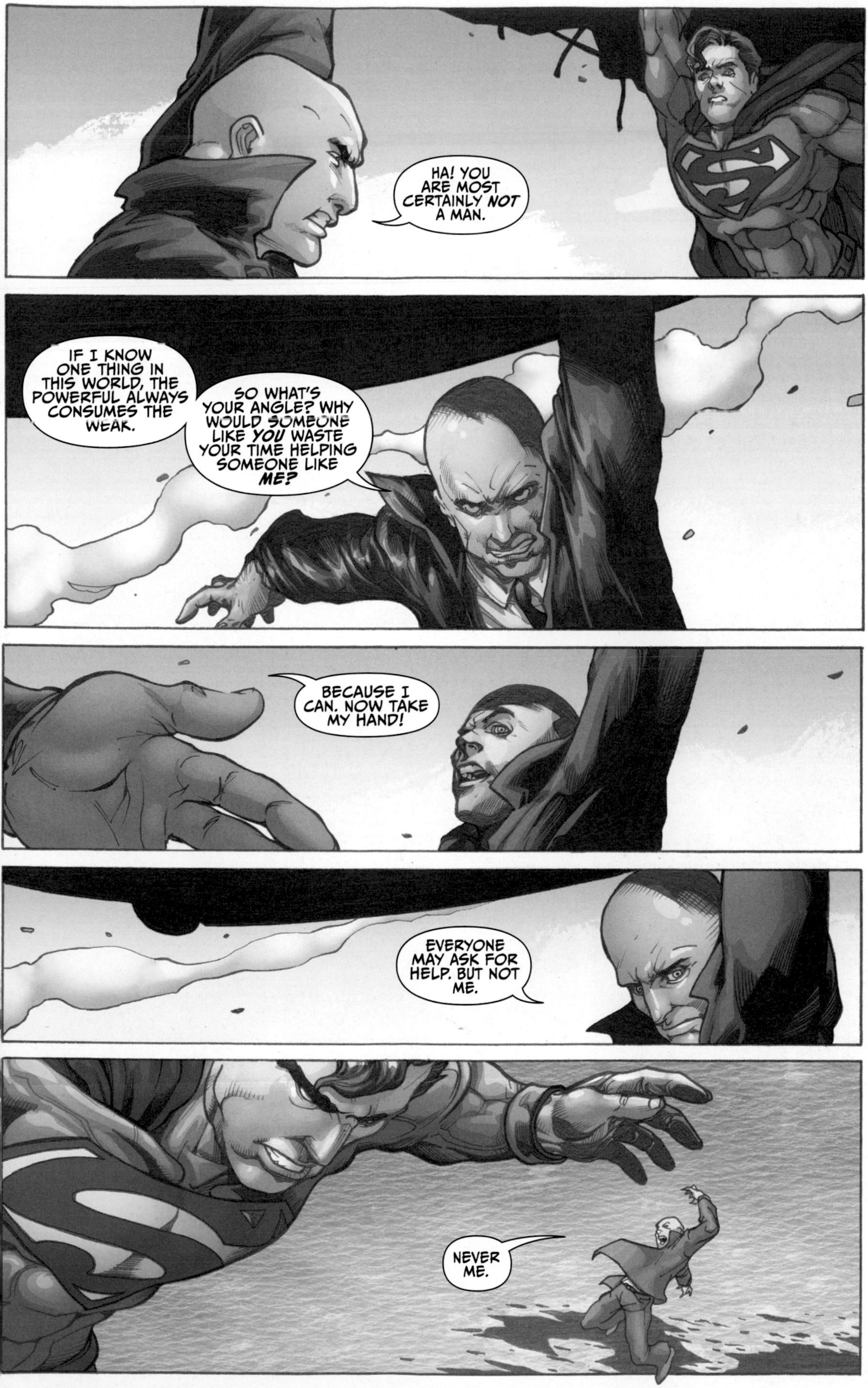
HA! YOU ARE MOST CERTAINLY NOT A MAN.
IF I KNOW ONE THING IN THIS WORLD, THE POWERFUL ALWAYS CONSUMES THE WEAK.
SO WHAT'S YOUR ANGLE? WHY WOULD SOMEONE LIKE YOU WASTE YOUR TIME HELPING SOMEONE LIKE ME?
BECAUSE I CAN. NOW TAKE MY HAND!
EVERYONE MAY ASK FOR HELP. BUT NOT ME.
NEVER ME.

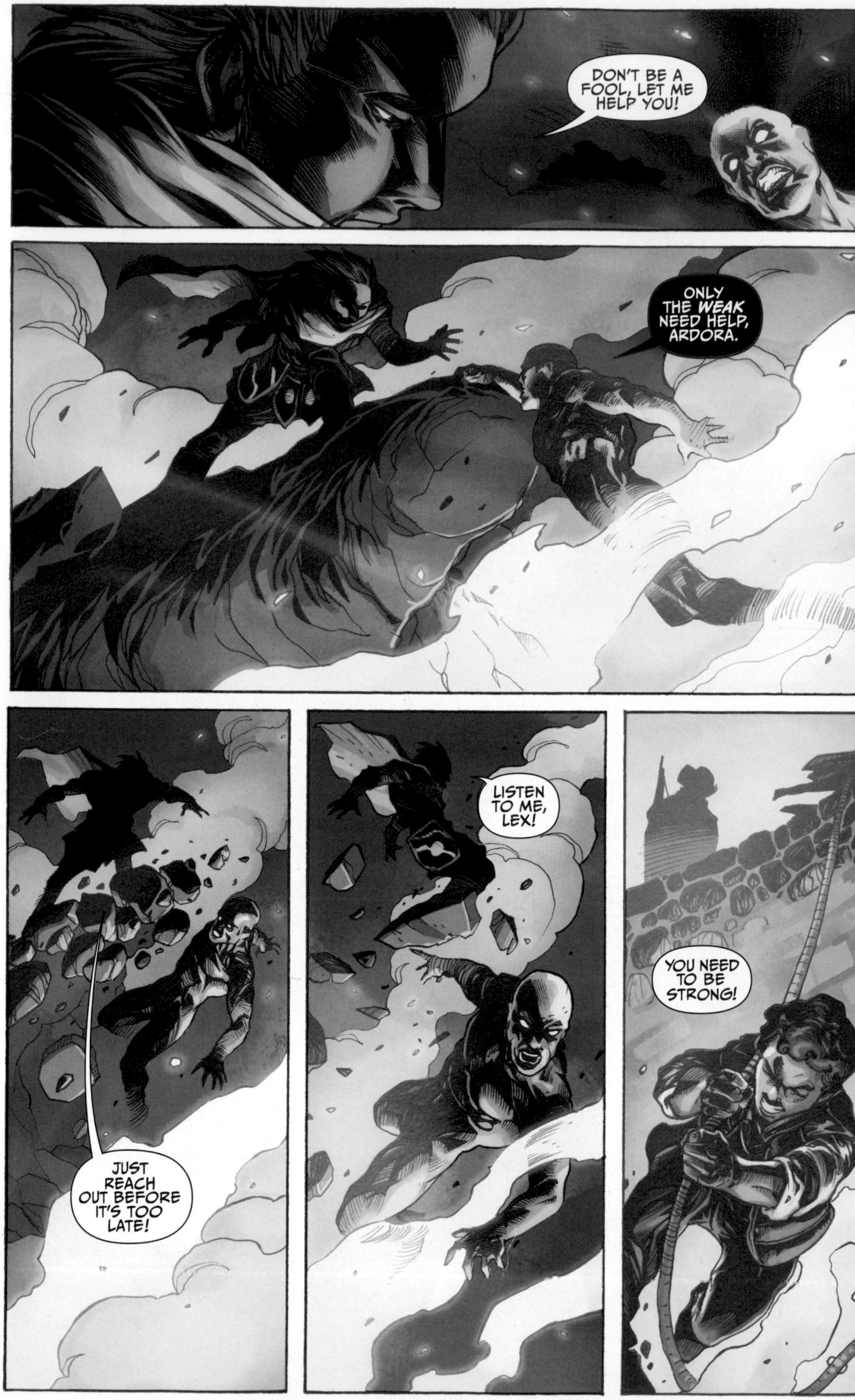
DON'T BE A FOOL, LET ME HELP YOU!
ONLY THE *WEAK* NEED HELP, ARDORA.
JUST REACH OUT BEFORE IT'S TOO LATE!
LISTEN TO ME, LEX!
YOU NEED TO BE STRONG!

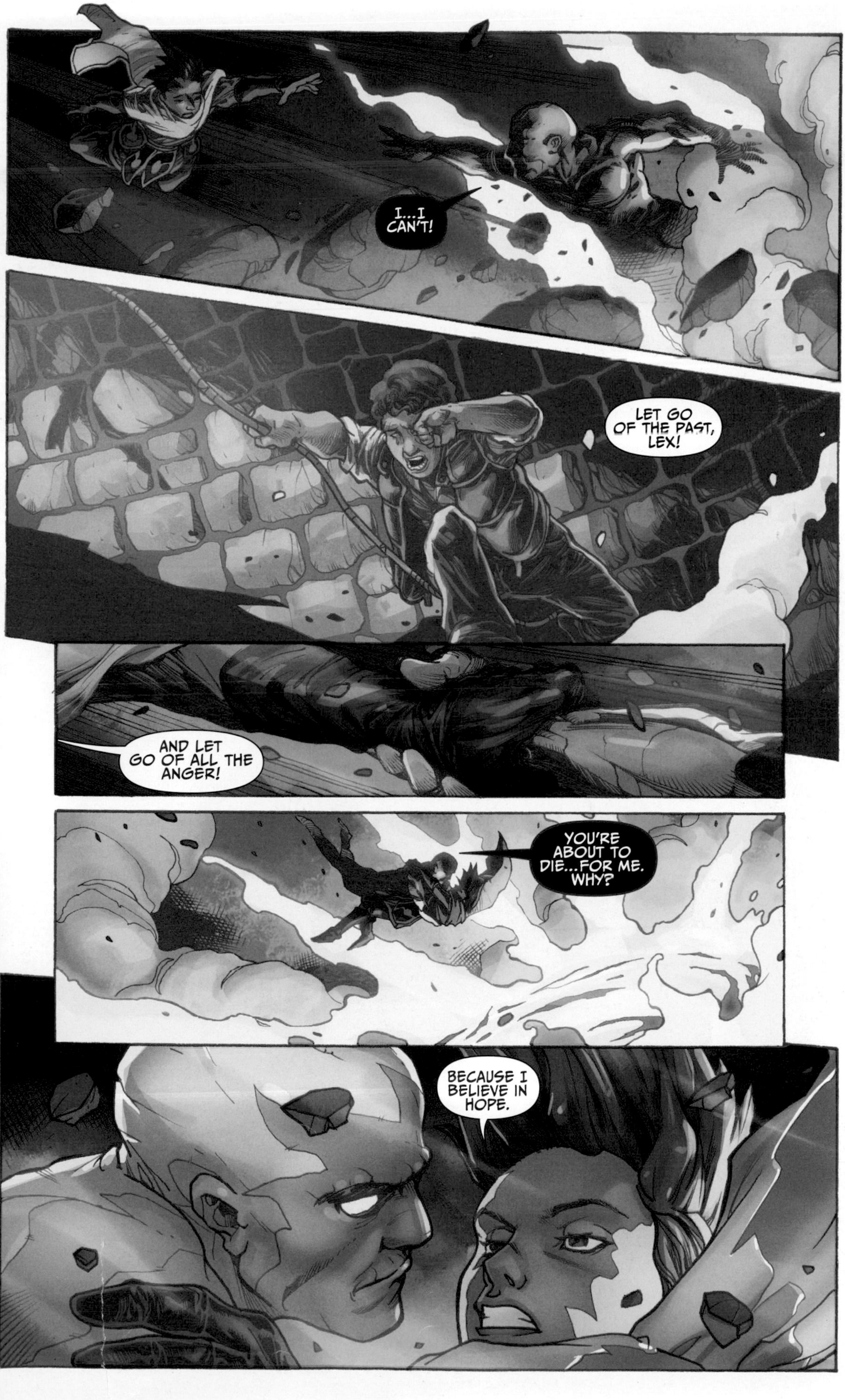
I...I CAN'T!
LET GO OF THE PAST, LEX!
AND LET GO OF ALL THE ANGER!
YOU'RE ABOUT TO DIE...FOR ME. WHY?
BECAUSE I BELIEVE IN HOPE.

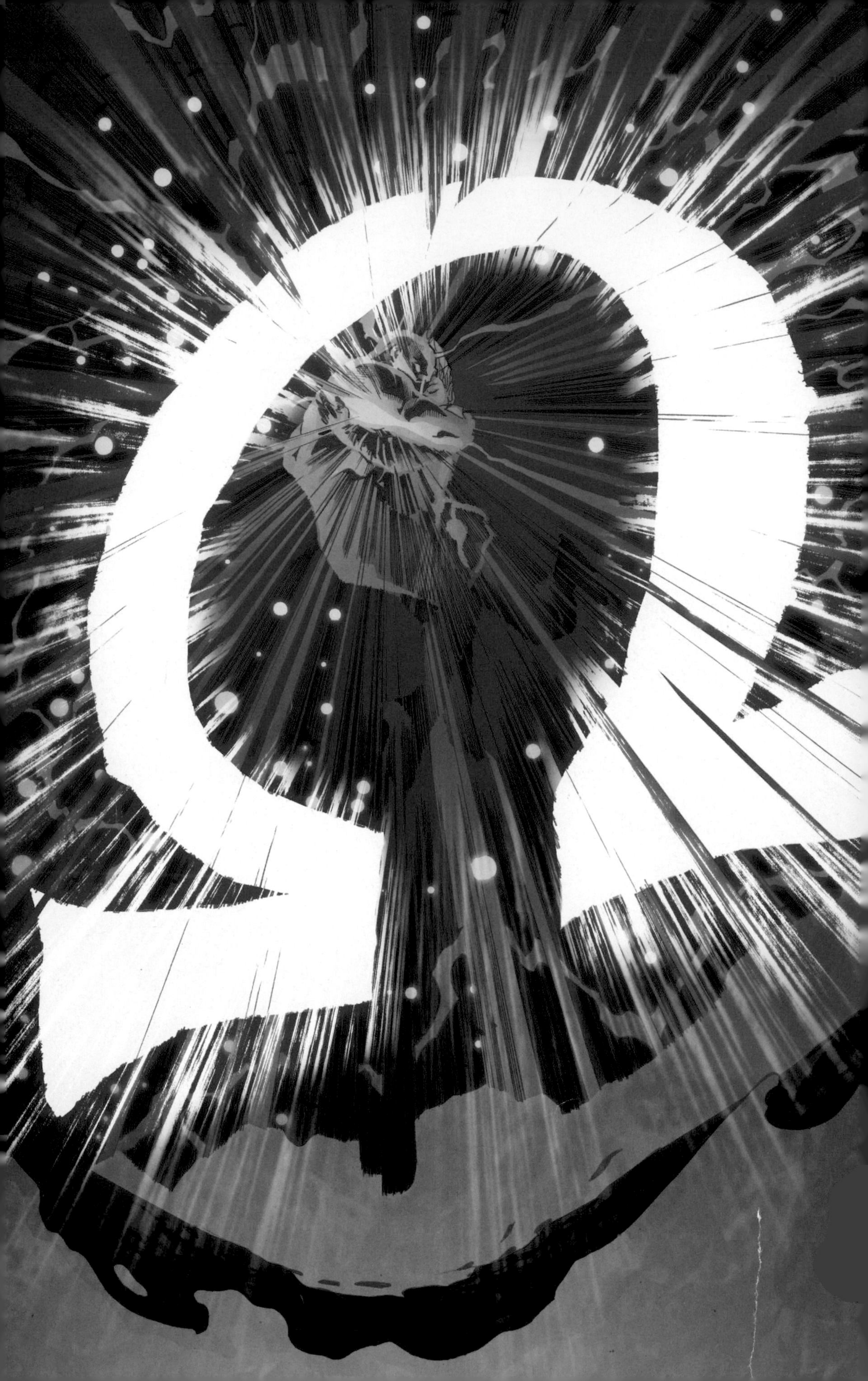

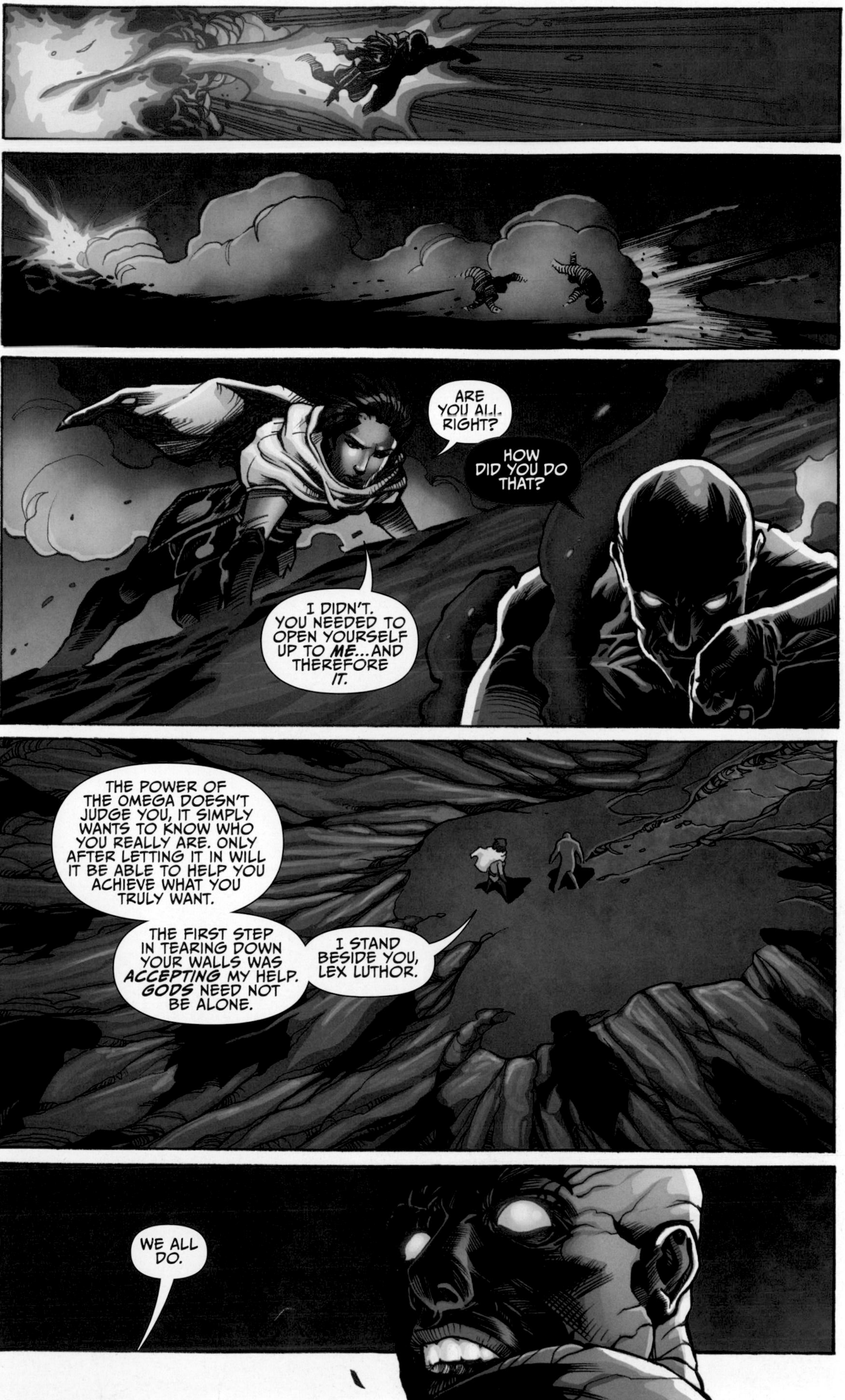
ARE YOU ALL RIGHT?
HOW DID YOU DO THAT?
I DIDN'T. YOU NEEDED TO OPEN YOURSELF UP TO *ME*...AND THEREFORE *IT*.
THE POWER OF THE OMEGA DOESN'T JUDGE YOU, IT SIMPLY WANTS TO KNOW WHO YOU REALLY ARE. ONLY AFTER LETTING IT IN WILL IT BE ABLE TO HELP YOU ACHIEVE WHAT YOU TRULY WANT.
THE FIRST STEP IN TEARING DOWN YOUR WALLS WAS *ACCEPTING* MY HELP. *GODS* NEED NOT BE ALONE.
I STAND BESIDE YOU, LEX LUTHOR.
WE ALL DO.

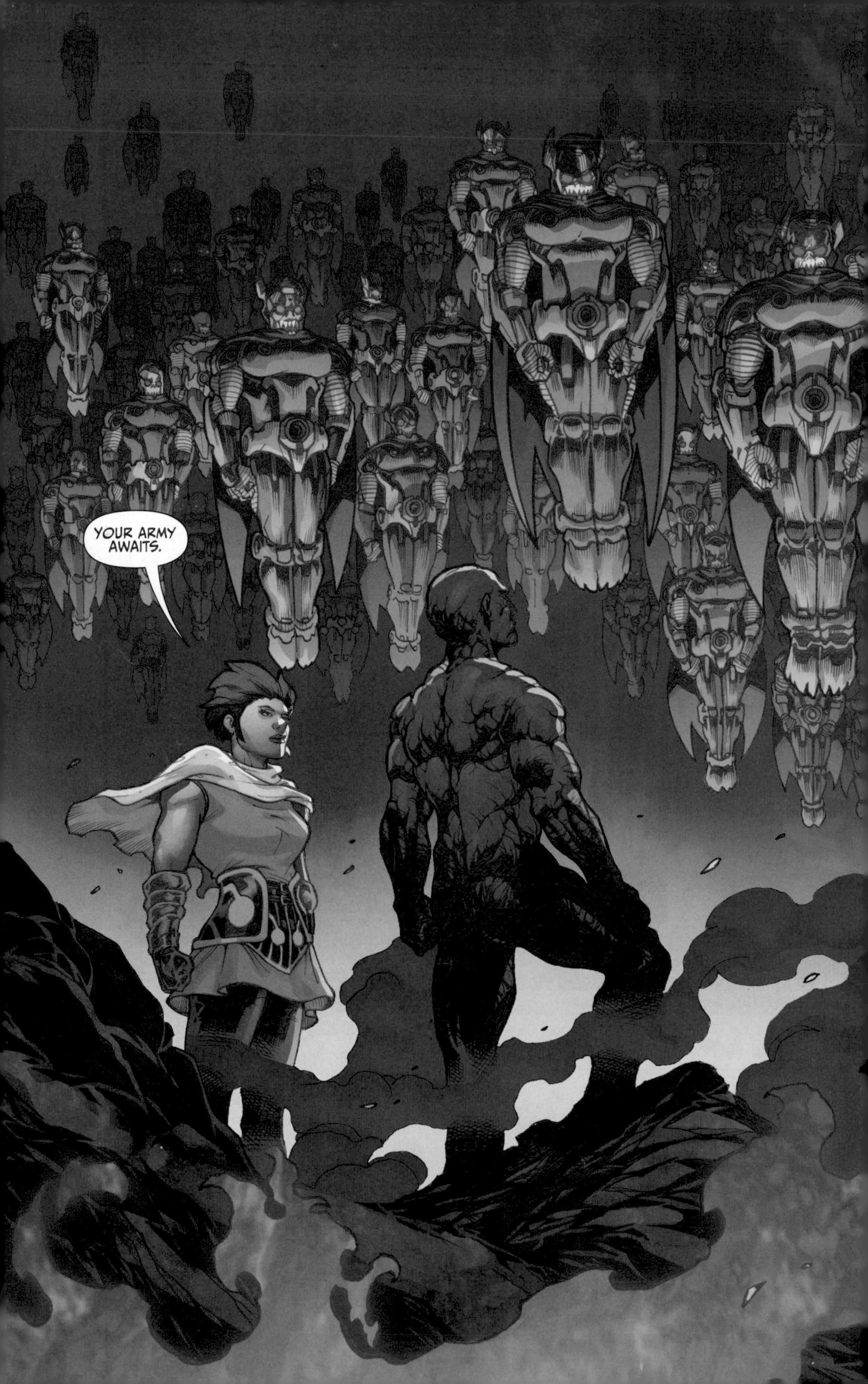
YOUR ARMY AWAITS.

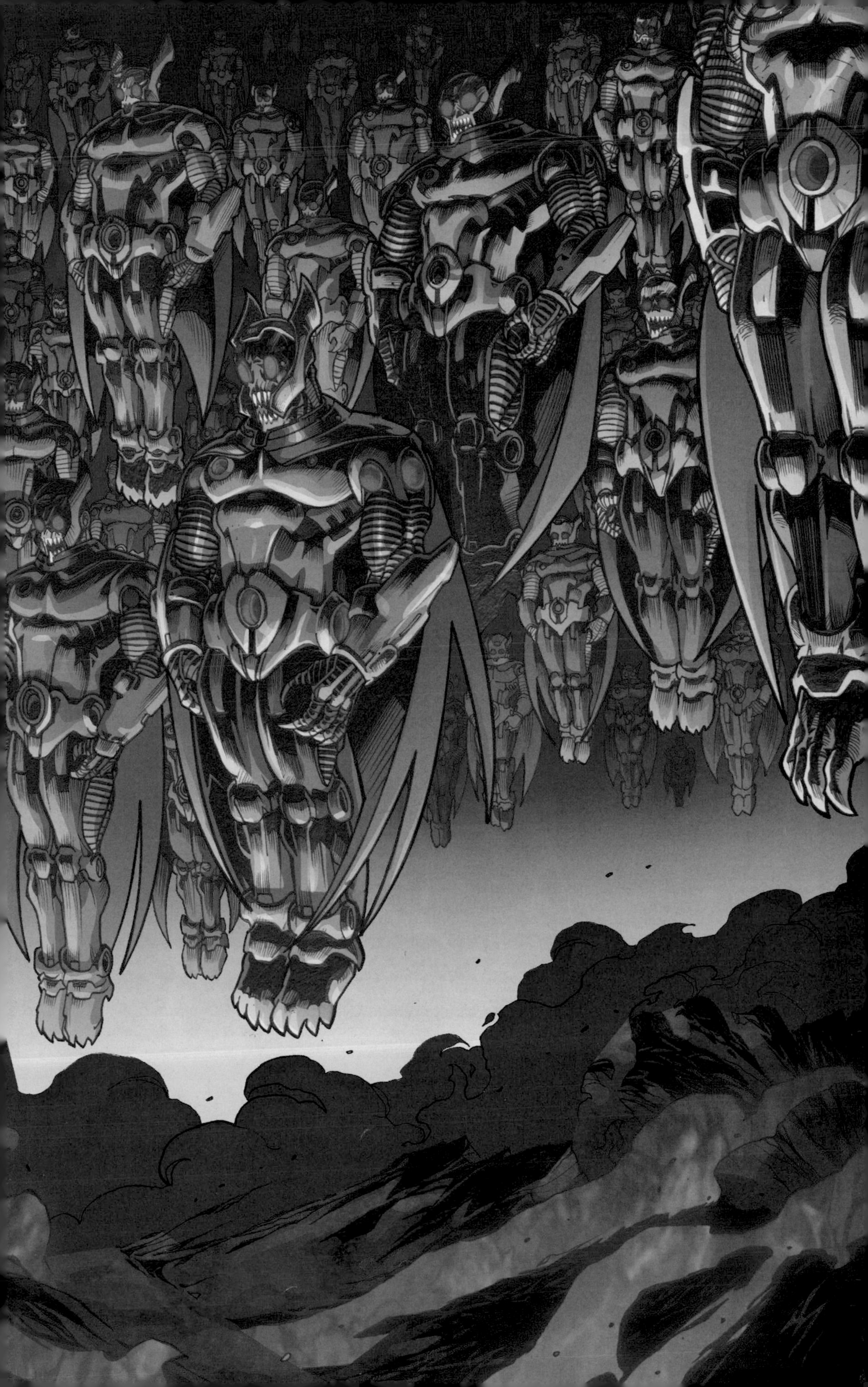

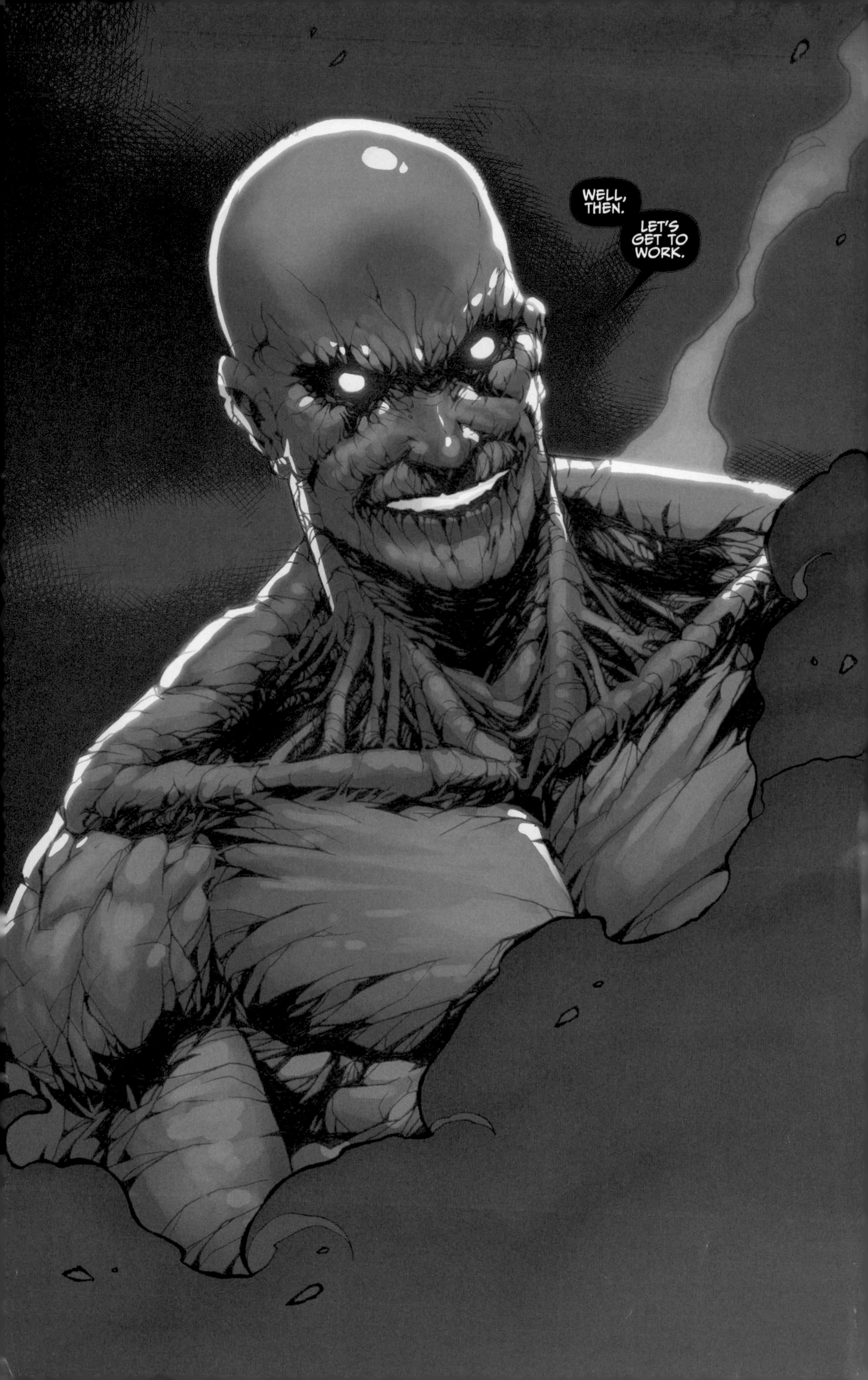
WELL, THEN.
LET'S GET TO WORK.

DARKSEID WAR CHARACTER DESIGNS
BY FRANCIS MANAPUL

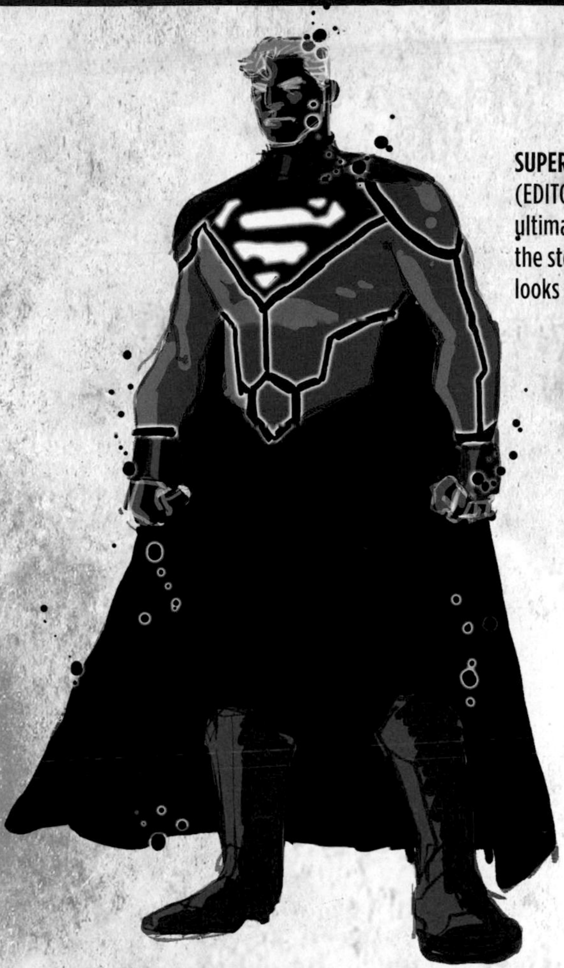

SUPERMAN: GOD OF STRENGTH
(EDITOR'S NOTE: Francis's Super-God costume was ultimately not used. There was no opportunity in the story for Superman to change costumes. But it looks so cool, we had to show it to you!)

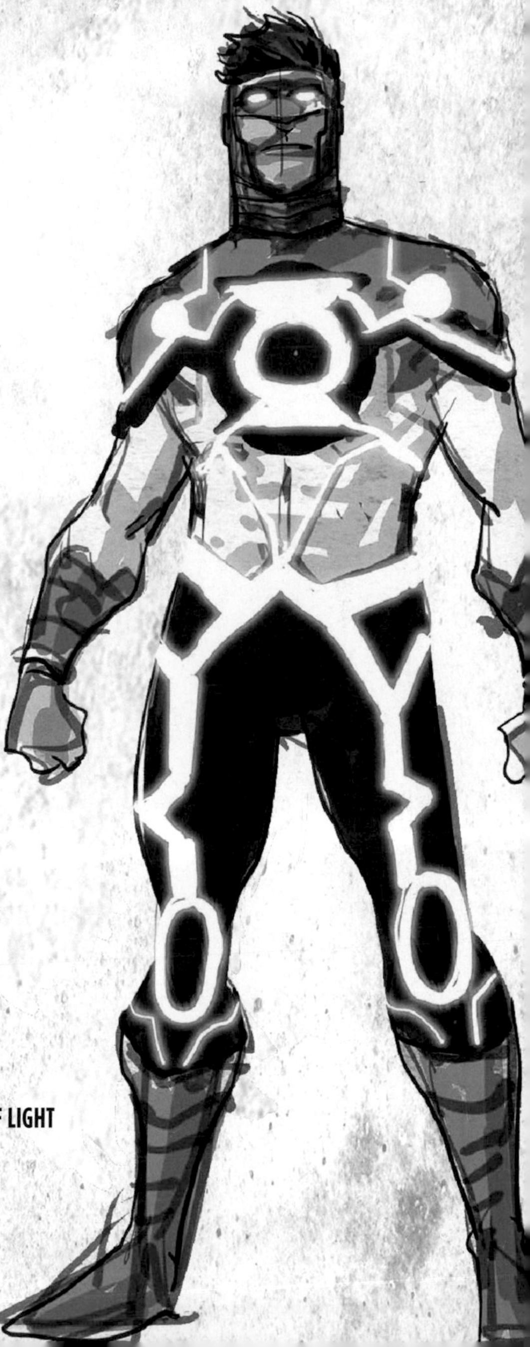

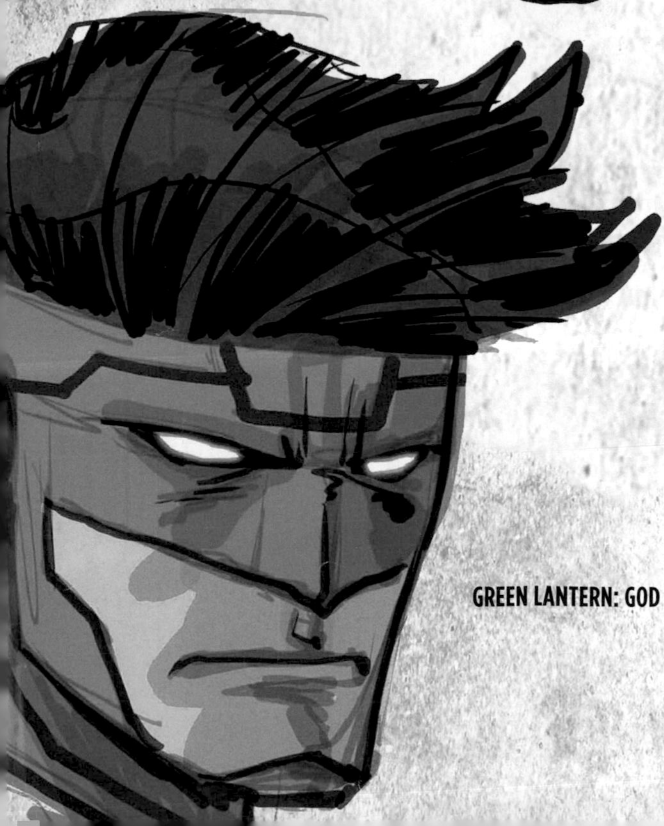

GREEN LANTERN: GOD OF LIGHT

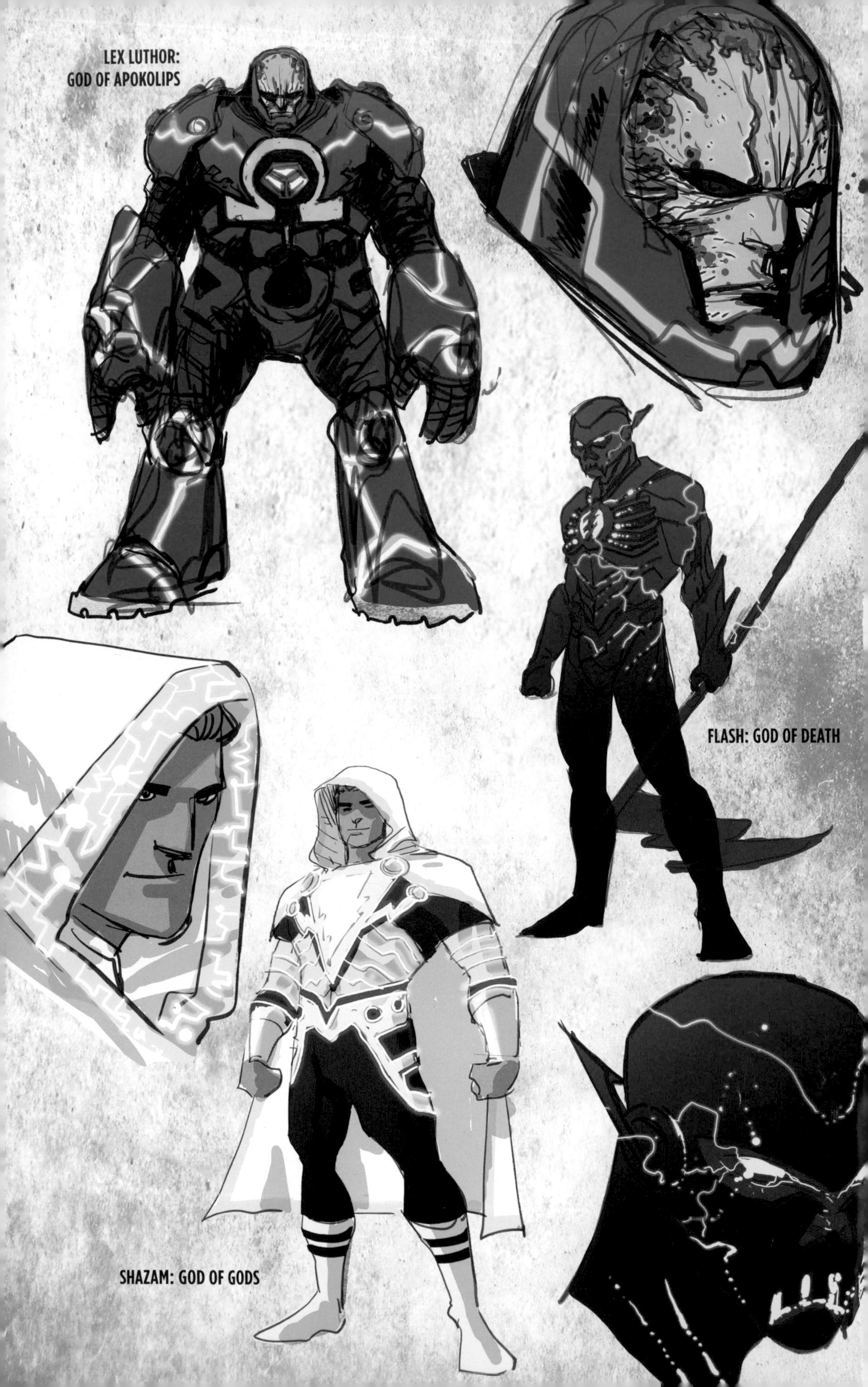
LEX LUTHOR:
GOD OF APOKOLIPS
FLASH: GOD OF DEATH
SHAZAM: GOD OF GODS